Antiques

THE SURVIVAL KIT FOR THE CANADIAN COLLECTOR

Antiques

HYLA WULTS FOX

Dundurn Press
Toronto & Oxford
1990

The writing of this manuscript and the publication of this book were made possible by support from several sources. The author and publisher wish to acknowledge the generous assistance and ongoing support of **The Canada Council**, **The Book Publishing Industry Development Programme** of the **Department of Communications**, and **The Ontario Arts Council.**

This book is loosely based on articles that appeared in the author's weekly *Toronto Star* column from 1976-1986 and in her freelance assignments, until August, 1990. They included some of the following publications: *The Maine Antique Digest; Canadian Living; The Financial Post: Moneywise Magazine; Century Home; Ontario Living; Antique Showcase; Chatelaine; The Medical Post; The Upper Canadian* and the now-defunct *Canadian Collector.*

J. Kirk Howard, Publisher

Editor, first edition: Leslie Wyle
Editor, revised edition: Mark Fenton
Design and Production: JAQ
Cover photo: Shin Sugino
Printing and Binding: Gagné Printing Ltd., Louiseville, Québec, Canada

Dundurn Press Limited
2181 Queen Street East, Suite 301
Toronto, Canada
M4E 1E5

Dundurn Distribution Limited
73 Lime Walk
Headington
Oxford OX3 7AD
England

Canadian Cataloguing in Publication Data

Fox, Hyla Wults
    Antiques, the survival kit for the Canadian collector

Includes index.
ISBN 1-55002-078-1

1. Antiques – Canada. I. Title.

NK841.F69 1990   745.1'075   G90-095732-8

Contents

This book is dedicated to my mother who nurtured and encouraged the creative spirit that has
so enriched my life, and to my daughter Shayne,
who has learned to live with it.

Preface

Like so many people, I got involved with antiques purely by accident. Two events within one year triggered what became an insatiable appetite and passion for things old, as well as a new career.

While visiting my former mother-in-law at her cottage on Lake Simcoe in the summer of 1969, I saw a clear-glass pitcher with embossed flowers. "It's an antique," she said. Not quite believing that something so clumsy-looking could have value, I drove to a nearby town and, wouldn't you know it, the first antique shop I passed had the exact same pitcher with a price tag of fifteen dollars. The dealer wasn't sure what it was. After asking a lot of questions and hounding libraries, I discovered it was a piece of depression glass in the Iris pattern. Having written numerous letters and visiting countless antique shops, I managed to add more than three hundred matching items to complete a dinner set for twelve plus serving pieces.

This initial brush with "antiquity" had made me into a habituée of antique shops, but I soon found out that there was more out there than just depression glass. However, the real turning point came in the winter of 1970 when my family and I visited friends in Quebec City who took us to rue St. Paul where we bought an early petite French-Canadian armoire. Although it has long since been traded away, it had taught me to appreciate early Canadian artifacts and decorative accessories. Gradually, my vision expanded as I discovered a myriad of other items — from jewelry to things loosely known as nostalgia or memorabilia.

This book is, first of all, the product of the knowledge I acquired since those early days. It is intended to take the fear and mystery out of collecting while demonstrating just how much fun it can be. It is not an exhaustive, encyclopedic examination of all forms of collecting and of all antiques but rather an introductory survey, a sourcebook and a guide for future study. It should help the neophyte to see things in a more discerning manner; to know what questions to ask; to stimulate respect for history, techniques of workmanship and the progression of styles and tastes. It points out the problems that can occur and the resources available to help solve them.

In short, this is the book I searched for and never found when I too was a beginner.

Hyla Wults Fox
Toronto, January 1983

Postscript:

In May, 1990 when Dundurn Press Ltd. suggested a revision of *Antiques* I was pleased because I felt there was a major gap in the literature. Every field needs a textbook and in the Canadian antiques world, we were missing such a basic publication. Nothing like it existed before my first book arrived on the scene and nothing like it has appeared since it went out of print sometime around 1985. Wherever I lecture, organize a course, visit a shop or show, people always asked where they could get a copy of my book. Unfortunately, I had to direct them to the antiquarian book shops. I am thrilled to be able to fill that gap once again.

When I initially began working on the new manuscript I thought it would be a snap since my basic philosophies proved, over the years, to be sound. But I forgot to take into account two factors: people and the marketplace. Not only have price standards changed in almost every category but even more important, a great many companies and individuals are no longer involved in the antique business or community.

A job that started with a smile and a chuckle, ended with a great sigh of relief. Not only has the entire book been given an overhaul, but every resource has been checked; a few have been omitted and many more added. At least 250 addresses had to be revised because so many North Americans changed venues. Both appendices have been totally redone and a new one added. Each chapter has had current stories, and information added and many have had a complete overhaul. Some, like the jewelry, folk art and textile chapters have had new photographs too. So, while we are calling this book a revision, it is more than that. It is a fresh look at the complicated marketplace and at the many resources available to help collectors, especially the novice, survive in Canada.

Hyla Wults Fox
Toronto, August, 1990

Acknowledgements

Words of gratitude must go first of all to Samuel and Sally Pennington, publishers and editors of *The Maine Antique Digest*. If they had not published my first article in their March 1976 issue, I would not have had the courage to try again.

I also am indebted to Dinah Kerr of *The Toronto Star,* who accepted my initial piece in November 1976 and keep asking for more and to Stratton Holland who became my editor in the early 1980s. They taught me much about writing and the newspaper business.

Special thanks must also go to Marlene Cook; Catherine and Carl Thuro and to Barbara and Rollo McDonald for their valuable 'antique' insights and support. Of course, I cannot fail to thank my long-time friends Nancy and Brian Willer who have always been there for me with unlimited amounts of friendship, creative suggestions and constant encouragement.

And to Shayne, to whom this book is dedicated, I really do owe it all. During her life she has added flavour, colour and texture to my world. In exchange she has endured either the sound of the typewriter or printer at all hours of the night; missed many meals while I was either writing or attending some antique function or other and has been my sounding board, listening to yet another potential 'opener.' For putting up with my crazy life, yet adding so much to it, I say an inadequate thank you.

Persons connected with various institutions have been most generous with their help; Ed Dahl, Curator of the Early Canadian Cartography Section of the Public Archives of Canada, Ottawa; Janet Holmes and Peter Kaellegren, Royal Ontario Museum, Toronto; Wes Mattie, Folk Culture Centre, Ottawa; Dr. Ted Brasser, Ethnology Dept., National Museum, Ottawa; Stanely G. Triggs, Notman Photographic Archives, McCord Museum, Montreal; Russell Cooper, Black Creek Pioneer Village, Downsview, Ontario; David L. Newlands, formerly of the University of Toronto, Museum Studies Programme and Max Allen, former curator of the Museum of Textiles, Toronto. In the United States, Eason Eige of the Huntington Galleries in West Virginia and Kenneth M. Wilson, formerly of the Henry Ford Museum in Michigan were most helpful.

Many auction houses and their staffs have generously contributed information for my columns, articles and this book. I especially thank the people at D. and J. Ritchie Ltd.; Waddington McLean Ltd., and Sotheby's, Toronto for letting me roam through their storerooms, ask questions, borrow photographs and drink their coffee. Geoffrey Joyner of Joyner Fine Art Inc., and Ronald Dupuis of Dupuis Auctioneers & Appraisers, Toronto have also been of valued assistance over the years. Robert W. Skinner of Boston and the world-wide branches of Sotheby's, Phillips and Christie's also were most generous in permitting me to use their photographs and other materials.

Toronto gemmologists, Laura Beard of Beardsley Enterprises and Jim Hurgle, of Ghcmz, both offered appreciated bits of constructive criticism for the jewelry chapter. June and Bob O'Neil of R.A. O'Neil of Toronto; Carl Booth of Glen Manor Galleries, Shakespeare, Ontario; Henry Dobson of Plattsville, Ontario and Don Lake of D. & E. Lake, Toronto, were always ready to come up with valuable insights, leads and suggestions (and yes, sometimes, even gossip). To all these people I owe a sincere thank you.

There are many others who have given freely of their knowledge and time:

The late Albert Aliman; Christopher Bashford; Michael Bird and his wife Terry Kobayashi; Bill Brethour of Yours, Mine & Ours, Toronto; Valerie Brown of Waddington's; Joyce Burne, Orangeville, Ontario; Cindy Calder of The Bead Goes On, Toronto; Dr. Paul and Joyce Chapnick; Alan Clairman; Elizabeth Collard; Mary Copeland; Joyce Taylor Dawson; Samantha Howard Fairbanks; John and Vicky Forbes; Ronald Fraleigh; Rudi and Barbara Franchi; Richard Fulton; Kip Gemmell; Agnes Gillespie; Marilyn Glazer Greenbaum; Dr. David and Jan Greyson; Pam Hanbury of Just Pam, Toronto; "Doc" John Hawkshaw; the late William Heacock; Rick and Holly Henemader; Christie Chidley Hill; Bill and Pauline Hogan; William Jackson; Jonny's Antiques, Shakespeare, Ontario; Louis Kernaghan; Ken Kershaw; Tami Jacobs Kligman; Betty Knowles; Vi and Rob Lambert; Uno Langman; Ed Locke; Mr. and Mrs. Ronald McLean; Duncan and Allister McLean; Christie Mills of Christie Mills Insurance, Toronto; Pat McHugh; Bob Ness of Obsession, Montreal; Steve Oltuski; Howard Pain; Dr. Ralph and Patricia Price; David and Marlene Ritchie; Gloria Rosenberg of Sawtooth Borders, Toronto; Michael Rowan; Barbara Rusch; James Snider; Bob and Brenda Star; Carol Telfer; Nick Treanor; Fred Tymoshenko; David Tyrer; Helen and Peter Vernon; Scott Wallace; Edith Weber; Ronald Windebank; Gary Wine; Paul and Grace Zammit and Charlotte Zuppinger.

Introduction

The word "antique" has come to be a catch-all term that means different things to different people. Some say it is an article that must be more than one hundred years old, perhaps because this time span is used by many countries to regulate the duty-free importation of goods made more than a century ago. Others disregard this custom house definition and instead use the year 1830 as the cutoff date. They believe that the only way to measure a genuine antique is to know that it was created by hand. The year 1830 is used as the time when the Industrial Revolution began and manufacturers started using machinery powered by the steam engine. It signaled the end of the "handmade" era. Many members of the Canadian collecting community look upon 1867, the year of Confederation, as crucial, although the Canadian Antique Dealers Association chose 1870 as decisive for determining when something becomes antique. Yet there are those who ignore all these fabricated dates, claiming scarcity as the sole criterion. To them, anything rare, no matter how recent, is worthy of attention and is, in fact, a collectible. Accordingly, newer items loosely lumped into the nostalgia and memorabilia categories can qualify as antiques.

My own definition closely parallels the last one. To me, an antique is something that is unique, that has a recognizable, known style, and is made wholly or partially by hand. A collectible, on the other hand, is something that is no longer being made and/or whose creator has since died; is machine-made, and evokes a nostalgic feeling.

Antiques, art, and collectibles should never be purchased because they might be "a good investment." Anyone who collects with that in mind is heading for disaster. Problems occur because private collectors usually buy at retail prices but end up selling at the wholesale level. Even when they dispose of goods through an auction house they must be prepared to lose at least 25 per cent on commission, insurance, photography and cartage payments.

There is no return on the "investment." Antiques and art bring neither dividends nor interest and, therefore, become a negative cash-flow situation. A lack of liquidity is another thing would-be collectors must consider. Not only are there expenses involved in selling pieces but it may take a long time to do so. Someone wishing to dispose of goods at auction may have to wait four to eight months for the appropriate sale to take place and when he has sold them he must be prepared to wait more than one month for his money.

While pieces are in collectors' hands, proper insurance, security, good storage facilities conservation and preservation must be provided. Beyond that, manipulations by certain shrewd investors who cause the market to fluctuate can play havoc with the value of antiques. When buying solely for investment, economic recessions and depressions must also be taken into account.

There only is one way to be safe. Samuel Pennington once said, "Buy what you love, take good care of it, put it together in an orderly, loving fashion and spend some time researching and learning about it. Maybe it will make your heirs rich!"

1

Collecting and Collectors

No one knows how many people are involved in collecting but conservative estimates show that in North America alone at least fifty million adults are engaged in the pastime, to a greater or lesser degree. Some of the items collected are as bizarre as barbed wire, paper dolls, beer cans, buttons, Adolf Hitler memorabilia, comic books, corkscrews, old poker chips, salt and pepper shakers, thimbles, playing cards, Dinky toys and even mouse traps. One California man has two hundred different vacuum cleaners he keeps in working order; a Canadian advertising executive concentrates on things that screw on tables — apple corers, for example; and a Toronto woman owns more than one thousand Avon bottles. There are connoisseurs of cookie cutters and manhole covers; and one Pennsylvania gentleman has the definitive collection of airline barf-bags. Even Prince Charles collects; according to a recent UPI story he is interested in old toilets or "loos" as they are called in Britain. Collecting isn't necessary to survival but it is so widespread that it must satisfy some part of the human psyche.

Why *do* people collect? Some say it is because the urge bears a relationship to sexual desires and emotions experienced during early toilet training. Accordingly, it's a kind of sublimation or substitution of a socially acceptable form of behavior (collecting) for one that is not acceptable (lack of control of bodily functions).

Dr. Nathan Wisebord, a Montreal psychoanalyst sees the prototype collector as someone who labels, organizes and categorizes to make his collection a particular field of study or endeavor. "It is an intellectual process rather than a passion." On the other hand, Dr. Zalman Amit, co-director of the new clinic for Behavior Therapy and Research in Montreal, suggests that hoarding is a perfectly normal preoccupation deeply ingrained in humans as well as in some animals. "Everybody has it, but in some it's more pervasive than in others."

To certain people, collecting is a way of surrounding themselves with the unusual and unique. Pat Rogal, library assistant in charge of the Picture Collections, Fine Arts Department, Metropolitan Toronto Library, collects all forms of early advertising because it amuses and pleases her. "As far as I'm concerned," says Ms. Rogal, "there is no need for any other justification."

Occasionally a collection begins without focus or planning; then it suddenly takes on shape and comes alive. A prime example of this is the oil lamp collection of author and lecturer Catherine Thuro who, twenty years ago, bought two oil lamps for twenty-five dollars because she liked the looks of them. Someone had recommended Loris Russell's *A Heritage of Light*, and she thought she would try to find examples that resembled those in his book. Until it was dispersed in three major auctions in 1989 and 1990 it was one of the finest oil lamp collections in North America. It included well over two thousand examples, the bulk of which were not in Russell's book. The more lamps she bought the more she realized he had barely skimmed the surface. Her direction began to change when she decided to write a definitive book on the subject. "My motivation to collect was solely to do the research, and lamps gave me a rare opportunity." The result was *Oil Lamps: The Kerosene Era in North America* and *Oil Lamps: Glass Kerosene Lamps,* monumental books that may be Catherine Thuro's bid for immortality.

The thrill of the search and the joy of discovery are other reasons for collecting. Some people like owning old things "made out of love or necessity;" to others finding their roots is important and many derive a sense of history from having antiques around them. It can also mean status or a way to decorate a home, allowing the collector to live with old things that retain their value rather than with new ones that depreciate as soon as they leave the store. Many collect because it fills their leisure hours with fun and helps them make new friends. A few admit they like "investing" in things they can love, use and appreciate every day rather than putting money in the bank or into stocks. Others collect to make themselves noticeable, unique. Being an expert on something, no matter how obscure, gives them credibility: a persona, if you like. Some just want items from their past, from their childhood because it brings warm memories or because they wanted it but couldn't have it back then. Interestingly, none of the people I interviewed ever mentioned investment as their sole motivation. (Investors "acquire" pieces in a cold and calculating manner, often solely out of greed. In many cases they don't even bother to scour the marketplace themselves but employ agents to do their buying for them. In my view these people are not collectors at all.) While everyone, it seems, collects for their own personal specific reasons, there is one basic constant — no one regrets it.

An unspoken code of ethics exists among collectors. By observing certain basic rules they create a feeling of brotherhood and even of conspiracy. Anyone who breaks these rules invites animosity and mistrust. To illustrate this point, I would like to relate a recent incident that involves two oil lamp enthusiasts, A and B. A asked B how much he should pay for a red "widget" he had uncovered in the Niagara Falls region. B told him he would figure it out, asking A to call him back later. Meanwhile B contacted every likely source in the area, located the particular article and arranged to buy it. When A found out about it he was furious. The entire "widget" collecting community now regards B as someone not to be trusted.

Of course, there is a great deal of legitimate, friendly competition and rivalry among collectors. When they get together, they openly discuss recent acquisitions, which dealer has what, as well as gossiping about upcoming shows, prices, cheque bouncers, etc., but rarely will anyone tell you exactly to whom they go for a specific artifact.

Twenty years ago, some friends who also happened to be collectors noticed that whenever they got together, they spent more and more time discussing their purchases and antiques. They would bring along newly acquired items and their social evenings became a grown-up version of "show and tell." Soon they decided to meet regularly at each other's homes. On the night I was invited, a Toronto veterinarian showed us his beer bottle cap and beer can collection, an interior decorator brought along a pair of art glass candlesticks and a primary schoolteacher let us admire a recently acquired decoy. I was impressed by their knowledge of Canadian history and the respect they had not only for their own but also for each other's collections.

Similar clubs can be established by any group. No membership dues are required, and no specific rules have to be observed; all it takes is a lot of enthusiasm and some genuine motivation.

Collecting for All the Right Reasons: Finding Freddie's Family

As discussed earlier, most die-hard collectors are not motivated by money or greed. Rather they are spurred by personal feelings and impulses. And so it was for Tami Jacobs Kligman when she found a brittle old photograph album, twenty-two years ago, in a Toronto antique shop. Although she had always loved antiques, especially more intimate and small-scale treasures such as photographs, autographs, Victorian valentine cards and diaries, she was particularly enthralled with this album. In fact, it launched her on a twenty-year-long hunt for the owners. This story is retold here because it illustrates in a dramatic, poignant way, the rewards of collecting and the positive features of being a passionate, creative and intuitive collector.

To Tami Jacobs Kligman, there was something instantly compelling about the burgundy velvet album; it had a genuine and nostalgic aura about it. She couldn't take her eyes or hands away from it. On the thick cardboard cover was a faded likeness of a young girl wearing flowers in her curly hair. A remnant of the original brass lock still clung to its side.

The album contained many original circa 1880 family photographs accompanied by pencilled inscriptions. Kligman found one shot

Freddie and his parents. *(Photo: HWF)*

particularly haunting: a grainy black and white photo of a man and woman wearing their finest Sunday clothes. Seated in front of them was a dignified-looking boy, four or five years old with a round face, a woollen cap, a lace-collared coat and some sort of military weapon across his chest. The subjects were identified as being Mr. and Mrs. J. W. McDonald and Freddie. "It only took Kligman a few seconds to decide that she *had* to own it. "I sensed the book was lost," says Kligman, "and that it was my duty to help find its way back home."

Kligman also valued the album because so little of her own family memorabilia has sur-

Tami Jacobs Kligman clutching the album before her visit. (Photo: HWF)

vived. "The oldest photo we have is of my great-great-grandmother in Russia," explains the 42-year-old Kligman, adding that it was one of the few shots her family brought with them when they fled the USSR in 1915. "What I would give to have an album like this of my family. I intuitively felt there must be someone who would treasure this book as much as I would were it from my family." She happily paid the $10 asking price.

Her twenty-year search began the day after she brought the album home. Most of the photos

in the volume were not of Freddie McDonald and his supposed parents but of members of a "Mitchell" family (who later turned out to be relatives of the McDonalds). Three towns were mentioned in the book's pages: Toronto, St. Marys and Emsdale. As the album clearly indicated the Mitchells were from Toronto. Kligman made that clue her starting point, and she spent hours searching through old city directories. The pieces, however, just wouldn't fit together, largely because finding the relatives of a late 1800s family with such a common surname in a large city was so daunting. Also, she couldn't find any clues in the St. Marys city directories and Emsdale didn't turn up in her searches through various maps and atlases.

Over the next two decades — a time that saw Kligman become a teacher and have a family of her own — the book remained part of her personal treasures. "The album was displayed in my home as if it were part of my own family. "It wasn't until February 1987, when she and her family bought a country home in Gravenhurst, that the mystery started unravelling. One day, while shopping, Kligman picked up a local telephone directory and noticed the first page was for a town called Emsdale.

A penny dropped. "Emsdale? There really is such a place? Flashing in my mind was the picture of that mother and father with the little boy in the lace collar." The following weekend, February 14, Kligman and her family returned to their country home with the album in tow. She also had a phone number for one J. F. McDonald from the Emsdale listings and she intrepidly decided to give the number a try. "My heart was racing as the phone rang," says Kligman. "How could I explain the story clearly? A woman answered. I told her my name, that I collected antiques, and that I had a photo album purchased 20 years ago containing a picture of a little boy named Freddie standing with his parents. She said I had a picture of her late husband, and asked how much I wanted for the album, not understanding that I just wanted to get it back to the rightful owners. Mrs. McDonald was thrilled. She said it was the best valentine present anybody could give her."

Months passed before a meeting could be arranged for the official handing over the album ceremony. When it finally came, one drizzly day in November, 1988, everyone was nervous. Kligman felt queasy all the way to Emsdale, a cross road community about 30 kilometres north of Huntsville. What would happen if the family didn't treasure the album as much as she did? Worse yet, what if she didn't like them, or they her? Over the years Kligman had developed a great attachment to both the album and the family to whom it belonged. It was crucial to her that everyone got along well. As it turned out, she needn't have been concerned.

Margaret Sinclair McDonald, obviously as excited as Kligman, answered the door wearing her best party dress, black patent shoes and pearls. She graciously ushered her guest into a clean, gold-coloured kitchen and introduced the assembled family members: Jean Laing, whose husband is Margaret's nephew, and Laing's daughter, Donna Gallant. All were treated to an afternoon tea party of sweets on Sunday-best china and quilted, lace-trimmed place mats.

What concerned those gathered was the mysterious way the album got out of the family. Kligman recalls being told by the antique dealer that it came in a box with a lot of other things. Perhaps it was acquired from an estate auction, where it is customary to lump items together to get rid of more merchandise. One theory they developed goes back twenty years when Gallant's aunt, Dorothy Laing, moved from a large house to an apartment. "Aunt Dot was the ulti-

mate collector," explains Gallant, a Toronto lawyer. "She had bags of photographs and material that she was always trying to get in order. She valued anything to do with the family. It's so ironic; she would never have let this album go out of the family. It had to have been a mistake." A mystery it remains.

While the cups were being filled, Mrs. McDonald was pressed to tell about her life, her marriage and, of course, her late husband, James Frederick Mitchell McDonald, the boy in the photo. "Her story", reflects Kligman, "was a time capsule of the history of that region. It put the whole album into a new framework for me. I especially loved the family stories involving the people I knew from the album."

Margaret McDonald was born in Harriston, a small town north of Listowel. When she graduated from Normal School (teacher's college) in Toronto in 1943, there was an oversupply of teachers and she ended up teaching in Northern Ontario for several years. Eventually she got a post in Emsdale, boarding at the home owned by Freddie McDonald's brother.

The young Miss Sinclair was fascinated with Freddie, the most respected man in the community. Not only was he on the school board but he was the postmaster, the first real estate agent in the area, the reeve and active in the Masons and the United Church. "He commanded everybody's respect. He was a presence," his widow remembers fondly.

The only problem was that he was 30 years older than Margaret. "It didn't faze me that he was older but it bothered him," she says. For the next three years, they remained friendly acquaintances. Finally, when Margaret accepted a teaching assignment in another town and it looked as though she would leave Emsdale forever, Freddie McDonald made his move. "He came over and told me he'd been talking it over with the minister who said our characters were right. I was mature for my age and he was young for his."

Even now, more than 40 years later, she blushes when she recalls that first kiss. "The next morning after the kiss he asked me if I was sorry, "she says, giggling girlishly. They were married April 29, 1946 — he was 60 years old, she was 30. The marriage lasted a full 30 years until Mac's death in 1976. Suitably, he was buried on Valentine's Day.

Theirs was a happy, loving relationship which might explain McDonald's reaction when she opened the album to the picture of her late husband and his parents. She started to cry. Kligman, too, began to weep, overwhelmed by the knowledge that she had not only given another person the perfect gift, but that she had finally solved a mystery that had nagged her for two decades. "I would look at the boy and speculate about what happened to him. Even then he looked so proper, so distinguished. What would he grow up to be? In my heart I knew he would be an important person."

Christina Duff Stewart

This is the story of how another Canadian collector, Christina Duff Stewart, turned her addiction into one of the world's largest collections. And, it all started with this little poem:

> Twinkle, twinkle, little star,
> How I wonder what you are?
> Up above the world so high,
> Like a diamond in the sky.

Is there anyone in the Western world who doesn't know this verse? But, and this is the ultimate trivial pursuit question, is there anyone who actually knows who wrote the original five stanza poem? Was it part of a Walt Disney pro-

duction? Did it appear in some anonymous turn-of-the-century nursery book? Or, was it handed down, by word of mouth, from mother to child as a folk tale?

If you chose any of the above you would be wrong. For it was actually penned by fifteen-year-old, Jane Taylor in 1806 just after she and her family moved from Colchester to Ongar, England. In writing to a friend she told of her joy at finally having her own 'space,' in the attic of her new home, where she could put "all the apparatus necessary for a poet ... a few bookshelves, a table for my writing-desk, one chair for myself, and another for my muse." Once, as she looked out the window, she wrote about how she would "roam and revel 'mid the stars .... When in the attic room, with untold delight, I watched the changing splendours of the night." That room, that window, that view, inspired "The Star," still one of our most beloved nursery rhymes.

It first appeared in a little book called *Rhymes For The Nursery*, published in 1806. She did not get credit for the poem nor did any of the other authors for their work. The book simply attributed authorship by noting it was "by the authors of Original Poems for Infant Minds" (published in 1804). And they were credited simply as "several young persons."

One of those "young persons" was her sister Ann, who wrote amongst other things, a poem called "My Mother." Although not as famous as "The Star," it might, even now, jog a few memories. At any rate, its sentiments are universal and timeless. In part, it went:

> "Who fed me from her gentle breast,
> And hush'd me in her arms to rest,
> And on my cheek sweet kisses prest?
> My Mother.

> Who sat and watched my infant head,

When sleeping on my cradle bed
And tears of sweet affection shed?
My Mother.

Who dressed my dolls in cloths so gay,
And taught me privy how to play
And minded all I had to say?
My Mother.

Who ran to help me when I fell
And would some pretty story tell
And Kiss the place to make it well?
My Mother."

But it wasn't just the two girls who were involved in the literary arts. Eventually all of the family members became writers and produced dozens of publications that included children's poems, of course, novels, history and geography books, travel guides, hymns, books about the law, as well as advice for servants, parents and teachers. The result was that they left historians, researchers and collectors — interested in documenting social history as well as the development of book binding, copper plate engraving, etc. — a legacy spanning the years 1790 to the 1920's.

The Taylors of Ongar, as they have come to be called, to distinguish them from another literary family of the same name in a different part of England, have fascinated Christina Duff Stewart, a book selector for the Graduate Research programme in English and Drama at the University of Toronto Library, for decades. In fact, her curiosity and interests led to a life-long addiction, which resulted in her amassing 750 artifacts, including books, manuscripts, art work and letters, pertaining to this family. Her gift, to Toronto's Osborne Library of her entire collection, has not only boosted their already significant holdings but made it the largest, most comprehensive research source, of Taylor material, in the world.

Ms. Stewart, a Canadian citizen and resident of Toronto, wrote her thesis, on the Taylors, in 1967, and sometime later, did research for a bibliography of Taylor books. "By that time I had bought a number of Taylor books which had come on the market," she said while trying to explain her addiction. "I had no idea what the bibliography entailed. It was a horrendous job because among them the family wrote 73 books and they all went into many, many editions ... some as many as over 100 each. I was trying to find everything I could that was anywhere, so that I could make the bibliography complete." When it was published in 1975 by an American company, she found that she had become, without her even realizing it, the Taylor expert.

In her research she discovered that some of the family still lived in England. She went to visit and was mesmerized by the wealth of their collection as it included paintings and original manuscripts. As only luck would have it, Stewart was contacted by a lawyer, some years later and told that the owner, a Taylor descendant, had "bequeathed the entire collection to me. By this time I had a room in my house, just for the collection."

After the publication of her bibliography people realized that Taylor artifacts were important. "Purchasing books got harder because people knew the books were rare. The prices got higher and higher and the books disappeared. Although it was great fun while it lasted, it did get to be a problem. I had to do something with the collection. I had offers from the States, but it meant that one institution would take the pictures, another the manuscripts and another the books. I couldn't do it. I decided since I had worked at the Osborne and loved it so much, this was where it should reside permanently."

Who were the Taylors of Ongar? According to Stewart, the first Isaac Taylor (1730-1807), was a publisher, bookseller and engraver who married a great-grand niece of Milton's mother. Their son, Isaac (1759-1829) was a non-conformist minister, also an engraver of note; he and his wife, Ann had: Ann, (1782-1866), Jane (1783-1824) Jeffrerys, (1792-1853) Isaac (1787-1865) and Jemima, who didn't write.

In 1798 Ann purchased the periodical, *Minor's Pocket Book*, for which she "unravelled enigma, charade and rebus, and forwarded the results to the publisher, William Darton. Jane followed suit and by 1803 Darton requested a volume of poetry from the sisters. By the time the second book was published, in 1806, the sisters were established as writers.

"They burst upon the nurseries, like a rocket," explained Ms. Stewart "people had never heard such poems before. They were moralistic but they had a new note in them; a freshness, a simplicity, a tolerance, a humour, a knowledge of children using subjects that little children would know about like washing, dressing and getting up."

Jane died about 1824 of cancer. "Ann had the most extraordinary courtship and married the Rev. Joseph Gilbert. Although she continued to write after her marriage, it wasn't significant. Jeffreys was almost a recluse. He was lame and very good looking. He married and had one child. Both Jeffreys and Isaac, who became a lay theologian, wrote for the young." As well, Isaac gained a reputation as a miniaturist and Bible illustrator. He was an inventor too. His beer-keg spigot was so unique that it was patented and used in Britain in all of the pubs. Their father, the Rev. Isaac, published a variety of books and his wife Ann wrote a series of manuals on conduct and behaviour."

Although Christina Duff Stewart obviously enjoyed writing, collecting, and amassing this monumental collection, her greatest pleasure, judging by the expression on her face when she talked about it, came the day she visited England and the Taylor's house which is now used by lawyers. "I went up to Jane's attic and saw the piece of sky that she was probably looking at when she wrote 'The Star.'"

The collection — including the books, an oil portrait of Jane and Ann Taylor, painted by their father Isaac in 1792, an album of drawings put together by Ann Gilbert, as well as a love letter from her husband, the Rev. Gilbert — is a tribute to collector Christina Duff Stewart for it shows how one person's curiosity, devotion, and committment can be of benefit to so many others. The Osborne Collection is part of the Toronto Public Library. (Boys and Girls House, 40 St. George Street, Toronto. Call ahead to make an appointment.)

The Art of Collecting

"I like antiques and would love to collect," wrote one of my readers, "but I am afraid. Can you tell me how to begin?"

There is no secret formula. Get involved and make it happen. When antiques were not as costly as they are today, you could simply blunder into an antique shop or participate in an auction sale, happily coming away with a five-dollar purchase. Those days are over, and when prices are high it is imperative to understand what collecting is all about.

First, question your motivations. Do you want to decorate your home with antiques? Do you want to collect just one group or several? If you wish to specialize, find the area that attracts you the most. Is it primitives, fine china, art deco, textiles, etc.? Are you becoming involved to accumulate assets or to be a connoisseur? When you have made your choice, learn the terms and vocabulary pertaining to collecting in

Above: Catherine Thuro, oil lamp collector and author of *Oil Lamps: The Kerosene Era in North America. (Photo: HWF)*
Right: "Doc" John Hawkshaw, Toronto antique dealer and teddy bear collector. (*Photo: HWF*)

general; head for the local library and read everything you can find about the area you have selected. If you plan to decorate with antiques, check books on furniture and look for styles that appeal to you.

Learn about fakes and reproductions, colouring and *how* specific items were made. Ask about countries of origin, about particular periods and when certain antiques were created. At the same time get out into the marketplace, visit shops, antique shows and museums. Find out about auctions and how they operate; talk to dealers and collectors you respect, and ask them about styles, prices and anything else that can help you increase your knowledge. Above all, handle the artifacts, examine them, smell and feel them!

I asked some of the most respected Canadian experts what their advice would be to someone about to begin antique collecting. Here are some of their comments and suggestions.

*Jack Kerr-Wilson, president,
Phillips Ward-Price, Toronto:*
Whenever anybody comes to me and says they would like to begin collecting I always tell them not to buy anything until they have gone around to the trade, the shops and auction rooms. After a short time, they will find out that their taste starts drawing them in a certain direction. They shouldn't be embarrassed at the way in which it goes. Just because someone says that a certain piece is hideous doesn't mean that it won't give you pleasure. The novice should buy what he likes because he has to live with it.

William Jackson, proprietor,
The Paisley Shop, Toronto:
I don't think novice collectors should buy at auctions. When I can't sell something or want to get rid of pieces because they aren't good enough for me I send them to be auctioned. They bring in more than I had marked them at my store. The novice collector gets caught up in the show business of it all. He sees his friends there and likes to be seen....

Henry Dobson, dealer in fine furniture,
Plattsville, and Toronto, Ontario:
Before I buy a piece of glass or a print — both areas outside my field — I make the necessary phone calls. I don't feel demeaned by doing it. A lot of collectors think that they are the lesser for asking advice. Not me.

The majority of connoisseur collectors I know went to the United States to take their training, not to make judgements of authenticity but to learn how to look at pieces. Canadians are at a disadvantage here; we just don't have the reservoir of "great" pieces. It may not be simple to understand what constitutes a "great" piece but then you're not buying wood or a clump of wool.

John Forbes, Canadiana and country dealer,
Guelph, Ontario:
When a new collector looks at a piece of furniture, he should consider condition first, then choose something that is aesthetically pleasing to him and yet has some market merit. He should also look for structural repairs, condition of paint, and so on. Remember, the general state should reflect the price.

Provenance is the least important factor. Where the piece comes from is irrelevant unless you are trying to collect Canadiana only, for example. That, by the way, I don't advise for novice collectors. Antiques from England and the United States have a better international market. Nor do I advocate collecting merely regional items. I will buy back anything from a collector, at the price that was paid. If it's three or ten years down the road, I'll even pay a profit. It is so difficult to find good pieces today.

Robert Russell, former general manager,
Waddington's, Toronto:
Rely on the opinions of reputable dealers and experienced collectors. Most academics aren't in the marketplace and don't handle or see as many pieces as dealers or advanced collectors.

One of my *Toronto Star* columns printed in 1986, entitled "Eight Great Tips if you're planning to build a collection" was a collaboration of advice from myself and Don Lake, proprietor of D. & E. Lake Ltd. and Lake Galleries in Toronto, specialist dealer in antiquarian books, maps, prints and art. We concluded that there were about eight important points for the novice to keep in mind. Here are some of the highlights of our conversation and the article:

1. **Do your homework.**
Besides reading everything ever printed on the topic, find and meet the best dealers. Interview them. Ask questions no matter how silly they might initially seem. Lake pointed out that dealers have a vested interest in helping collectors: "It is the role of the dealer to create great clients; to make them sophisticated and in a sense, to play a leadership role in developing connoisseurship."

2. **Define Goals.**
After deciding on your collecting purposes, choose a subject according to its availability. Remember some things are not only difficult but impossible to acquire today. Be realistic. After goals have been established, learn who the

movers and shakers are in your particular area. Seek out the very best. Be aggressive.

3. Buy quality.

Buy the best you can afford from the dealers who handle the best. The last few words are important, Lake says, because, "the difference between a good dealer and an average, everyday dealer, is that the good dealer worships quality and he buys and sells only the best. "An average dealer's best might be just mediocre quality, especially in the international marketplace. As well, when it comes time to liquidate, the best sells fast. Great artifacts live forever. It is much harder to dispose of medium quality pieces.

4. Have self-confidence.

You must be able to rely on your own good taste, your own judgment, your own intuition. Don't buy what is trendy. Buck the fads. Learn to make them yourself. Never buy anything on someone else's suggestion. Buy only those things you truly love and can't live without.

Also, new collectors must be aware of the way the market fluctuates. A great deal depends on the state of the economy. In addition, the market always moves in cycles. When Oriental rugs are hot, it's either the time to learn about another field or stop buying them altogether. Now, for instance, rugs on on a downslide. The market is sluggish. It might be a good time to learn about the area and consider buying.

5. Condition is important.

In Lake's experience, condition is almost always the most important factor in determining the item's value. Try to buy not only the best, but artifacts that are in perfect condition; things that don't need an apology. The difference in price between a mediocre artifact and a superlative one can be 100 percent. Condition, no matter what the kind of artifact, from baseball cards to paintings, is crucial.

6. Rarity.

"This," says Lake, "can't be based merely on the experience of one dealer. Rarity is an absolute word. It comes from the cumulative experience of the entire marketplace." Of course, condition becomes secondary in a rare or unique item. A truly rare piece will live forever. There will always be a buyer. No matter what the price.

7. It's costly.

Sure the experts might be able to fluke a bargain here or there, but most of us who dabble will never find one. "Don't think about bargains," says Lake. "In the long term, if you buy quality, what is not a bargain today, will be tomorrow."

And remember, there is a downside to being a collector. Unless you are a dealer or an expert, you cannot expect to make a profit on your collection in the short term. You must be prepared to hold on to your purchases for many years. (See page 10 for more details on this subject.)

8. Protect your yourself.

Don't buy from dealers who hold things on consignment. "If they can't afford to own the items, then you probably can't either," says Lake. Also, make sure the dealer has clear title to the piece. Protect yourself from buying stolen or faked goods. Get a bill itemizing all the details the dealer has verbally stated. In addition, get an independent appraisal of very expensive items. Make sure you get what you have paid for. Don't rely on the dealer's word alone. After all, he has a lot at stake.

Establishing Provenance

Not long ago I received a telephone call from an acquaintance who had just acquired a piece of furniture with a signature hidden in the back of one of the drawers. His first words to me were "You know how to research; teach me how to do it!"

Researching is neither easy nor cheap, but it is part of the fun of collecting. When writing letters of inquiry always include a stamped, self-addressed envelope (SASE) or an international stamp coupon when you are dealing with a foreign country.

To research a specific name in Canada or the United States, begin by contacting the local genealogical society. Most Canadian provinces have their own organizations and many publish bulletins for their members. For a list of major Canadian genealogical societies see the end of this chapter.

Canadian church records, cemetery stones, wills, birth and death certificates can also yield a great deal of information. Read at least one of the following: *In Search of Your Roots, A Guide for Canadians Seeking Their Ancestors; The Genealogist's Encyclopedia;* or *Your Family History.* (See page 23.)

You can also hire a genealogist. They are usually familiar with records and material in their own geographical areas. Most charge approximately $20 per hour, plus mailing and photocopy expenses. To find a genealogist, contact historical societies, archives and museums in localities you are investigating. Generally, they will send out lists of genealogists' names, leaving the ultimate choice to you.

Old newspapers contain a wealth of information. They list marriages, deaths, curious happenings, advertisements and events which could involve the people you are researching. Most Canadian museums, archives and libraries have their old newspapers on microfilm; reading them is tedious but well worth the effort.

Mika and Hunterdon House Publishing Company specialize in old and rare book reprints at a significantly lower price than the originals but just as good for research purposes. To obtain a list of current titles contact Mika, Box 536, Belleville, ON K8N 5B2, and Hunterdon House, 38 Swan Street, Lambertville, NJ 08530.

Antiquarian books provide a wealth of information. Hundreds were written by local genealogists or historically minded individuals.

Archives and museums are other valuable areas to investigate, as they hold unpublished manuscripts, letters and diaries. Generally, they will not provide a detailed outline but will advise if they hold anything of interest. A list of these institutions is included on page 24. Finally, if you are overwhelmed by the whole genealogical research maze you might to contact the following organization for help:

The Genealogical Research Library
86 Gerrard St. East, #8E
Toronto, ON M5B 2J1
Phone: 979-1782

Bibliography
Books
On Collecting and Collectors (some are out of print but likely available from antiquarian book dealers. They are worth the hunt!):

Behrman, S.N. *Duveen*. Random House, 1952.

Hood, Dora. *The Side Door*. Toronto: Ryerson Press, 1958.

Rheims, Maurice. *The Glorious Obsession*. Souvenir Press, 1980.

Sack, Harold with Max Wilk. *American Treasure Hunt: The Legacy of Israel Sack*. Little, Brown and Co., 1986.

Stillinger, Elizabeth. *The Antiquers*. New York: Alfred A. Knopf, 1980.

General References
Baxter, Angus. *In Search of Your Roots, A Guide for Canadians Seeking Their Ancestors*. Toronto: Macmillan of Canada, 1978.

Leonoff, Cyril Edel. *Pioneers, Pedlars and Prayer Shawls, the Jewish Communities in British Columbia and the Yukon*. Victoria, BC: Sono Nis Press, 1978.

Matthews, C.M. *Your Family History*. London: Letterworth Press, 1976.

Pine, L.G. *The Genealogist's Encyclopedia*. New York: Collier Books, Macmillan Publishing Co. Inc.

Rottenberg, Dan. *Finding Our Fathers: a Guidebook to Jewish Genealogy*. New York: Random House, 1977.

The following books list genealogical societies, museums and archives in North America:

Directory of Canadian Records and Manuscript Repositories, published by the Association of Canadian Archivists, Ottawa, ON KIA ON3.

The Official Directory of Canadian Museums, 400-280 Metcalfe St., Ottawa, ON K2P 1R7. ($60) (Over 1, 900 Institutions listed.)

Journals.
The Canadian Genealogist, 172 King Henry's Blvd., Agincourt, ON MIT 2V6. Quarterly, edited by Elizabeth and George Hancocks, well-known Canadian genealogists.

The Nova Scotia Historical Review, Public Archives of Nova Scotia, 6016 University Ave., Halifax, NS B3H 1AV4. Published quarterly.

Toledot, published four times a year by the United States journal of Jewish Genealogy, 808 West End Ave., Suite 1006, New York, NY.

Genealogical Societies

Alberta Genealogical Society, Box 12015, Station A, Edmonton, AB T5J 3L2.

Genealogical Association of Royal Nova Scotia, Box 641, Station M, Halifax, NS B3J 2T3.

B.C. Archives and Records Service, 655 Belleville Street, Victoria, BC V8V 1X4.

British Columbia Genealogical Society, Box 94371, Richmond, BC V6Y 2A8.

New Brunswick Genealogical Society, PO Box 3235, Station B, Fredericton, NB E3A 2WO.

Ontario Genealogical Society, 40 Orchardview Blvd., St. 251, Toronto, ON MYR 1B9.

The North American Black Historical Museum, 277 King Street, Amhertburg, ON N9V 2C7.

Prince Edward Island Genealogical Society, Box 2744, Charlottetown, PEI C1A 8C4.

Quebec Family History Society, Box 1026, Postal Station, Pointe Claire, PQ H9S 4H9.

The United Empire Loyalist Association, Dominion Headquarters, 23 Prince Arthur Ave., Toronto, ON M5R IB2. Their *Loyalist Gazette* is published four times a year.

Canadian Jewish Historical Society, Congregation Beth El, 2525 Mark Ave., Windsor, ON N9E 2W2. Bulletin published twice a year.

The American Jewish Historical Society, 2 Thornton Rd., Waltham, MA 02154.

The Jewish Historical Society of British Columbia, 950 West 41 Street, Vancouver, BC V5Z 2N7.

The Jewish Historical Society of Western Canada, 402-365 Hargrave Street, Winnipeg, MB R3B 2K3.

Directory of Canadian Archives

Canadian Council of Archives, Secretariat, 344 Wellington Street, Room 5078, Ottawa, ON K1A 0N3.

Public Archives of Canada, 395 Wellington St., Ottawa, ON KIA ON3.

Provincial Archives of Alberta, 12845-102 Ave., Edmonton, AB T5N OM6.

Provincial Archives of Manitoba, 200 Vaughan St., Winnipeg, MB R3C OP8.

Provincial Archives of Newfoundland, Colonial Buildings, Military Rd., St. John's, NF AIC 5E2.

Public Archives of Nova Scotia, 6016 University Ave., Halifax, NS B3H IW4.

Archives of Ontario, 77 Grenville St., Toronto, ON M7A 2R9.

Public Archives of Prince Edward Island, PO Box 1000, Charlottetown, PEI CIA 7M4.

Archives Nationales du Quebec, CP 10450, Sainte Foy, PQ G1V 4N1.

Saskatchewan Archives Board, 3303 Hillsdale Street, University of Regina, Regina, SK S4S 0A2.

Archives Branch, Government of the Northwest Territories, Prince of Wales Building, Yellowknife, NWT XIA 2L9.

Archives of the Yukon Territory, PO Box 2703, Whitehorse, YK YIA 2C6.

Some Recommended Antiquarian Book Dealers

About Books, 280 Queen Street W., Toronto, ON M5V 2A1.

Acadia Books, 232 Queen Street East, Toronto, ON M5A 1S3.

Another Man's Poison, 161 John Street, Toronto, ON.

Atticus Books, 84 Harbord Street, Toronto, ON Bjarne's Books, 10005-82nd Avenue, Edmonton, AB T6E 1Z2.

David Mason Books, 342 Queen St. West, Toronto, ON M5V 2A2.

D & E Lake Ltd., 239 King St. East, Toronto, ON M5A 1J9.

Hugh Anson-Cartwright, 229 College Street, Toronto, ON M5T 1R4.

Huronia-Canadian Books, Box 685, Alliston, ON LOM IAO.

Joseph Patrick Books, PO Box 100, Station V, Toronto, ON M6R 3A4.

McBurne and Cutler, 698 Queen Street West, Toronto, ON M6J 1E7.

Michel Brisebois-Libraire, CP 246, Station B, Montreal, PQ H3B 1J7.

Old Favourites Book Shop Ltd., 255 Adelaide St. W., Toronto, ON M5H 1X8.

J. Patrick McGahern Books, 763 Bank St., Ottawa, ON KIS 3V5.

Princeton Antiques Bookfinders, 2915-17-31 Atlantic Ave., Atlantic City, NJ 08401. Outstanding Book Search Service.

Robert Dalton Harris & Diane DeBlois, PO Box 175, Wynantskill, NY 12198.

St. Nicholas Books, PO Box 863, Station F, Toronto, ON M4Y 2N7 (Children's Books and Related Material).

Stephen C. Lunsford Books, PO Box 86773, North Vancouver, BC V7I 4I3.

The Village Bookstore, 239 Queen St. W., Toronto, ON M5V IZ4. (Also a good source for contemporary books on antiques.)

2

The Business of Buying and Selling Antiques

High interest rates, the stock market and the general state of the economy directly affect the antique market. When times are good and collectors with money are plentiful, antiques carry high price tags. Museum quality artifacts disappear quickly from dealers' stocks as collectors compete for an opportunity to buy the best. This, obviously, is not the ideal time to make large purchases. When the economy is sluggish, dealers are anxious to turn over their stock and some may be receptive to offers, trades or on-time payments. Many outstanding pieces become available when collectors encounter cash-flow problems and are forced to raise money by disposing of items in their collections. Some are even willing to accept significant losses.

While economic ups and downs are important, there is no doubt that antiques and collectibles move in cycles brought about by museum exhibitions, books and magazine articles. The trick is to spot these trends before they burgeon into fads.

Samplers are an excellent case in point. For years, no one paid much attention to these small pieces of needlework that dealers were giving away for as little as $75 and $100 per piece. Yet, there were collectors, mainly in the United States and in England, who did acquire sam-

plers, and when in 1978 New York's Museum of Folk Art exhibited Theodore H. Kapnek's collection, it was extensively covered by trade magazines and newspapers. Kapnek had assembled his samplers over ten years and an imposing book-catalogue had established them as an area of collecting worthy of attention. When Kapnek died in the summer of 1980, his much publicized collection was offered in January 1981 at a spectacular auction sale. Prices soared because everyone who ever had heard about his samplers and had seen them illustrated wanted to own just a small piece. As a result, it became difficult to buy a single good sampler in the United States. Competition still is vigorous, and prices, to say the least, are very high.

Not only is it sensible to buy certain items when they are not fashionable but it is also prudent to sell them when prices are at their peak. If we could examine the records of various auction sales, we would soon see that advanced collectors and astute dealers sell at the top of the cycle when investors attracted by high auction prices buy. Perhaps that is one reason why some collectors ultimately do well financially, even though they are not directly responsible for these developments. As one observer explained, "Collectors buy primarily because they love art and prefer to buy it as cheaply as possible. They are turned off by rising prices, because the consequence is less art for the money."

Since each geographical area has its own particular "hot items," it makes good sense to buy in locations where collectors have not yet become aware of the specific pieces, merchandise is easier to come by and prices are lower. For example, antique lighting fixtures dating back to the early days of electricity were in demand in Quebec City well before Ontario collectors paid much attention to them. Similarly, collectors in the American Midwest paid high prices for 1920 oak furniture at a time when there was virtually no demand for it in Canada. In these instances, pickers and dealers become transporters, moving antiques and collectibles to areas where they will fetch the highest prices.

A dealer's truck after "picking" Nova Scotia. Someone playfully gave him the "yard sale" sign. *(Photo: HWF)*

How Antique Dealers Buy

According to what is shown on television and described in books, antique dealers' shops should be located in seedy, rundown neighbourhoods where buildings are decrepit, store interiors dark and dingy and everything is covered with dust. The owners usually are depicted as strange, at best, and sinister, at worst. Many of the problems besetting the antique market today flow from these misconceptions.

Contrary to public belief, antique dealers do not wave magic wands to make their merchandise appear from nowhere. In England, "knockers" (people who literally knock on doors looking for merchandise) and "runners" (people who run from shop to shop offering goods to shop owners) are the middlemen of the antique business. The North American equivalent is the "picker" who does two jobs, for he is a broker as well. The pieces he picks are taken by truck from shop to shop, from town to town. Rarely

does he keep stock for long nor does he have a fixed business address. He knows what will sell where and for how much.

Each dealer has a favourite picker and tries to buy from him whenever possible so that his shop will be the picker's first stop the next time. Competition among dealers for that initial call is fierce. Some even arrange to pay premiums to well-known pickers, guaranteeing to buy everything they offer in order to remove them as sources for competitors.

A story is told about an Ontario dealer who tried to get to a Quebec dealer's picker just before he was to bring in a load of merchandise. The Ontario dealer waylaid the truck about a mile down the road from the Quebec dealer's shop and proceeded to skim off the best pieces. The Quebecker got wind of it and set out to teach the Ontarian a lesson. He purchased a fake diamond-point armoire and placed it in a nearby farmhouse. One night, the Ontario dealer, duped by the picker, agreed to pay a hundred-dollar premium for information about the cupboard's whereabouts plus the cost of the piece. He picked it up at night but when he examined it in broad daylight realized he had been fooled.

Because of the scarcity of truly good pickers, their identities are closely guarded secrets. Although, as a rule, they do not deal directly with the public, there are occasions when they come out of the woodwork. The most notable exception is the Bowmanville Spring Antique and Folk Art Show where select pickers are allowed to participate. Occasionally a few even set up booths and display their merchandise in the parking lot, much to the displeasure of the professional dealers, and because their overhead expenses are lower than those of regular exhibitors their prices generally are lower as well.

Dealers also acquire merchandise by buying complete estates for a fixed amount. Among the "treasures" they acquire are things they will reject, possibly because of lack of expertise in a particular area. In these instances, an advanced collector may find a bargain, especially if he is more familiar with their value than the dealer.

Goods also can be bought sight unseen from abroad, usually in containers, shipped from Great Britain to a Canadian wholesaler and then forwarded to a dealer or an auction house. Although labelled "antiques," they often consist of goods manufactured well after World War I. It is easy to recognize these pieces as they frequently are poor imitations of well-known furniture styles as well as a lot of new brass artifacts such as spittoons and car horns.

Occasionally, a dealer is called to a home to view items a prospective client wishes to dispose of. If he is reputable, he will appraise them fairly, advise the client of their value and either make a verbal or, in the case of a genuinely precious article, a written offer to purchase which the owner can accept or reject.

Auctions are another source where dealers can acquire stock. However, many find it difficult to compete with those collectors who are new at the game and often willing to pay prices that are inconsistent with the market. Some dealers shun auctions altogether because they see them as competition or places where articles can be overexposed and, therefore, become less desirable. On the other hand, there are dealers, especially in the United States and in England, who view auction sales as events that will benefit them and their businesses. They believe that if they are seen there paying record-high prices for certain items and the transactions are subsequently reported in the press, the resulting publicity will enhance their credibility and result in an influx of new customers.

Buying from Antique Dealers

All it takes to become an antique dealer is the desire and the ability to fill out the proper papers for a tax exemption permit. They do not have to pass exams and may enter the business without much experience and previously acquired knowledge. There are no policing agencies to check the possible presence of fakes and reproductions in shops or at shows. Apart from standard consumer protection organizations there are few, if any, agencies that collectors can turn to for help in case of trouble.

Before choosing a dealer consult trade magazines and newspapers. Check the advertisements to find out whether a particular dealer has a high profile in the community. Does he participate only in prestigious shows avoiding flea markets and shopping malls? Look at his library. How large is it? Is he trying to broaden his knowledge? Is he mentioned in the acknowledgements of books dealing with the collecting area you have chosen?

In other words, select your antique dealer as you would a dentist or a lawyer. Check with local collectors, experts and museum curators for references and recommendations. Who do the experts go to when they need advice? Do journalists specializing in antiques repeatedly quote certain dealers' opinions in newspapers, trade journals and in magazine articles? (Ignore ordinary staff writers of daily newspapers; they usually turn to the dealers with the highest visibility and the nicest looking antique shops.)

The novice collector would do well to consider a dealer with a well-established business as opposed to one who merely travels the show circuit, although there are exceptions. A reputable shop owner may allow you to take home an item on approval and may be quite happy to arrange term payments if immediate total cash settlement is a hardship. For your protection, insist on a detailed bill of sale, listing any restorations, provenance, age, value, complete description and a money-back guarantee, just in case the piece has been misrepresented by the dealer.

These services are not available when purchasing from an auction house. This is one reason why antiques may cost a little more than when they are bought in a shop. The novice collector is better off spending those extra dollars than risking possible loss. The following stories illustrate this point.

Some time ago, David Tyrer, former Canadiana specialist at Waddington's, Toronto, was asked to appraise a dining-room suite belonging to a certain real estate broker who mistrusted and refused to do business with antique dealers. Tyrer told him the set was relatively new, had a top retail value of about $3,000 and would bring about $2,000 at auction. This was not happy news for the owner who had purchased the suite from his aunt for $8,000! Because he had neither bill of sale nor return privileges he was stuck.

A similar case involves a young couple who, totally unfamiliar with the antique marketplace or textiles, one day found themselves looking at Oriental rugs in an elegant carpet shop. Without ever having read a book on the subject or visiting another store, they put down $7,000 as deposit on a rug valued by the vendor at $17,000. Because they were in the midst of moving they decided to leave it at the shop until it could be delivered to their new home. A month later they began to have second thoughts about their purchase, especially after consulting an expert who felt the rug was vastly overpriced. They tried to recover their deposit but the shop owner refused to return it. The couple sued and spent about three days in court but ultimately lost the case on the grounds that theirs had been a normal business transaction and therefore did not entitle them to a refund.

This last case illustrates the importance of comparison shopping, especially for items you are not familiar with. Also, the dealer with the smartest shop located in a trendy part of town is not necessarily the one to give you the best service, merchandise or price.

Buying at Antique Shows

Die-hard antique enthusiasts feel the same excitement and pre-curtain jitters before the opening of a great antique show as opera buffs do before a Placido Domingo concert or sports fans before a Stanley Cup playoff game. In fact, when passions and emotions are stirred there isn't much difference between a crazed hockey fan and an addicted antique collector. Manners? Etiquette? What are they anyway?

Antique dealer, Henry Dobson recalls one incident that took place in the early 1970's when he participated in the prestigious Canadian Antique Dealers Association Show. "There was a

29

long line-up before the show. Several of the big collectors were after something in my booth. One of them was so anxious to get to it that when the show opened, he knocked down the security guard, jumped over him, and made a lunge for the piece. That was a memorable event, all right."

Collectors remember a similar experience at the 1979 Kingston Antique Show when an Ontario dealer bullied his way to the front of the pre-show line-up, pushed aside a portable divider just as the show opened and ran ahead of everyone else. In his blind haste he knocked over a dealer's child, causing his head to hit the concrete floor. Observers claim he didn't even look back. He just charged ahead and grabbed a burl bowl from a young girl's hands. She moved over to a ship carving and held the tag. At that point the mad dasher, as he came to be called, touched the other end of the carving and boomed out: "I have it!"

Such behaviour sparked discussions of show etiquette. How should collectors act when they first come into a show? What is the proper way to buy if two people are after the same piece? Should customers have signed, blank cheques in their hands in case this kind of situation arises? Or, should they have sold stickers and simply slap them on the pieces as they go round the show? Although there hasn't been a rigid procedure laid down, show promotors started becoming aware of 'potential' situations and have taken steps to make certain that no one could butt-in on people who had queued, sometimes for twelve hours before show time. Too, dealers became hawk-eyed; aware of the first people in their booth. They were determined this sort of thing would not continue.

Now, collectors after a specific item try to be the first in line, even if it means hiring someone to hold their spot. Often, they make a consious

effort to look calm and sedate. Furthermore, a few show promotors try to discourage buying between dealers before the show opens—in order that collectors feel their wait in line is worthwhile—by writing into the contracts that this practice is not allowed. Although it isn't as blatant, a few dealers still do it quietly.

How to See a Show

Antique shows, especially the very large ones can be confusing, with so much material to consider. One experienced collector has the solution to handling this overload." First, get a general idea in your mind of the layout of the building. I usually walk it, like a Loblaws store up and down the isles. I never buy anything the first time around. I try to allow myself at least two hours for a major show. The first sixty minutes to digest everything and the second to give my favourite things another look." In addition, she approaches a show with an idea of what she is looking for: furniture for a specific spot in her house, a piece of jewelry, a birthday gift for her husband. Then, she concentrates on that when she is going around.

Henry Dobson has another suggestion. He says collectors shouldn't just buy or look at their favourite dealer's stock. Rather, they should explore the entire show, especially the new dealer's booths. As an example he talked about a recent experience. "A couple came into my shop in Plattsville, Ontario and asked why they had never seen or heard of me before. I found that fascinating since I had taken part in shows, for years, right next to their favourite dealer. But they said, at shows, they only bought from him. They didn't notice or look at anything anyone else had."

Ask dealers, if you are looking for something special. "They might have just what you want back in their shop or in the bottom drawer of the showcase," says Kip Gemmell, antique jewelry specialist based in Lindsay, Ontario. I've had collectors go from dealer to dealer asking for a specific item and the very serious ones have special want cards printed, with their names, addresses and phone numbers."

Also, she advises that if you fall in love with something but need time to rethink your finances, or figure out where to put it, "ask the dealer to put the item away or hold it while you stop for tea." Dealers are usually quite happy to comply with this, especially if it might prevent tears as happened at a recent antique show.

Barbara McDonald, a dealer in folk art and nostalgia, tells the story about a seventeen-year-old girl who fell in love with two vintage teddy bears in her booth. "She couldn't make up her mind which one she should buy and decided to go for a walk. When she came back, minutes later, one of the bears had sold. That was the one she had decided to buy. Naturally. The poor kid just stood in front of my booth and cried." Had she known to ask, Mrs. McDonald would have been pleased to hold both bears for a while.

A Dealer's Point of View

What is an antique show like from a dealer's prospective? Without exception, the dealers interviewed all had the same reaction. They used words like "exciting and fun" as well as "exhausting, boring, frustrating and aggravating." The one thing that universally upsets them is the frequent comment, "My grandmother had one just like that but she threw it away. If only I had it now." There is only one answer to that. Some ubiquitous soul said it best on an unsigned poster:

THE ONLY ONE INTERESTED IN WHAT YOUR GRANDMOTHER HAD WAS YOUR GRANDFATHER

Second on the dealer hate-list has to be the way most people think dealers price their goods. Says Toronto dealer, R.A. O'Neil "It is a fallacy that dealers put their prices up at shows. If anything we keep them realistic because we want to sell the stuff, not show it." He violently objects to the way some individuals try to get prices down. "There is a nice way to dicker with a dealer — Can you do any better? What will you let it go for? What is your best price? But don't tell me what you'll give me for the piece. Forget it."

On the other hand, many dealers are no longer reducing their prices. "I don't give discounts anymore," advised one well-known show dealer who asked to remain anonymous, "because this stuff is getting too hard to find and it takes so much time out of my life to find and buy the really great stuff. It annoys me to think that people ask for discounts." Almost as an afterthought she added that "these same people don't expect discounts from Eatons or Simpsons, so why should they from me?" What she didn't say was that expenses at antique shows are steep. Booth rental can go as high as $1,500 a show. Add costs for food and accomodation, if the show is out of town as well as travel costs, moving exenses, and so on. No wonder discounts annoy some dealers.

In addition, when customers ask for a better price and then don't want to pay tax, dealers see purple. As Kip Gemmell says, "Why is it that people think we pocket the tax? Don't they know we have to pay it just the same as everyone else?" Others complain about collectors who quibble about the price, get it down as low as possible and then pay by credit card causing dealers to loose an additional 5-6% in fees to the card company.

Yet another dealer suggested that the whole situation has gotten out of control. According to her, many of her colleagues mark their goods up 10 to 20 percent to account for the bargain hunters. In the end, she says, it's the polite buyer, who suffers because he pays the full price. She didn't have an answer to the pricing dilemma but suggested that people who insist on wheeling and dealing on prices would be best off attending shows just before closing; when dealers might be anxious to sell, especially if business has been slow.

Selling at Shows

Many collectors eventually become dealers, even if they don't set out with that in mind. As they become sophisticated, improve their tastes and acquire more knowledge, they see better artifacts than their own. So they sell from the bottom to add to the top. Shows are the ideal places to do this kind of business, for dealers are there to buy as well as sell. The only rule is to approach the dealers when they are alone. No dealer wants customers to know his source, nor would he welcome your advances if you ruined a sale.

If you are serious about selling your treasure have clear photographs with you so that the dealer will know if he should take the time to make a house call. Before you offer the piece to a dealer, know what it is and have a price in mind. Don't expect a dealer to make an offer or to give you a free appraisal. Dealers buy at the wholesale level because they have to cover their expenses and make a profit.

Remember, that antique shows are excellent places to begin learning about antiques, for they offer the services of numerous specialists and can, unlike museums, provide the novice with an opportunity to handle the goods.

For some people, however, antique shows are ideal spots to meet people. Antiques are almost an after-thought. "The individuals I have met at various fairs over the years, have added colour and richness to my life," says one well-known but anonymous Canadian collector. Others agree saying they are real social events. "You get to know the dealers and the collectors on a personal level. Its wonderful to share a cup of coffee, a bit of gossip and information," added Michael Bird, noted Ontario-based, folk art collector and author of five books. In fact, for Bird, this club-like atmosphere, is just as important as the show itself. He compares antique shows to movies and concerts. "Part of the enjoyment is savouring the experience, comparing notes with others, sharing the highlights. It isn't just the enjoyment of the moment; it is the after-effect."

Buying Privately

While newspaper advertisements often sound tantalizing, buying privately has been successful for only a handful of collectors. People with inherited antiques to sell usually ask unrealistically high prices because their value judgement is either coloured by what a friend has told them they should charge or because precious memories are connected with the piece. Whatever you do will be wrong in this situation. If you offer too much, you'll be "taken," and too little will hurt and offend the owner. It might be better to let professionals handle such transactions.

The Business of Selling Antiques

Disposing of antiques is part and parcel of being

a real collector and perhaps more difficult and more complicated than acquiring them. Yet, in order to buy well you must know how to sell. The story known as "The Cupboard in the Junk-room," which I originally wrote in the *Maine Antique Digest*, dramatically illustrates what can happen when selling is done without understanding antiques or the market.

Some years ago, Grant Temple, a farmer from Selkirk, Ontario, dropped into Peggy's Antique Shop in nearby Stoney Creek, to invite the proprietors, Mr. and Mrs. Spera, to look at some of the old bottles and sap buckets on his farm. The Speras agreed and while wandering through the farmhouse discovered a cupboard on the top floor that Mrs. Spera liked so much she offered to buy it, not for resale (as she later testified) but to put in her bedroom. Although Mr. Temple told her he was not interested in selling, Mrs. Spera returned to the farm a few more times in the hope of changing Mr. Temple's mind.

Finally, on October 9, 1975, he consented and the two parties agreed on a price of four hundred dollars — half the amount payable immediately and the balance before delivery in December of that same year.

A few days later, Mr. Temple heard that a similar cupboard, not as large nor in as good a condition as his, had been sold at a nearby auction for two thousand dollars. He brought in Nick Treanor, proprietor of Adam Haynes Antiques in St. Catharines, to view the piece. Treanor gave him a written appraisal and even offered to purchase the item for six thousand dollars. Failing to mention the Spera deal, Mr. Temple told him it was not for sale.

Shortly thereafter, Mrs. Spera arrived at the farm, pressing the balance of the purchase price on the owners who reluctantly accepted it but refused to let her have the cupboard when she returned to pick it up.

On December 16, 1975, Mr. Temple's lawyer informed the Speras that his client had decided to keep the piece for sentimental reasons, offering one hundred dollars as compensation and asking them to forget the whole deal. They refused to accept the money and immediately began legal proceedings against the Temples.

In the action for specific performance of a contract, heard in the Cayuga County Court before Judge W.W. Leach on April 2 and 3, 1979, antique dealer Henry Dobson appeared on behalf of the Speras. He described them not as experts but as people who pick up used furniture for resale to dealers. Nick Treanor, on the other hand, himself a specialist in Niagara Peninsula furniture, told the court that the plaintiffs were antique dealers like many others and, in fact, quite familiar with the particular style and type of furniture under dispute which, by now, had been correctly identified and labelled as "a six-foot-high walnut Niagara Peninsula Chippendale style linen press."

Despite arguments from Temple's lawyer that his client had the right to rescind the transaction because Mrs. Spera had knowingly misrepresented the cupboard, the judge ruled in her favour. In his written statement he concluded that "it is clear from the evidence that the parties entered into a contract for the purchase of the cupboard. The plaintiff has fulfilled her obligation under the contract and paid four hundred dollars. The defendants have defaulted as they refused delivery and still have the funds."

Judge Leach's decision, the only one of its kind in North America, also said that "the law says buyer beware *(caveat emptor)*. To this should be added seller beware. These cautions are particularly applicable in buying or selling antique furniture."

The Temples launched an appeal that was soon abandoned in favour of a settlement. Value of the piece at the time of the Judge's decision was estimated at between $8,000 and $10,000; today the cupboard would have a retail value of about $12,000 to $15,000.

A few years later, in the fall of 1981, several Ontario dealers were anxious to acquire a cupboard from another farmer. He refused to sell to any of them because he "didn't want to make mistakes." Suddenly, the cupboard was spotted in a local country auction by two knowledgeable dealers who agreed not to bid against each other. The piece went under the hammer for $1,000 to the one and his buddy immediately gave him a

The Temple family and the now-famous "Cupboard in the Junkroom." *(Photo: HWF)*

$250 profit. The dealer who had bought it for $1,250 sold it the next day to a third dealer for $8,000. Not even one week later, without spending a cent on restoration, the third dealer sold it to a fourth for a reported price of $17,000. Had the farmer initially dealt with any of the reputable dealers involved he would have made between $6,000 and $8,000. Instead he received $1,000, less the 25 per cent auctioneer's commission.

Both cases dramatically illustrate the real need for understanding what you own. However, learning to assess the value of an item is another matter because it is worth only as much as someone is willing to pay for it. The best way to test values is to place the antique into a well-advertised, big city auction. You will know what it is worth the instant it has been sold. Appraisers can tell you its approximate replacement price which generally is much higher than the amount you would receive if you sold it. My rule of thumb is that in the retail market an article is worth approximately 40 to 60 per cent less than its insured value. Most auction companies will base their appraisal on the amount they think the item will bring at auction. Retail prices usually are higher than that, although there are exceptions.

To sell an antique the following options are open to you:

Selling to a Dealer
Selling to a reputable dealer may be the best way to dispose of goods, as they move quickly, instantly recognize quality, and know how much to offer for an object. The vendor will be paid immediately, but the price he receives will not be as high as if he sold to a private customer because dealers must allow for overhead, interest on money while the piece is in their possession and profit. Unlike the general retail mer-

chant the antique dealer rarely doubles his cost. For exceptionally good pieces his mark-up will be about 35 per cent.

The dealer you choose should be a specialist in the object you are trying to sell. Don't expect an expert in Canadian furniture to be equally knowledgeable about antique gold jewelry. To ascertain who is right for you, visit shops, attend shows and make inquiries of those who are involved in the marketplace. Check trade magazines and newspapers to find out who is dealing in similar artifacts.

Selling Privately

You may find it difficult and time consuming to locate the person who might be interested in your particular "widget." Advertising in newspapers and magazines is expensive; not to mention the inconvenience, when you do get a reply, of having people walk in and out of your home to view the item you wish to sell. Some collectors don't seem to mind that; to them it is just part of the game.

Selling Through Auction

People, especially those who want or need money within a six-month period, find auction sales the best alternative because they are able to get rid of all their treasures at once and receive one lump sum in return.

The auction you choose should be widely publicized and well attended. No one wants to be left with a piece at reserve prices or at prices resulting from low bids. Before entering an item to be auctioned, allow for storage, cartage, photography and commission expenses. (See chapter on Auctions.)

Becoming a Dealer

You can, of course, set yourself up as a dealer at a local flea market. This method, more than any other, will teach you something about the marketplace. You need a sales tax exemption license before you start, and remember that even part-time dealing involves keeping books and filing monthly or semi-annual tax returns.

Donating to a Museum

As a last consideration you might like to donate your piece to a museum providing it is within their collecting needs and they are interested in owning it.

The one quarrel I have with giving antiques to museums is that it permanently removes ahem from the marketplace and from collectors who no longer can enjoy them. In many cases the pieces simply disappear into the museum's basement, never to be seen again. (See chapter entitled Antiques and the Government.)

It is important to remember that nothing lasts forever and while we may adore the things we collect in our lifetime, our children may not feel the same way about them. Your heirs should know how to properly dispose of your collection. Your records should be up to date and kept together with other important documents, including receipts, names and addresses of experts and detailed instructions concerning disposition.

3

Auctions

One toilet set, six pieces, as good as new, cost three dollars and a half. Sir? No, sir, they are not broke but the man selling them is; fifty cents-half a dollar-fifty-five, fifty-five, fifty-five-thank you, Madam-seventy-five, going eighty-five, that's right. One dollar-cheap-one dollar, one dollar and a quarter? Thank you, one and a quarter, make it half; thirty-five-yes, Madam, worth three and a half-fifty-one and a half and fifty-five, in time; fifty-five, fifty-five, fifty-five, sixty; one dollar and sixty cents, not half price. All done. Sold!*

That staccato, repetitive chant of the auctioneer is familiar to everyone, and although his words and style may differ from auction house to auction house and from country to country, everything else is the same — the drama, the suspense and the atmosphere. In fact, it is legitimate to compare auctions to games of chance because all the players are gamblers — the consignor, never certain how much money he will make or lose; the bidder, never certain how high he will be forced to bid and who he is bidding against; and the auctioneer whose income directly depends on how much the goods will fetch.

If things are that speculative, what is it that continuously draws the crowds? Is it the lure of a possible bargain, the chance to acquire something others want or is it the quality of the merchandise itself? For some it means social interaction; to others, satisfying their ego to be seen at certain prestigious sales. Those caught up in the drama will make sure they are noticed bidding on certain high-priced items, although

auction houses will never divulge the names of successful buyers.

There is a kind of "high" people experience inside an auction room. Some label it excitement while others describe it as "auction fever," a contagious disease which inexplicably causes those stricken with it to bid irrationally high on pieces they cannot afford or, worse, will not even want when they are in full control of their senses. It can affect anyone, but it generally is the neophyte who, unfamiliar with existing market prices and auction practises, drives up the bidding to unprecedented heights. Auctions, like everything else, are governed by laws, conventions and rules. To understand and observe them is fundamental to surviving in the antique business.

The Catalogue

Terms of sale usually appear either in the front or at the back of the catalogue. They include stipulations regarding bids and other auction procedures. Contrary to popular belief, the auctioneer does not have to accept every bid and

---

*Quoted from Powers, A.D. *How to Conduct an Auction.* Chicago: E.L. Fantus Co., circa 1900.

can withdraw an article from sale. He also can reject an increase after having acknowledged an opening bid if, in his opinion, it is not high enough. The auctioneer can change his mind before or even during the auction and has the right to withdraw an item prior to the sale if he suspects it to have been stolen, damaged, faked or misrepresented by the consignor.

When the auction hammer falls, the lot is considered sold and the bidding is over. Some catalogues state that on the fall of the hammer, title to the offered lot shall pass to the highest bidder who may be required to sign a confirmation of purchase and pay the full selling price. After the hammer has fallen, the purchaser generally assumes full risk and responsibility for the lot he has purchased. This means that even if the article is damaged by the auction house's staff *after* the bidding is concluded, the bidder must pay the full hammer price. The purchaser, therefore, is well advised to pay for the goods and take possession of them as soon as possible.

Most catalogues contain clauses to protect the gallery against claims by purchasers regarding damage done before or during the preview. One particular catalogue clearly states that "each and every lot is sold by the Vendor with all faults and defects and with all errors of description and is to be taken and paid for whether genuine and authentic or not, and no compensation shall be paid for same." Another advises that:

while the auctioneer has endeavoured to catalogue and describe correctly each lot to be sold, guarantee is not made of the correctness of the catalogue or other descriptions of the physical condition, size, importance, authenticity, attribution, provenance, exhibitors, literature, historical relevance of any lot and no statement

anywhere shall be deemed such a warranty, representation or condition and no sale will be set aside on account of any imperfections not noted. Every lot is sold 'as is' and without recourse.

One recently published Toronto catalogue tried to make the term slightly more palatable:

if within ten (10) days of the sale of any lot, the purchaser gives notice in writing to (........) that the lot so sold is a deliberate forgery and if, within ten (10) days of such notice, the purchaser returns the lot to (.......) in the same condition as at the time of sale and proves beyond a reasonable doubt that the returned lot is a deliberate forgery, considered in the light of the entry in the catalogue, the sale of the lot will be rescinded and the purchase price only will be refunded to the purchaser. The consignor agrees to be bound by the auctioneer's decision.

Consider the foregoing clause carefully. It is virtually impossible to find an expert who will provide, in writing, "complete documentation" of anything within a ten-day period, especially if a chemical analysis is required. Whose opinion counts in the decision whether or not a piece is a forgery? The purchaser's or the gallery expert's? Exactly what does "deliberate forgery" mean? (I've never heard of an accidental one.) By stating that "only the purchase price will be refunded," does it mean the purchaser loses the buyer's premium if the gallery agrees the price is a forgery?

This same catalogue goes on to warn that "by the making of a bid the buyer acknowledges his acceptance of these conditions and the terms of any notices and other conditions in the catalogue." Auction catalogue descriptions often are confusing and purposely obscure. Does it state that the artist was actually A.Y. Jackson, for instance? or is the painting merely attributed to him? D. and J. Ritchie of Toronto are one of the few Canadian auctioneers who have tried to clarify this point by printing a "Glossary of Art" at the back of their catalogues.

"In the style of" is another phrase that can trip up novice collectors. It does not mean that a piece is attributable to a particular source, only that it could have originated there but likely did not. It, therefore, should be interpreted to mean that the piece *resembles* work done by a particular factory, for example, but, in fact, was made elsewhere and probably at a later date. (It even could be a recent copy or reproduction.)

Not only are terms of sale governed by the material listed in the catalogue but also by announcements made at the beginning of an auc-

Glossary of Art*

Forename and Surname of Artist

The terms and statements shown in the glossary are qualified statements and are made subject to the provisions of the conditions of sale.

a) Cornelius Krieghoff
(The artist's first name or names and last name.)
In our opinion a work by the artist.

b) C. Krieghoff
In our qualified opinion a work which may be in whole or part by the artist.

c) Krieghoff
In our qualified opinion a work related to the style of the artist.

d) School of Cornelius Krieghoff
In our qualified opinion a work by a pupil or follower of the artist.

e) After Cornelius Kriegoff
In our qualified opinion a copy of the work of the artist

f) Signed
In our qualified opinion is the signature of the artist

g) Bears Signature
In our qualified opinion may be the signature of the artist.

h) Dated
In our qualified opinion was executed at about that date.

i) Bears date
In our qualified opinion may have been executed at about that date.

*Reprinted by permission of D. & J. Ritchie Ltd.

tion. As far as the gallery is concerned such announcements (additions or deletions) are part of the terms of sale, even if the bids were made by mail or over the telephone. As no one has ever challenged this practise in the courts, the legal implications are not clear, although they would be worth investigating.

While Canadian catalogues are full of disclaimers, it is not certain that these disclaimers can effectively release auction houses from liability. They can be compared to the tickets issued by parking-lot owners and the notices posted on their premises, repudiating all responsibility for articles stolen or vehicles damaged. Yet, Canadian courts consistently have held these people liable regardless of what is written on the ticket stubs or is posted on their property. One wonders what the courts would decide about the responsibility of auction houses regarding their disclaimers.

What about the people who authenticate the merchandise to be auctioned and those who compile the catalogues? They are, in Canada anyway, underpaid employees (except for a few at one or two auction houses), considering the hours they put in, setting up and dismantling shows and assisting during previews and sales. Henry Dobson, a respected Ontario dealer, believes that "by the very nature of the business, the auction houses attract certain academically trained, security-minded individuals, many of whom have very little experience with antiques and are not really experts on anything."

One particular auction was a prime example of Dobson's assessment. In the spring of 1981 a reputable auction company held a Canadian Heritage sale in Toronto. Most pieces had been documented by a cataloguer with little knowledge of the field. Artifacts were incorrectly catalogued, poorly documented and full of other errors and omissions. Estimates were unrealisti-

cally high. Lot 447, for instance, a Quebec diamond-point armoire, was not described as having been heavily restored and the high gallery estimate between $8,000 and $12,000 — indicated to the novice collector, at least, that it was a fine piece of furniture. Without doubt, that same armoire would be sitting in someone's antique shop, looking for a buyer at $3,500. Interestingly, bidding stopped at $5,500, and the lot was bought-in by the auction house. Needless to say, the auction was a total fiasco, as a large percentage of the items remained unsold.

While most others are not as problem ridden as this one was, many things can happen through carelessness or even because of honest error. Prudent prospective bidders, therefore, must first assume that pieces may be damaged or spurious and then set about proving to themselves that they are as described in the catalogue.

Two theories exist about the way objects are placed in the catalogue. The first is that items listed at the beginning often are teasers used to encourage those who still are a little shy and hesitant when the bidding opens. In fact, these early lots may be the best buys of the entire sale. The second theory is that high-priced items offered early in the sale will set the tone, indicating to prospective buyers that those to follow will command equally high prices.

About twenty years ago, two Van Gogh paintings were offered at a Sotheby Parke Bernet auction in New York City. When John L. Marion, the company's chairman, was asked why the more important of the two had been listed first and why both were sold early in the sale, he replied, "If you begin with the less valuable, people tend to hold back, whereas if the major picture is put up first, all the unsuccessful bidders can try for a second time."

To keep interest high and obtain good prices for mediocre items some auctioneers hold back the better pieces until halfway through the sale. Generally, the auction crowd begins to thin out about that time or perhaps a little later and many of the people who remain in the room's stuffy atmosphere are either too drowsy to participate or too busy gossiping with friends. This is prime buying time and possibly the best opportunity to pick up bargains.

The Preview

Never go to an auction without first attending the preview. There you can examine the pieces, compare them with catalogue descriptions, check whether repairs and damages were accurately noted and whether the estimates are realistic. Avoid weekends and evening hours, as they generally are too crowded to make close inspection possible. The best times are mornings or early afternoons when the gallery's experts are on hand to show the goods and answer questions.

Note the length of the preview time. Does it allow you to consult books, magazines and museum personnel? Can you bring in your own experts to authenticate pieces? Is a complete catalogue available at least one week prior to the auction?

During the preview make notes in your catalogue about interesting lots and check off pieces you consider marginal. Guess what they might fetch at the sale.

The Bidding

A bid constitutes the offer which an auctioneer is free to accept or reject. The sale is not complete until the auctioneer's hammer has fallen. Before that time a bidder can change his mind and withdraw his bid. According to Canadian contract law, he merely has to communicate to the auctioneer before the hammer has fallen that he wishes to retract his bid. If you are new to the game, by all means, attend the auction but *do not bid*. See what happens to the objects you have marked in your catalogue during the preview. Did they fetch what you had estimated? Or what the gallery had estimated? Watch the auctioneer; does he try to extract bids by embarrassing or needlessly prodding bidders? How does he increment bids? Observe the bidders and watch their style. Note whether more bids come from the front, the middle or the back of the room.

After examining several auction catalogues and attending a few previews and sales, you may feel sufficiently confident to participate in the actual bidding. Before entering the auction room, you will be handed a bidding number or "paddle" and a member of the gallery staff will ask for your name, address and possibly your driver's license number; some houses may insist on noting your banks name and address for a quick credit check. When you have successfully bid on an object, hold up the number so that the auctioneer can record your purchase properly.

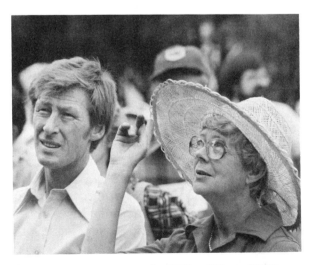

An anonymous country auction bidder. *(Photo: HWF)*

Proper positioning in the auction room is important. Upfront bidders may get a better view of the goods as well as being able to observe the auctioneer more closely. Sitting at the front may be clever strategy if the room is filled with friends and colleagues, as it leaves the onus on them to stop bidding against you, not the other way round. However, it may be a drawback not to be able to see who is bidding against you — a dealer, a true connoisseur or an absolute rookie. In many cases the novice will indicate by a shaky hand, a whisper or a furtive look to a neighbour that he is about to stop bidding. That's the time to hang in for a few more increments, and chances are the item will be yours. On the other hand, the novice may flaunt his paddle, stand up and smile smugly to indicate that he plans to go on bidding forever.

Subconsciously, the rookie will likely seat himself in the middle of the room to have the security of others around him. "Some people take encouragement from spontaneous bidding," says veteran auctioneer Ronald McLean. "It gives them confidence knowing that what they are bidding on is worthwhile because others want it. But the dealer or collector who really knows his stuff isn't affected by this at all." Many experienced auction goers will *stand* at the back of the room or off to one side from where they can survey the scene. This allows them to decide, on the spur of the moment, whether to hold back or be obtrusive. The experts usually bid conspicuously, although discretion does have its advantages. I remember wanting a particular signed and numbered print being offered at an auction. Knowing that *the* collector of that particular artist would be present, I realized that if he saw me bid against him the price would jump dramatically, and I would be out of luck. I, therefore, arranged to bid by telephone. During the auction the contest

was between the two of us, and the collector, unable to figure out who was bidding against him, finally gave up. When I told him, months later, who had been his "hidden" opponent, he said if he had known he would never have stopped bidding.

Novice collectors often complain that dealers cause high prices at certain auctions. Nothing is further from the truth; if anything, they keep prices realistic because they must allow for overheads and profit margins. Should you be lucky enough to bid against a dealer, be aware that he must cut off at the wholesale-retail dividing line. If you can get in your bid at the next highest increment you'll have a good buy. On the other hand, when a dealer acts as agent or has several clients in mind for a particular piece his bid will exceed the current retail price.

You, the collector, ought to have an upper limit in mind which you must never be tempted to exceed. Do not let anyone within earshot hear what that limit is, especially while you are in the midst of bidding. If you glance at your mate or hold a quick discussion, the auctioneer will notice your hesitancy and egg you on by any means at his disposal. Signs of indecision also warn your opponent that you are about to stop.

Some people like to open the bidding and stay in to the bitter end. Occasionally, this pays off in a "fast knock," a tactic used by some auctioneers to hold the audience's attention, especially if it seems restless or appears to be losing interest. They will offer a lot, accept a ridiculously low bid and strike the hammer quickly. Since everyone hopes to have the same luck the next time, the tempo quickens. Others feel that entering the bidding too soon may draw in too many bidders and cause prices to rise. They believe that waiting until the bidding has almost finished allows them to jump in with better chances of success. The danger is that the auctioneer may let the lot go for less to the bidder who has been in the running since the beginning; there also is the possibility that jumping in late may prompt others to restart their bidding.

Contrary to popular belief, people rarely bid with the wink of an eye, the tug of an ear or similar signs. Ronald McLean says it sometimes does happen when dealer bids against dealer. "If they both specialize in the same thing, the first one may have asked the second to hold off bidding. He may have agreed but since he really needs the piece he could come to me beforehand and say, 'I don't want to make trouble but when I'm sitting with my legs crossed, I'm bidding.'"

Another tactic is changing seats. Marlene Ritchie of D. and J. Ritchie Limited gives the example of the important dealer who bids obviously at the beginning of the sale to make others think it must be a good piece because Mr. Big is after it. "But when Mr. Big drops out, people in the audience assume he has decided the piece is not worth that much and they also stop bidding. Eventually Mr. Big, having quietly moved to another location in the room, collects his prize because the auctioneer has responded to their prearranged sign.

Auctioneers also have their own tactics; some start the bidding at a price they think they should get and when they can't, they continue to drop the amount until someone bids. Others start at one third or half of what they expect to receive and gradually coax up the bidding.

Order or Book Bids

When a collector is unable to attend the sale or believes his presence might hurt his chances to acquire a certain artifact, he can make use of the book or order bid. This means he authorizes the auction company, either by phone or by letter, to bid on his behalf, up to a specified amount.

David and Marlene Ritchie, Toronto, disposing of a silver tea set at one of their Toronto sales. *(Photo: HWF)*

These bids are normally secretly arranged between the gallery and the bidder and executed by one of the gallery employees. Some auctioneers open the sale with the book bids, mainly to save time. Many collectors find this practise annoying because it plays their hand too soon and leaves them exposed. When this happens the book usually loses.

Before leaving a bid with any auction gallery, make sure their methods are acceptable to you. If you are not satisfied, pay a local dealer a small commission (usually between 5 per cent and 10 per cent) to do the bidding on your behalf.

Reserves, Buy-Ins, Estimates

Reserves set by the consignor are the amounts below which he will not dispose of his goods. To protect the consignor, the gallery agrees to sell the merchandise only if the bidding exceeds the reserve, an amount only known to the gallery and the consignor. If the auctioneer fails to elicit bids equal to or exceeding the reserve, he will buy back the goods or "bring them in." The term most often used in this context is "buy-in." Almost every auction house has a specific buy-in fee which can be as high as 10 per cent of the reserve; it is always charged back to the consignor.

Because the reserve is set beforehand the consignor does not need to attend the auction. In most places it is against the law to bid on your own goods and most consignor-dealer contracts contain a clause to that effect.

In the event that the auctioneer disregards the reserve and disposes of the piece for less than the required amount, he is obliged to pay the consignor the difference between the selling price and the reserve figure.

Virtually everything sold by major auction companies has reserves. Many art and antique collectors are opposed to the system because they believe it makes a sham of the entire auction. Some even are hoping to lobby the auction companies to publish the reserve figures or, failing that, to open the bidding at the reserve.

Trading standards officers in London, England are currently examining the reserve system as they feel estimates set below the reserves established by consignors may be in violation of the Consumer Protection Act. The officers are probably correct in their thinking. It just doesn't seem right to have the catalogue estimate state that an artifact might go, for example, between $20,000 and $25,000 when in fact they know that the reserve is $22,000. It means, of course, that the auction house has purposefully mislead the auction goers. Should the English change the law, watch to see if it spreads to North America.

Generally, reserves are between 60 per cent and 90 per cent of the low estimate, never above the high. These estimates are set by the gallery, mainly to provide a guide to the novice. They may be purposely low because the gallery wants to tempt the bidders or purposely high to elicit

more money. It also should be remembered that most catalogues are prepared at least two months before the auction which means that the estimates may be totally outdated by the time the sale takes place. The January 1980 gold/silver price rises are a good example. When catalogues were prepared in November 1979, no one could have foreseen that a few months later these metals would reach the heights they did.

Lots that do not meet their minimum reserve or the figure the auctioneer considers adequate are "called back" or "bought-in" by the house. Some auctioneers don't want the public to know how many pieces were not sold and will simply call "sold to number 184," for example. This may be the house number and the only way to learn it is to note, beside each lot, the successful bidder's name or number. After a while, a certain number will likely reappear. It could be an individual's or the one belonging to the house.

If you were able to note the lots acquired by the house and decided after the auction that you might like some of these pieces after all, the company will sell them to you privately, provided you meet the reserve. This little known fact has resulted in some great bargains. In the mid 1980s, Sotheby Parke Bernet of Toronto offered a Quebec corner cupboard with an estimate ranging between $1,500 and $3,000. But because an important antique show took place at the same time not a single dealer attended the auction and there was no response from the participating public who had not recognized the cupboard's rarity. It was passed but when a certain antique dealer got wind of it he called the auction company and acquired the cupboard for around $2,600 (the reserve). It was not long before it appeared at an antique show with a $20,000 price tag.

After the sale, check with the auctioneer to learn what was sold and what was passed. As well, a list with sale results is usually mailed to catalogue subscribers about three weeks after the auction. Any lot numbers not included would indicate that the items were passed or bought-in.

Auction Games

"Auctions can be jam-packed with mysterious subtleties, quirky twists of fate, emotional cross-currents and instances of manipulative chicanery that defy scientific analysis," wrote the three authors of *Americana at Auction*. I would go one step further and say that some of the "games" played at auctions cheat not only consignors and auctioneers but also the participants.

One trick I call the "bad-mouth" routine (although officially referred to as "chill" or "damp" bidding) is used when an expert, either a dealer or a collector, pretends to find fault with an object. If you believe he knows more than you do, you will shy away from bidding because you don't want to look foolish. The "expert," however, by eliminating such competition, can sometimes buy the piece at a fraction of its real value.

Another ploy is the "big bid" technique. Someone after an expensive item may inform everyone within earshot that he knows that a government agency or large institution will enter a big bid on a certain piece. This intimidates the competition, and the originator of the story can acquire the artifact for far less than its value.

Then there is the old "fake-em-out" bit. A well-known dealer or connoisseur sits in a prominent spot during the auction and bids on a fine piece of porcelain, for instance. He goes to approximately one third of its value, dramatically scratches it off in his catalogue, shakes his head and stops bidding. Another person, at the back of the room, jumps in and buys the piece at a bargain price. Everyone else had been tricked

into thinking if the expert doesn't want it, what is the matter with the piece, anyway? The person at the back of the room was the expert's junior assistant.

There is the story about a New York jewelry dealer who boasted to his friends that he had just pulled a wonderful scam. He had a diamond bracelet in his shop which he couldn't move. Having bought it for $20,000 he would have sold it for that amount just to get his money out. Because he was in a jam and needed money in a hurry he decided to put the bracelet into a New York City auction, with a $40,000 reserve. It was bought-in by the gallery for $38,000, and the jeweler happily paid the nominal buy-in fee. Later, a man from Houston, Texas, walked into his store asking to see "something special." The jeweler showed him the bracelet and told him he had bought it for $38,000 but would sell it for a mere $2,000 profit because he needed the money quickly. The Texan, after examining the bracelet and the auction catalogue where it had been illustrated, described and estimated, bought it for $40,000.

Rings, Pools, Syndicates

Another way that bidders defraud galleries and consignors is by participating in rings, pools or syndicates. These began in England more than a century ago when auctions were attended almost exclusively by dealers who found they could buy cheaper if their bidding efforts were coordinated. The book *Confessions of a Dealer,* by Thomas Rohan published in London in 1924, explained the procedure:

> Suppose ten dealers have formed themselves into a Ring, that is to say, into a conspiracy to cheat owners of property out of the true value of their possessions and suppose that these ten conspirators attend

a sale and there find a picture which is worth a fortune. The usual procedure is as follows: A meeting is held before the sale, and the matter is debated. How much is the picture likely to fetch in this auction? Let us say that it is agreed the price will be around £100. It is then settled that one of the dealers who wants the picture shall bid for it, and he is styled the King of the Knock-Out.

The picture is put up, lot 21, let us say, and the nervous bidders glance at the formidable dealers from London to try to discover what they think about it. Those professional faces express indifference, contempt, or active dislike. At last someone bids £50. The King of the Knock-Out, as if he is willing to risk a few pounds on a doubtful picture, makes an advance of £5. The bids proceed, the rest of the dealers laughing or jeering among themselves, and at last the valuable picture is knocked down to the King for, let us say, £100.

After the sale the group would hold their own private auction, probably somewhere far removed from the scene of the original sale, to divide the piece equally or to compensate those who had refrained from bidding. In the private auction, the painting might fetch £2,000. The new buyer would give that amount to the ring, the king would take out the original £100 he had paid to the gallery, and the ring participants would share the remaining funds equally.

This practise was considered fraudulent manipulation of the market and declared illegal in the United Kingdom in 1927. Despite many complaints it wasn't until the summer of 1981 that someone was actually prosecuted for the offense. Nine antique dealers (excluding the ring leader who incidentally escaped) were convicted for being involved in the West Wales Price Ring and subsequently banned from British auction rooms for a six-month period. Each was fined £500 and also had to pay the prosecution and defence costs of between £800 and £1,500.

In Canada there are no specific laws dealing with rings but any such operation would be considered illegal here as well, if only by provisions set out in the Canadian Criminal Code under the conspiracy and fraud section.

"I've never seen a really successful ring operation in Canada," says Ronald McLean. "It may be because unlike the English houses who sell in greater percentage to the trade, we sell a lot to private collectors in this country." McLean did mention, however, that there was some difficulty with rings when Canadian art first appeared on the market. "But that has not happened for years because so many private buyers are involved." What we may see in Canada, as well as elsewhere in the world, are "conspiracies" of several dealers or collectors who collectively may decide not to bid on one particular item to allow someone else to go ahead.

Ronald McLean, president of Waddington, McLean Ltd., Toronto, prior to an Eskimo and ethnographical auction. *(Photo: HWF)*

Buying Stolen Goods at Auction

Most consignor-auction house contracts stipulate that the vendor has clear title to the goods. Even so, it is conceivable that the seller may have stolen the work. The question then arises, who compensates the purchaser? The auction house, the seller, the original owner or no one?

In July 1978, Beresford Willcox, an English art collector, bought a painting of the Madonna and Child from Christie's in London, England, for £19,000, plus 10 per cent buyer's premium. Later, the police confiscated the painting on the grounds that it had been stolen from a church in Lincolnshire. In March 1982, the seller of the painting was convicted of receiving it, knowing or believing it to have been stolen. Willcox approached Christie's demanding his money back, plus £1,000 spent on restoration. The auction company refused, stating that as agents they were not responsible. He launched legal action for the return of all his money claiming that the auction house was duty-bound to ensure that the seller had good title of the property.

Christie's relied on the conditions of sale in their catalogue. It clearly stated that neither the seller, Christie's nor any of their employees had authority to make or give representation or warranty in relation to any lot, nor were they responsible for any statement in the catalogue. The auction house claimed that they had not been a party to the contract by which the painting was sold and that the premium of £1,900 was part of the purchase price retained by the defendant in terms of their contract with the seller. Unfortunately, an out-of-court settlement was reached and all parties agreed to keep the results secret.

Country Auctions

Generally speaking, country auctioneers know little about antiques. As they are not attached to an established house nor operate at a permanent location, they have nothing to do with pricing organizing sales. Their job is to place ads in the local press, announcing a forthcoming auction. After they have called the sale, they dispose of the goods and collect the proceeds for which they are paid a commission of between 15 per cent and 25 percent on the hammer price.

The old-time dispersal auction is, by and large, finished in North America. Few farms or country estates are still being liquidated as they once were — from livestock and barn to the farmhouse's basement and attic. When a family does dispose of its assets, they seldom sell their heirlooms or antiques. This means that most country auctioneers had to rethink their roles.

Knowing that the antiques and collectibles crowd are avid auction goers, they get the family to put a few heirlooms into the auction. The city folk come to bid on the old dry sink, the family bible or the painted blanket box, only to discover that they were outbid by family members who have made prior arrangements with the auctioneer. Other country auctioneers look for farm owners who have themselves frequented auctions in the past and have acquired not a valuable collection but a group of old objects that will be advertised as the "Final Dispersal of a Fine Old Canadian Estate." All that collectors will see are odds and ends someone has assembled, not because he had an eye for beauty or quality, but because he had been able to buy them at bargain prices.

Country auctioneers also sell merchandise given to them by dealers; some even go out and buy stuff solely to auction it at a forthcoming sale. At these sales we can see reproductions such as horse brasses, car horns and brass spittoons as well as old stock or "mistakes" sent out by big city dealers to be offered to city folk who wouldn't look at them in their local antique shops.

A few so-called "country auctioneers" buy containers from abroad and have them shipped to an old vacant farm house to be auctioned off quickly. These containers, mostly from England, include many 1940s pieces, miscellaneous reproductions and some new merchandise.

Country auction ads are designed to have the sale and draw the crowds. Everything is made to look rare and unique. Because there seems to be no control over the ads, the auctioneers get away with misleading and confusing descriptions. The novice should not put too much faith in flyers, posters or country auction ads, nor should he go too far out of his way to attend such sales for they could well be a waste of time.

No catalogues are printed for country auctions. Goods are not identified, nor statements of authenticity issued. Things are always sold "as is," and the auctioneer accepts no responsibility for their condition. No significant preview times are allowed; during set-up time, the consignor will drag boxes from the house that have never been examined by anyone. For the most part this is a frustrating, time-consuming activity but it has been known to be fruitful. Once, while attending such a sale with a non-auction-going friend, I was surprised to hear him bid fifty cents for a box containing part of a toilet seat, a telephone book, a cookie tin and an old beat-up brass fixture. He was successful. The crowd, including me, laughed. He carried the box to a nearby patch of grass, tipped it over and rummaged through the junk. Suddenly he held up a tiny heart-shaped box that contained a small diamond ring. No one laughed then. The brass fixture cleaned up nicely, was rewired and now hangs in my home.

When attending a country auction take the time to poke around the piles of boxes, cartons and packages. If you discover a treasure, do not take your eyes off it. Boxes get shifted from

Two of Canada's colourful country auctioneers: Ontario's Max Storey (top) and Nova Scotia's Chris Huntington. *(Photos: HWF)*

place to place, and your piece may get sold to someone else.

Weather is important. When it is sunny and warm, people come out in droves, and prices rise accordingly. But when it is either very hot or very cold, they stay away from country auctions. Once I attended a sale on an extremely hot and humid Saturday afternoon. During the last quarter of the bidding the only people left were the auctioneer, two dealers and me. My purchase was a three-quarter-size brass bed with the original rails for thirty-five dollars.

When you do go to a country auction take along a folding chair, a blanket, warm clothing and a raincoat. Don't forget a rope for tying large purchases to the roof rack of your car, reading material to help while away those boring hours and some food if no concession stands are nearby.

Mock Auctions

Mock or fake auctions take place from time to time in almost every major North American city. They usually are held in motel rooms or unmarked and empty stores — rugs being the favourite merchandise sold. The set-up is easily recognizable because there seldom is a large crowd. To make the sale appear legitimate, "shills" or "ringers" are scattered throughout the room, occupying the rows of empty chairs. Their numbers mostly exceed those of the authentic bidders in the audience who, as bona fide customers, were lured to the scene by glitzy newspaper ads, knowing nothing about rugs, the market and auctions.

The difference between mock auctions and the real thing is that the mock auction organizers always own the goods and that their sales rarely are held twice in the same location.

When I was a columnist for the *Toronto Star*

a reader phoned to tell me that he and his daughter had accidentally stumbled into an antique rug sale at one of Toronto's largest and most prestigious hotels. "I was stunned to see one woman write a four-figure cheque for a rug that looked new to me and worth no more than a few hundred dollars," he said. Another collector who attended a similar auction reported seeing a shill bid, buy and pay for a rug, leave the store (with the collector secretly in pursuit), walk around the block and return to the auction through the backdoor. "He deposited the rug, donned a new hat and coat, ran around to the front door and meandered into the store only to repeat his performance," my informant told me.

How to Sell Through Auctions

Disposing of a whole estate, a complete collection or even a single antique piece is not simple. Of the three choices open to you selling privately, selling to a dealer or selling through an auction house — the latter seems to be the easiest and requires the least amount of time. However, the consignor must know exactly what he owns and what similar items would fetch in the retail trade. He also must be prepared to accept a hammer price that is about half the retail figure, although it may be considerably more.

Choosing the right auction house is equally important. Some concentrate on particular areas or hold sporadic, specialized sales, while others have weekly, general auctions. Specialized items do better at specialized sales or at houses that specialize in one area, such as dolls, rugs, etc.

Compare prospective auctioneers to see who can offer you the best deal. Take your time. Most mistakes are made when the sale is put together in a hurry and things are given to the auction house to be sold "as is." Pieces can end up in the wrong type of sale, wrongly positioned in the catalogue or they may be lost altogether.

Examine various auction house contracts and remember that most are negotiable. Everyone wants your collection, especially if it is of top quality.

After you have chosen an auction house that meets your needs, list every item, describing in detail possible flaws, repairs or restorations. State whether an illustration or description of the piece you wish to sell has appeared in a book or magazine or whether it ever has been exhibited in a museum. This usually enhances the provenance and results in a higher price. Make sure the right people at the gallery receive this information. Do not let the auction company take physical possession of your goods until the very last minute before the sale. Not only can damage occur in their storerooms, but once they have the goods, they are in control. After the sale, ascertain that each item in your lot has reached the auction block, was sold and for how much.

Before signing a contract consider the following questions:

Should I sell my entire collection as one lot?
Some feel placing many similar pieces in one sale will flood the market and cause prices to drop. Auction goers also may become confused when confronted with too many pieces of a similar nature; lower prices may result. On the other hand, a specialized sale of one particular type of artifact can attract collectors and dealers from around the world. It is a fact that like objects, put together over the years by a discerning collector, always do better than a few randomly placed artifacts.

How soon after the sale does the auctioneer pay out?
Standard time is thirty days; some houses will settle sooner if special arrangements have been made beforehand. (In Alberta, auction houses are legally bound to pay out fourteen days after the sale.)

What are the commission rates?
Some houses charge consignors a straight 10 per cent, while others may ask more. (See listings of auction houses, Appendix 2, pp. 221-229.)

Are there other deductions?
An auction house can deduct cartage fees and many charge to insure the goods while they are stored on the premises. (See listings of auction houses, Appendix 2, pp. 221-229.)

Do I have to pay commission on the reserve if the artifact falls to sell?
(See listings of auction houses, as this varies from company to company, Appendix 2, pp. 221-229.)

What are the other charges?
By charging the consignor for photographs, the gallery tries to recover the cost of publishing the catalogue. Some charge anywhere from a few dollars to six hundred dollars per photograph. (See listings of auction houses, Appendix 2, pp. 221-229.)

Do I have input as to the position of my goods in the catalogue?
Most auction houses do not allow consignors a choice in this regard. Owners of valuable collections should insist on some input *before* signing a contract and *before* the goods are in the gallery's hands. Catalogue placement is less important for goods of lesser value, and the consignor may have to abide by the auction house's decision.

Auctions and the Law

Legally, the auctioneer is the agent for the consignor and, much like a real estate broker, is accountable only to the vendor. Auctioneers and auction houses are paid by the consignor, a commission of between 10 and 25 per cent depending on the quality and quantity of the merchandise.

In 1975 many auction houses restructured their commission rates after Sotheby's and Christie's of London initiated the move, at a time when galleries were vying with each other to attract good quality merchandise. They felt that by lowering the commission rates to vendors from 20 percent to 10 per cent they would make it more enticing for consignors. The balance was made up by charging buyers a 10 per cent premium, on top of the hammer price. (Sales tax is applied to the total figure.)

Despite opposition by antique collectors, dealers and art personnel, this policy, known as the "10 and 10," subsequently was adopted by most of the world's large auction houses. The Society of London Art Dealers and the British Antique Dealers Association proceeded to take legal action against these houses claiming, first of all, that by acting collectively they were, in effect, establishing a monopoly and, secondly, were not providing a viable service for this new charge. As well, they felt the auction houses were dramatically increasing their revenue by taking percentages from both the seller and the buyer. The case was settled out of court in the fall of 1981 when Christie's issued a press release, stating that "as a gesture of good will and in the interests of preserving London's position in the international art market, the plaintiffs had decided to withdraw the action."

As a result, a joint committee of the antique trade and the auction houses was formed to consider "an auctioneer's and dealer's code of conduct, the improvement of legislation covering rings," and any other matters of mutual interest. All future post-sale lists would have to show aggregate prices instead of or in addition to hammer prices. Each of the defendants contributed £37,500 toward the plaintiffs' costs, estimated to be about £150,000. Despite the settlement, the Office of Fair Trading in London decided to investigate the matter, dropping it entirely in the spring of 1982 by stating that they had no real case against the auction houses.

On reflection, it seems everyone missed the point. Auction houses are still taking commissions from consignors which would indicate that they are acting on their behalf. Yet, by taking another 10 per cent from the buyer, they may be, in effect, equally obligated to him. The question remains whether the courts will find or imply that an auction house does have an obligation to the buyer because it is collecting money from him. In a rising market no one ever goes after the seller. But when it falls the buyer must look to the seller to make up for defective goods or other losses.

The law books of Canada are almost devoid of any mention of auctions. Generally, this country treats them like other sales of goods. Alberta is the only province that has a Sale of Chattels by Public Auction Act; while in England, auctions have been the subject of litigations for centuries and consequently have generated a body of common law precedents. Whenever Canadian or American lawyers (United States auction houses are, for the most part, unregulated) have to deal with auction problems not covered by provincial or state statutes, they must turn to the precedents set by English common law.

Halsbury's Law of England is a reference book of precedents for lawyers that sets out the basic points of English law pertaining to auctions and auctioneers as established in the various cases over decades. Here are some of their more interesting conclusions:

1. That an auctioneer may sell property of his own as principal, and need not disclose the fact that he is so selling, since he is not the agent of the purchaser.

2. An auctioneer has no implied authority to conclude a sale by private contract, even if the sale proves abortive and he is offered more than the reserve price. If, however, the vendor accepts a purchaser introduced by the auctioneer, and himself concludes a sale to that purchaser by private treaty, the auctioneer has a right to claim remuneration.

3. In some cases, where property has not reached its reserve and has been bought in, and immediately afterwards the auctioneer has sold the property at the reserve price to a person present at the bidding, the sale has been held good as, in effect, a sale by auction.

4. Any place at which a public auction is held, even though a private house, is for the time being a "place of public resort" for the purposes of the criminal law.

5. It is an offense to promote or conduct or to assist in the conduct of a mock auction.

6. The advertisement of an auction is merely an intimation of an intention to sell, and therefore, in the absence of fraud, intending purchasers who attend an auction have no right of action if the property is not put up for sale. Even when the property is put up, it may be withdrawn before the fall of the hammer. When, however, the advertisement amounts to a representation of fact that the auctioneer is authorized to sell, and this representation is fraudulent, persons

incurring expense on the faith of it can sue the auctioneer in tort.

7. The conditions of sale will generally be held to have been sufficiently communicated to bidders if they are exhibited legibly in the auction room.

8. A sale by auction may be notified to be subject to a reserve price and a right to bid at an auction may be reserved expressly by or on behalf of the seller.

9. Unless notification is made, it is illegal for the vendor or any one on his behalf to make a bid, or for the auctioneer knowingly to take such a bid, and any sale contravening this rule may be treated as fraudulent by the purchaser.

10. Verbal statements made by the auctioneer may or may not form part of the contract of sale. Verbal statements made to the purchaser by the auctioneer before the sale may amount to conditions or warranties which override the written conditions of sale.

Alberta is the only province to specifically deal with auctions and auctioneers in its Sale of Chattels by Public Auction Act, Revised Statutes of Alberta, 1980. It states among other things:

1. No one may hold sales or be an auctioneer unless they hold an auction sales business license or an auctioneer's license.

2. At the commencement of a sale by public auction, or if a sale is adjourned, at the recommencement of the sale, and before any chattels are offered for sale by public auction, the auctioneer shall read the conditions of sale or have them read and shall announce the name of the auction sales company holding the sale and his own auctioneer's license number.

3. No chattels purchased at a sale by public auction shall be removed from the place at which the sale is held unless the purchase price of the chattels has been paid to the auctioneer or auction sales company or other arrangements satisfactory to the auction sales company have been made for the payment of the purchase price.

4. A person who has chattels offered for sale by auction shall before the sale is held, deliver to the auctioneer or auction sales company holding the sale:

   a) if the chattels are in excess of $10 in value a statutory declaration, and

   b) in other cases a statement in writing, made or signed by him or by some other person authorized by him and who has knowledge of the facts, setting out whether or not any of the chattels offered for sale are subject to, a mortgage, charge, lien or encumbrance and, if so, the full particulars thereof.

5. An auction sales company shall keep a record of every auction sale held by him and retain each original record so kept in his possession for two years after the day of the sale to which the record relates.

6. An auction sales company shall within fourteen days after an auction sale, deliver to the person for whom the sale has been held and to each person having an in interest in or charge on chattels sold as disclosed by the statutory declaration or statement required by section 12, an itemized statement of the chattels sold and the amounts received therefor. (Author's Note: This fourteen-day settlement time is vastly different from practise in any other province, state or country. Normal practise is to pay out between thirty and thirty-five days after the sale.)

7. An auction sales company shall place all money it receives on account of a sale it makes into a trust account in a bank, treasury branch, credit union, trust company or other institution recognized under the law of Alberta and hold it separate from the money that belongs to the auction sales company in accordance with the regulations and disburse the money it receives or holds in trust in accordance with the regulations and the terms of the trust governing its use.

8. A person who contravenes this Act or the regulation is guilty of an offense and liable to a fine of not less than $100 nor more than $1,000.

9. A prosecution under this Act may be commenced within two years after the commission of the alleged offense but not afterward.

In Ontario, auctions are governed by the Sale of Goods Act. Its function and purpose are to provide a legislative environment for the control of commercial transactions per-formed in the usual course of business in an attempt to protect consumers and regulate the free market. Because there are no special laws governing sales by auctions in Canada we are forced to rely on the Sale of Goods Act. The laws that govern any sale applies to sales by auction. In part it says:

a) Where goods are put up for sale in lots, each lot is prima facie the subject of a separate contract of sale.

b) A sale is complete when the auctioneer announces its completion by the fall of a hammer or in any other customary manner, and until such announcement is made any bidder may retract his bid on behalf of the seller, it is not lawful for the seller to bid himself or to employ a person to bid at such a sale, for the auctioneer knowingly to take any bid from the seller or any such person, and any sale contravening this rule may be treated as fraudulent by the buyer.

c) A sale may be notified to be subject to a reserved or upset price, and a right to bid may also be reserved expressly by or on behalf of the seller.

d) Where a right to bid is expressly reserved, but not otherwise, the seller, or any one person on his behalf may bid at the auction.

Specifically related to auctions is Nova Scotia's law requiring auctioneers to purchase an annual license in the town, city or municipality where the auction is to be held. The fee varies from nothing to as high as $150 in the city of Halifax.

Quebec is the only province to have a 1 per cent provincial auction duty which is levied in addition to the 8 per cent provincial sales tax and the 10 per cent buyer's premium charged by most Quebec auction houses.

Conclusions

Below are some areas that I believe need serious consideration by Canadian lawmakers.

The 10 per cent vendors' and the 10 per cent buyers' commissions should be better regulated and more clearly defined as to whether there is any liability by the auctioneer to the purchaser.

- Penalties should be imposed for employing shills and holding mock auctions.
- Rings should be defined and penalties imposed for participating in them.
- The time for final settlement with consignors should be standardized.
- Standard terminology should be used in catalogue descriptions.

- If auction houses claim to employ "experts," they should be made to guarantee the authenticity of the goods they offer for sale.
- Auction companies' "terms of sale" clauses in catalogues should be standardized and better defined.
- The names of cataloguers, together with their qualifications, should be listed in auction house catalogues.
- The above recommendations are far from complete. Many auction-related problems could be solved if only some suggestions were implemented.

Glossary of Auction Terms

aggregate price — the hammer price plus the buyer's premium, excluding taxes.

as is — everything sold at auction is purchased just as it is. The buyer is responsible for examining the goods beforehand, noting damage, repairs and restorations.

book bid — also, left bid, absentee bid, order bid, execution bid. Usually employed when the potential purchaser is unable to attend the sale in person. Can be done by letter, telegram or telephone.

buyer's premium — usually a 10 per cent charge added to the hammer price to make up the auctioneer's commission.

buy-in — also, buy-back or bid-in. Occurs when an auctioneer cannot obtain a bid, at least up to the reserve price set by the consignor. The lot is not sold, although it may appear to be.

estimate — the selling price anticipated by the auction house, usually shown at the back of the catalogue.

hammer price — also, knockdown price. Amount called out by the auctioneer as he drops the gavel at the end of bidding.

lot — one or more pieces sold as a group.

not sold — total of hammer prices for all lots sold. Does not include premiums, taxes or prices for unsold lots.

paddle — bidding number given to auction participant at the start of the sale. Used to identify the bidder and to record his bid after the sale.

reserve — lowest price at which consignor will sell.

ring — also, pool or syndicate. A group of people who agree before the auction not to bid against each other but who may later sell the goods in private auction among themselves. An illegal practise that cheats consignors and galleries.

running-up — a tactic used to push bidders to spend more than they intended. Employs shills, book bids and other unethical methods.

shill — also, puffer or ringer. Usually employed to attend auctions run by unethical auctioneers and galleries. His function is to drive up prices by bidding against legitimate bidders. Considered illegal in many places.

underbidders — a person whose bid is second to the successful bidder's.

withdraw — to take out a lot before or even during an auction sale.

Bibliography

Pennington, Samuel, Thomas M. Voss, and Lita Soils-Cohen. *Americana at Auction*. New York: E.P. Dutton, 1979.

Powers, A.D. *How to Conduct an Auction*. Chicago: E.L. Fantus Co., circa 1900.

For a list of major Canadian and U.S. auction houses, see Appendix 2, pp. 221-229.

4

Fakes and Reproductions

I may pertinently be asked how the well-meaning collector is to escape the forger? Escape absolutely he never can. Even the expert buys his experience at the cost of his purse and his vanity. He can only hope to avoid being too grossly deceived if, having a definite passion as well as a talent for the subject, he devotes himself seriously to training his eye to distinguish quality. Let him not imagine that a practical acquaintance with last year's forgeries will prevent his falling victim to this year's crop. Moreover, let him not pay the slightest attention to supposed pedigree or provenance, nor to the various papers and documents and alleged traditions that purport to guarantee the genuineness of a work of art, for these are much easier forged than the work of art itself, nor is there anything to prevent a picture being painted or a marble carved to correspond with a description in a perfectly authentic document.

Art historian Bernhard Berenson
in a letter to *The Times* of London, c. 1920

Fakes

Fakes are objects that have been altered, restored or newly fabricated in order to defraud or deceive. They encroach on every area of collecting, from fine art and antiquities to collectibles. As prices rise, so does the volume, the level of expertise, the creativity and the craftiness of the faker.

Fakes affect private collectors as well as institutions. Museums, in the past, kept their mistakes secret, disposing of their forged artifacts at obscure auctions or reporting them "missing." Now they are putting them on show for everyone to see.

Dealers, too, are more willing to talk about how they got "hung on one" years ago, and some actually are pleased to acquire a fake to display alongside the real thing.

Counterfeiters are rarely identified, charged and held for trial. However, when it does happen, the story becomes front page news. One of the most interesting in a long line of famous scoundrels was the English artist Tom Keating who faked a series of Old Masters, as well as work by Cornelius Kreighoff (1815-1872). When he took the stand at his trial in January 1979, he provided some rare insights into his own motivations, as well as those of other imitators. "Some painters say it's spiritualism," Keating told one English newspaper. "I am not a spiritualist, but there were times when the Master came down and took over the painting. It was

terribly difficult to tell the difference between his work and my own. I have had that experience about twenty times in my life. It happened with the Goya. That was so good I marked it in white lead so if it was X-rayed it would be seen that it was not a Goya."

Most of Keating's "imitations" deliberately provided hidden clues so that the people scrutinizing them would have no trouble spotting them as fakes. He wrote messages on the back of pictures, used new materials and often painted modern items into a supposedly eighteenth-century work. Reading Keating's life story is a must for anyone involved in collecting art. He claims not to have cared about whether or not his "sextons" had taken in anybody:

> I've simply made them and sent them out
> into the world to have a life of their own. If
> someone likes them enough to hang them
> on his wall, that has always been satisfac-
> tion enough for me.... It is not my fault if
> they sell them for a few shillings in the
> nearest junk shop, or that some posh bloke
> flashes past the shop in his Bentley and
> catches a glimpse of what he thinks is a
> long-lost masterpiece....

Keating's trial ended abruptly on February 28, 1979, because of the defendant's failing health. Following the trial, English dealers, auction houses and art gallery owners demanded that a committee of experts be set up to act as a watchdog over the ethics of the trade." Although the idea was good, nothing significant ever came of it. In fact, in the spring of 1981 *The Times* of

Top left: The now famous Brewster-La Montagne "faked" chair. *(Collection and photo: Greenfield Village and the Henry Ford Museum, Dearborn, Michigan.)*
Left: An authentic Brewster chair owned by the Pilgrim Society, Plymouth, Massachusetts. *(Photo: The Pilgrim Society)*

London discovered another person who was just as adept at creating "pastiches."

Janice Thompson, a young mother of two, worked for a Brighton art restorer who had a contract with a New York company for ten thousand paintings. Mrs. Thompson was instructed to produce vintage looking pictures that had "no grey skies, no cows, no rough seas or storm clouds." She removed any "offending" sections from original paintings and replaced them with more "serene" views. Also, as many required some kind of signature, she simply inserted random names at the bottom of the canvas.

A *Toronto Sun* article quoted her as saying, "It was all done openly, anyone could walk in and see us at work." Mrs. Thompson denied that her paintings were fakes, maintaining that she had never signed a famous artist's name to any of them. She suggested, however, that greedy salesrooms had misrepresented her and, therefore, should take the blame.

While Mrs. Thompson's art may have been created without malicious intent, eventually similar works will cause serious aggravations to collectors, as their provenance will be forgotten or purposely concealed.

While Keating and presumably Thompson both worked for money and experience; in other cases fakers were motivated by loftier aims. Armond La Montagne, a former Rhode Island policeman as well as an accomplished wood carver and sculptor, made and sold several reproductions of seventeenth-century furniture. When he discovered that his pieces had "aged" considerably within a short period and subsequently increased in price, he decided to design and manufacture something that would cause those "lazy and unquestioning" experts all over the world to sit up and take note. La Montagne first wanted to create a piece of furniture, get it into a major museum and then publicly reveal its true provenance. He decided on a heavy chair with turned spindles under the seat and to name it after Elder William Brewster (1567–1655) who was said to have owned one like it.

Two genuine seventeenth-century "Brewster chairs" exist. They were made from ash with an even number of spindles, whereas La Montagne purposely used oak for his master piece giving it an odd number of spindles. He then submerged it in the ocean a few times, took it apart, put it together again, smoked, torched, bleached, gouged and painted it, covered it with thinner glue and finally dusted it with the contents of a vacuum cleaner. In case he ever needed proof that he was, in fact, its maker, he carefully removed a piece of one leg as well as two spindles.

In the end, he just gave the piece away. It passed through the hands of three Maine antique shop owners, the last one selling it to a well-known and highly respected New Hampshire dealer who concluded it was a rare piece. Now known as the famous "Brewster chair" he offered it to none other than the prestigious Henry Ford Museum in Dearborn, Michigan, who bought it in the late 1970s for an undisclosed amount. It was placed on exhibit there as well as on the cover of a major catalogue entitled *American Furniture 1620-1720*.

Later, the members of the museum's curatorial staff discovered they had actually bought a fake. Katherine Hagler, the museum's curator of furniture, described in a letter to me exactly how the forgery had been uncovered.

At two different times we heard rumours that the chair had problems. We had the chair X-rayed and thoroughly examined by our chief conservator and one of his assistants. They found then that the spindle holes had been drilled with a modern spade bit.

But it was the editor of the *Providence Sunday Journal* who actually discovered La Montagne was the manufacturer of the "Brewster chair" and who, according to Ms. Hagler, "was trying to prove to the world that a chair could be made today, equal in quality and craftsmanship to those made in the seventeenth or eighteenth centuries." She also suggested that "La Montagne was miffed by some slight he presumably had received from some museum curator." Rather than return the chair to the vendor who had expressed a willingness to take it back, the museum kept it and periodically puts it on show as an example of a typical fake, as well as a reminder that anyone can be fooled.

Every medium, not just art and furniture, can be threatened by fakers. Look at the case of Peter Ashley-Russell, an English goldsmith. In May, 1986 he pleaded guilty to six counts of false hallmarking of silver and gold flatware and to obtaining money by deception. His sentence, 21 months in jail with half of the term suspended seemed light in view of the fact that many of his forgeries will never be traced. No one knows how many fake pieces he sold in his Portobello Road stall to unsuspecting tourists.

The prosecutor told the court that Ashley-Russell, then 38, gave the police a guided tour of his facilities, revealing a secret panel in his workshop that contained forgeries, tools, and hallmark punches which he made over the last few years from melted gold coins. These he used, on many occasions, to make himself an estimated $80,000.

He was discovered by accident, when a beautifully engraved gold rat-tailed spoon and three-pronged fork with the marks of William Mathew, 1689, were sold by Christie's London in the summer, 1985 for 48 pounds. The purchaser, Spink & Son, bidding on behalf of a client, asked the Goldsmiths' Hall to examine the pieces. It was subsequently found that they were forgeries and the works traced back to Ashley-Russell through Christie's.

Since the forgeries were uncovered, other pieces have come to light. Apparently a collector with 23 years' experience bought a fake Charles I spoon for £600 after it had been authenticated. Another 17th century faked gold spoon was sold to a dealer on Portobello Road for slightly under £8,000. The prosecutor, David Waters, said that the dealer later resold the spoon for £18,000 without knowing it was a forgery.

Cut glass has recently come under the gun too. An outstanding article appeared in the March, 1990 issue of the *Maine Antique Digest* clearly illustrating how rife the cut glass market is with fakes. According to the author, Ian Berke, as many as a thousand pieces of newly cut glass with a market value as high as $5 million has been sold to unsuspecting collectors of American brilliant cut glass, in the last few years. Although no one knows where the fakes are being created and by whom, it is a fact that they have found their way into many of the most important collections.

In his article, Berke outlined some of the collector's guidelines for recognizing these fakes. He warned that "nearly all genuine American brilliant period cut glass will fluoresce a pale lime yellow under long wave ultraviolet light (blacklight), while the newly-cut glass fluoresced a distinct purple-pink." He also suggested that newer pieces, for whatever reason, attracted dust faster than the authentic, old examples. He did, of course, give many other clues to watch for. If you are involved in the collecting of brilliant cut glass, get a copy of this article and/or join the American Cut Glass Association (see Appendix 3, page 235.)

Canadian museums are no less vulnerable. In the spring of 1976 the Ethnology Department of the Museum of Man in Ottawa was offered four Northwest Coast Indian masks. A spokesperson for the museum admitted that they had been bought knowing that they may be fakes.

The vendor had claimed that they were pre 1900, made of native Canadian material and had lain buried under a cottage since the turn of the century.

R. Scott Williams in his report to the Canadian Conservation Institute and the Canadian Ethnology Service in Ottawa stated that four sets of tests were run on the masks. The wood was examined and compared with vintage examples in the museum's collection; the paint was sampled and subjected to chemical analysis, and the tool marks were studied. He concluded that the masks were recent carvings by "Ksan artists and had been doctored to make them appear old." The National Museums of Canada chose to keep them for future study.

When, a forged map surfaced in central Ontario, cartography collectors had a rude awakening. Up until then this area of collecting had been relatively free from imitations.

Early in November 1978, Edward Dahl, curator of the Early Canadian Cartography Section of the Public Archives of Canada, was offered an Ortelius map by an Australian dealer. The

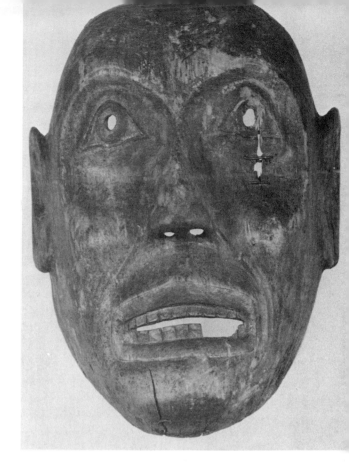

Top right: One of the four fake masks owned by the National Museums of Canada, Ottawa. *(Photo: National Museums of Canada, Canadian Conservation Institute, Ottawa)*

Right: A vintage Tsimshian wooden face mask acquired by the National Museum of Man in 1911. *(Photo: Canadian Ethnology Services, National Museum of Man, National Museums of Canada, Ottawa)*

price was three hundred dollars. Because the Archives already owned a copy of this particular map, they passed on the information to Ken Kershaw, proprietor of The Mappery in Ancaster, Ontario, one of Canada's most prestigious map dealers. He realized that an Abraham Ortelius map from the 1586 (or later) edition of the atlas *Theatrum Orbis Terrarum* would be worth upward of at least two thousand dollars. Thinking that the Australian vendor might not have been familiar with North American prices, Kershaw decided to purchase the map. In the meantime, Edward Dahl learned through a dealer in France that several forgeries of this particular map had turned up on the Continent. He immediately conveyed this information to Ken Kershaw who at that time was eagerly awaiting the map's arrival. Would it indeed be a forgery good enough for him to be fooled?

He almost was. After examining it, he contacted Edward Dahl at the Public Archives, and they both decided to send it to Ottawa for further examination.

There were many clues that led them to conclude the piece was a fake.

Clue One: when held up to a bright light or exposed to ultraviolet rays, the map clearly showed that, at some point in time, someone had written by hand on the paper before the map had been printed, although the writing had been carefully bleached out. However, Dahl pointed out that in 1587 when the map would have been made, the engraver could have run out of paper and may have bleached a sheet so that it could be reused.

Clue Two: the map was approximately one third of an inch smaller than the original. However, Geoffrey Morrow, the Archives' prints and drawings conservator suggested that if the paper had ever become wet, it could have shrunk by that much.

Clue Three: the paper on which the map was printed showed perforations spaced about six inches apart, down the centre of the map. This indicated that it had, at one time, been sewn or bound into a ledger. (Vintage maps were seldom sewn directly into the binding of the book but were attached onto guards which then were bound into the volume. This technique allowed maps to lie flat when the book was open.) Of course, someone could have obtained a single sheet of the map from the printer to be sewn into a book at a later date.

Clue Four: when Dahl examined the map under magnification, he found that the tiny ridges or "hills" made by the ink were missing. These ridges are caused when the paper is pressed into a copper plate; they are always present on vintage maps. Again, this was not 100 per cent proof of a forgery because the ridges could have been flattened in the conservation process.

Clue Five: modern printing methods and machines cannot duplicate the clean sharp lines and fine effects achieved by the early engravers. On original maps, the crosshatching (lines going vertically and horizontally and almost, but not quite, touching) is distinctly black and white. On this example, the lines were not as clear and, in fact, many of the areas were totally black.

Clue Six: on the "reproduction map" the plate mark — the depression line caused by the copper plate being pressed against the paper during the printing process — extended three eighths of an inch beyond the neat line, the outer margin of the map. Original vintage maps in the Archives' collection had the plate marks extending only one eighth of an inch beyond that line.

Clue Seven: Edward Dahl, writing in *Archivaria,* the journal of the Association of Canadian Archivists (Issue No. 10, Summer

Detail of the forgery. *(Photo: the Early Canadian Cartography Section, Public Archives of Canada, Ottawa.)*

Detail of a 1587 Ortelius map in the collection of the Public Archives of Canada.

1980), stated, "when a plate is inked, some may adhere to the edge of the plate and leave a fine line when printing occurs. On an original, this line would, of course, coincide with the plate mark." Since the plate mark occurred one eighth of an inch beyond the line, he felt that a photographic process must have been used to reproduce the map. "The plate mark was added later by simply pressing a metal plate slightly larger than the map image against the paper. Without a plate mark, the producer of the map or vendor could have had little success in passing it off as an original engraving."

One of the problems in making a map of this type is locating the right kind of paper.

Paul Stoney, a noted Virginia map enthusiast,

remembers going to the markets in Madrid where dealers would sell books containing old hand-made, unused plain paper that could easily be acquired for such purposes. Walter Reuben, a respected map dealer in Texas, further explained the difficulty in forging rare maps. "You just cannot entirely get from a photographic process the engraver's effect, no matter how clever. It's only two dimensional."

Colour could be another clue. While the fake Ortelius map was not coloured, many fakes are. Graham Arader, noted American dealer, reports that the forgery he owned showed very poor colouring, something an experienced collector/dealer would notice right away when comparing it to the real thing.

The fake sampler. *(Photo:* The Maine Antique Digest)

Although no one yet is certain who is actually responsible for these fake maps, or where they are being manufactured, rumour has it that someone in Italy, after locating a bundle of old church records and documents, is bleaching out the ink and printing maps onto the old paper by a photo-offset process. This theory has been substantiated by many of the other clues and errors found on the Ortelius map. Apparently the going rate in Europe for this same forgery is about eight dollars (U.S.).

It was only a matter of time until textiles, too, would be subjected to the faker's hands. Since samplers reached extraordinarily high prices in

the United States, collectors became more and more concerned about protecting their investments. In January 1981, a few weeks before the record-breaking Kapnek Auction in New York City, Samuel Pennington, editor of *The Maine Antique Digest,* wrote about several suspicious-looking samplers that had recently surfaced. They all were dated between 1820 and 1835 and, as in the map case, no single clue was sufficient proof that the samplers were indeed fakes, although the sum total of evidence did point a finger at a serious problem.

Connecticut antique dealer Kathy Schoemer offers the following pointers to help collectors verify the authenticity of their samplers.

Fakes usually are small (sometimes 6-1/2" x 8-1/2"). Most are plain in design and inferior in quality or workmanship. The reverse side looks messy with much thread wasted. Imitations may have rough selvedges, crude deep hems or no hems at all, never found on genuine pieces. The thread on the reverse of old samplers is rarely the same colour as on the front, as the back is never exposed to light and, therefore, should be much brighter and crisper looking. Regarding the formation of the letters, Ms. Schoemer observed that "almost no serifs were used" and that all the fake examples she saw had simple cross-stitch borders.

The sampler illustrated here had been acquired by Samuel Pennington for research purposes. When I examined it, I noticed that the maker had not bothered to count the threads which means that each letter is slightly larger or smaller than the next and that the letters are not equally spaced. The number of motifs in the borders at top and bottom do not match, although the motifs on the two sides are the same. The sampler had been sewn into a needle case, yet there are no marks or creases to indicate that it had been folded for 150 years. Any fabric that is subjected to pressure for so long must show crease marks or signs of ripping and shredding along the fold lines. In this particular case the ground is completely flat. All these things rarely, if ever, happen on vintage pieces.

Folk art is a whole area where fakes have started running rampant. Carelessness and of course, inexperience on the part of the buyer, can very often lead to some fatal errors. The following tale about a modern weathervane, illustrates this point clearly.

Not too long ago, Marshall Stone, a retired newspaperman and part-time antique dealer, was reading a glossy American antique magazine when he spotted an advertisement for an exhibition of folk art at a prestigious New York City gallery. Featured in the half-page colour spread was a wooden weathervane carved in the shape of a snake. When he called the gallery, he learned that it had been sold for $7,500. Stone was furious.

He knew the weathervane was not antique as implied in the ad. He was certain about the age of the piece because he himself had made it in 1976 — implanting his initials, MLS and the date, 76, on the underside of the head — to replace a vintage weathervane stolen the year before.

Apparently, after Stone moved away from Maine and left his weathervane residing on the roof of his former home, he received reports from old neighbors that many people had been trying to buy the vane but were deterred when told it was quite new. A few years later, the snake was split in half by a strong wind and it toppled from its post. The new owner of the house simply threw it into the barn and forgot all about it.

Along came a dealer, who realized the vane was new but still wanted to own it. He paid $40 cash and quickly sold it to another Maine dealer for $275 and it just disappeared into the marketplace. Early in the summer, 1983, it was spotted at a flea market and went through the hands of two dealers until it was purchased by Joel and Kate Kopp, respected New York City folk art dealers and proprietors of *America Hurrah*. They sold it in due course for about $7,500.

The Kopps did not know that the vane was new. And, to be fair, without having the provenance of the piece, it is difficult to judge the age of a wood that has been exposed to the elements. Paint weathers first and can look old in just a few years. Wood takes longer to weather and can be protected from age patination with many coats of paint. In addition, the very nature of folk art causes problems to the vendor. Since most of it was made by unknown craftsmen, the trade is more likely to accept a piece like this without asking for provenance. And even if they do, the picker or owner, often knows little about it. No one told the Kopps about the weather vane's past until they had advertised it in *Antiques*, placed it on a postcard, taken it to a prestigious American antique show, had it described in the *New York Times* and sold it.

But as soon as the Kopps realized what had happened they cancelled the sale. No real harm was done. The story has not only warned everyone, yet again, to be careful of such situations but has suggested that if Joel Kopp can be fooled or mistaken, it can happen to anyone.

"We all thought it was a smashing thing and were so happy that it came at a perfect time for our sculpture show and from a very careful buyer. None of us did what we should have done. We didn't really look at it and make it prove to us it wasn't a fake. We can't be too cocky, too sure, or take anything for granted. We can't let a piece talk to us. We must ask it to prove its authenticity."

Kopp said that if he had looked at the paint on the vane with a jeweler's loup, he "would not have dated it at the turn of the century but put it in the 1930s or 1940s and would not have paid what he did for it, asked what he asked, or presented it in the way he did." He said, also, that the date, 76, had been gouged out and the initials were inset in 19th century manner.

It is interesting the way in which fakes sneak into the marketplace and how, in many cases, they start off innocently but are shoved into consumer's hands by people other than the creator. That is exactly what happened to Torontonian Craig Black's creation.

In 1974, Black flipped through a copy of a newly published book—*The Flowering of American Folk Art 1776–1876* — chronicling a landmark exhibition at the Whitney Museum in New York City — he was fascinated by a black and white illustration of a carved wooden blancing toy. So intriguing was it to Black that he decided to make one for himself, just for fun.

After turning the sculpture on a newly acquired ninety-year-old lathe, he finished it by hand and painted it the appropriate colours. Then it went into the bottom of a laundry tub for a few years.

Because Black was never really happy with the piece it stayed hidden in the basement of his house. Years later, after he opened his own furniture restoration company, the balancing toy resurfaced and was placed, with the rest of the collection, in the bathroom. An antique dealer saw the carving in the late 1970s and offered Black $175.

"There was no secret about it, no pretense of it being old," said Black. "I told everybody I made it." Even with that information the dealer was still interested and Black made the sale, agreeing to wait for his money.

Black never did get paid for the piece and actually lost track of it for ten years. But then, in 1984 he rediscovered it in ads placed in two prestigious American antique journals. Vendor Bob Bonner, proprietor of Bonner's barn, Malone, New York was obviously proud of his newest acquisition.

Although Black phoned Bonner and warned him that the piece was new, Bonner didn't believe him. In fact, Bonner was so taken with the toy that he decided not to part with it; placing it in his own private collection where it remained until the spring of 1988 when it was placed in a liquidation auction, four months after Bonner's death.

The fourteen-year-old balancing toy went under the hammer for $3,750 and was purchased by a curator for a major American museum. Craig Black is still shaken by the whole experience.

"I do restoration work, quite a lot of it, and that balance toy is an embarrassment. It was made as a whimsy, for my own enjoyment and now it has become a piece of valuable folk art?"

Concerned about the variety of fakes entering the marketplace and the problems they create, Samuel Pennington, editor/publisher of *The Maine Antique Digest*, in conjunction with New York's Museum of American Folk Art and the Hirscl & Adler Folk gallery, sponsored the first catalogued exhibition of folk art fakes. The month-long event opened April Fool's day, 1988, in New York City, amidst much hoopla and fanfare.

While many dealers were upset about the focus — feeling it would scare would-be collectors away and at the same time, educate the fakers — others were thrilled. For they were grateful to see the real piece beside the fake; they were happy to have all the little tip-offs pointed out and explained. If the show did anything it warned collectors to be alert.

Perhaps the key-point to aid in the identification of fakes, as Pennington pointed out in the catalogue, is that although fakes and forgeries might look good, their prices generally give them away as they are very often priced significantly lower than current market values.

"Fakes," he wrote, "appeal to the bargain hunter; to the collector who doesn't want to do the research necessary to know the good from the bad; to the collector who thinks he's smarter than professional dealers. And he stated that, "there's an adage in the trade that every buyer of a fake has failed to heed. 'If it's too good to be true, it probably is.'"

Shortly after the April Fool show closed, the Cartier Foundation in Paris mounted an equally intriguing exhibition, Real Fake, on view from June to September, 1988, consisting of all manner of forged goods including fake currency, stamps, art and counterfeit branded goods such as industrial products of foodstuffs, pharmaceutical products, toys, cassettes and discs, designer clothes, luxury goods and of course, watches. Their purpose in mounting the exhibition was to show how fine the dividing line between genuine and fake objects in our everyday lives and how deadly a problem it has become.

What can consumers do to protect themselves from making costly mistakes? Here are some suggestions:

1. Do your homework. Before you buy anything study the marketplace, visit museums and read every book pertaining to your particular area of interest. Visit the antique shows and shops. Develop your tastes and your eye.
2. Deal only with the best dealers and auction houses. To learn their identities ask friends whose judgement you respect in other areas; read the trade papers to see who the experts call upon for quotes, information.
3. Get a written guarantee from the vendor, describing the piece, its history, age and the price paid. Remember if you buy at auction there really aren't any guarantees.
4. Visit the reproduction shops in various museums. Know what is being sold.
5. Stay away from bargains; if it's too cheap, there is probably a reason.

If you missed the fake exhibition in New York, an illustrated catalogue, entitled *April Fool: Folk Art Fakes and Forgeries* is available for $15 U.S. from *The Maine Antique Digest*. (See Appendix 1, page 219 for their full address.)

Reproductions

Although reproductions start innocently enough, they play havoc with the market when they fall into wrong hands. Believe it or not, many North American museums do damage by carrying reproductions in their gift shops. These institutions feel that the public, especially people who are leery of getting involved with the intricate world of antiques, should have a chance to enjoy living with old-looking pieces.

Regrettably, however, these reproductions are not often properly marked to warn future generations that they are, in fact, facsimiles. What happens is that a so-called "legitimate" reproduction eventually seeps into the marketplace, causing trouble for collectors, especially those who are new at the game.

Pieces of furniture can be made to look older than they are by burying them in manure piles, letting them sit in the ocean for a while, or beating them with chains. Paintings can be "cracked" by heating them in ovens; prints can be "smoked" or ivory "boiled;" and bronze or brass objects will have an "antique" look after submerging in potassium nitrate for a while.

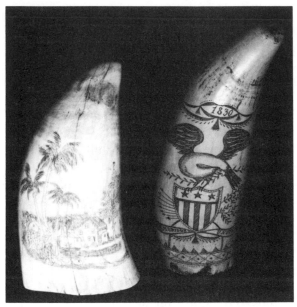

Under ultraviolet light the genuine whale tooth at the left fluoresces while the plastic fake at the right does not react. *(Photo: Gene Myers. Courtesy Mystic Seaport Museum Inc., Mystic, Connecticut)*

Unmarked or improperly identified reproductions frequently change hands and eventually lose all connection with their origins. In some cases, pieces that were once clearly labelled had their logos or manufacturing dates deliberately removed or covered.

One of the easiest methods of identifying a reproduction is to check major museum gift shops for their catalogues. For this kind of detective work, a publication offered by Greenfield Village, Henry Ford Museum, Dearborn, Michigan, is one of the best. Simply called *Reproductions,* it illustrates and describes over one hundred items, many of which have been spotted at some of the best antique shows in North America. Painted toleware document boxes, glass candlesticks, goblets, hooked rugs and wrought-iron "early" lighting devices are but a few of the things known to have acquired over-

night fame and at least a century's worth of antiquity.

Other good guides for the novice are the antique magazines that carry reproduction ads. Under the heading "Fine Classical Reproductions and Collectibles" one issue of *The Antique Trader* listed the following articles at random: "Dolls and lamps, brass and copper, clocks and weathervanes, banks, spittoons, fireplace fixtures, candlesticks, picture frames, bed warmers and more." Other ads feature reproduction jewelry, fixtures, cigar-store Indians, and even Diamond Dye store cabinets — all described as "detailed" and "just like originals." Someday, they too will find their way into the legitimate marketplace. In April 1980, a collector walked into the offices of Phillips Ward-Price Auctioneers in Toronto, clutching a piece of decorated whalebone (or tooth). (Known as scrimshaw, these artifacts were usually carved by eighteenth- and nineteenth-century sailors.) The collector wanted to have his particular piece appraised with a view to selling it. David Tyrer, then the auction gallery's expert in Canadiana, folk art and collectibles, took one look at the scrimshaw and knew it was a fake.

The owner was astonished as he had just been told by the Royal Ontario Museum's ethnographical and mammology experts that this "fine example" of a whale's tooth was more than one hundred years old. Tyrer subsequently took the piece to the museum. A small section was trimmed off for analysis and it was proved that it had been made of plastic within the last five years.

Intrigued by the origin of these problem pieces of scrimshaw, Richard C. Malley, assistant registrar of the Mystic Seaport Museum in Connecticut, spent a great deal of time researching and investigating them. His work resulted in a detailed and illuminating article in the

Maine Antique Digest of May 1980. In it he writes about Artek, Incorporated of Antrim, New Hampshire, describing one of the largest United States manufacturers of some very beautiful and accurate scrimshaw reproductions. Selling from about $25 to $50 each, all are carefully stamped with the company's name, the word "reproduction" or "replica" and the initials of the respective museum that owns the originals. These pieces, so easily purchased from museum gift shops, surface on the open market all over the world minus identification. Another company based in London, England, produces "polymer plastic" scrimshaw pieces. Unfortunately, they show no markings or labels to identify them.

Experts have come up with various means to warn collectors, especially novices, about scrimshaw fakes and reproductions. Writing in *Art and Antiques* (May-June 1981), Daniel Prince points out that under ultraviolet light true whalebone will fluoresce, while polymer will not. He advises collectors that under a jeweler's loupe tiny perfectly round air bubbles appear, scattered around the ends of the tooth of plastic scrimshaw. Similar holes in real scrimshaw would be irregular in shape.

Joyce Burne of Orangeville, Ontario, a specialist in oil lamps and goblets, is concerned about the number of new and reproduced pieces flooding the North American glass market. One bit of advice she gives to new collectors before buying is to place the glass on top of a pure white piece of paper. "Old glass should have a hint of colour, whether it's pink, grey or purple. New glass has no colour or tint at all." She also stresses that collectors should know and understand how old glass was formed so that they can spot the new machine-made pieces.

When pressed glass was made a gather (lump of glass) was cut and blown into a mold. The line where it was cut with the tool will always remain somewhere in the old piece. The only exceptions are pieces that have been refired, to add another layer of glass. The line could be in the bowl, on the side, or in the stem. A new piece of glass won't have that fine hidden line.

Joyce Burne once acquired a collection of goblets including a clear glass Maple Leaf pattern piece. Her instincts told her something was wrong but she packed it away until she could prove her case one way or another. About a year later she bought a vaseline-coloured Maple Leaf pattern piece. By comparing the two, her worst fears were confirmed; the clear goblet was a fake.

The design on the old piece was more prominent, while the new one looked skimpy and light. Looking down into the glass, the new one seemed to have the stem attached with three large blobs or three large holes on the bottom, while the old glass had three small notches. The reproduction had a very thick stem, whereas that of the old one was slimmer. Also, the imitation had a thick, clumsy edge. The old one was delicate and smooth. The new goblet was much heavier in weight with pronounced seams, compared to the old goblet's, which were smoother and much finer.

Joyce Burne now takes both pieces to shows as a teaching tool and to remind collectors how easy it is to make mistakes. Her vintage piece (circa 1880) is marked at $295, while the clear glass reproduction is priced dramatically lower at $20 She never intends to part with her fake, lest it fall into wrong hands.

A third example on Mrs. Burne's shelf is a Westward Ho patterned goblet. The frosting on the new one is even and precise, whereas on the vintage piece it appears much above the cut line reaching into the plain glass border or rim at least a quarter of an inch higher than it should.

A pair of reproduction beds, sold as vintage, which turned up at one of the C.A.D.A.'s show/sales. *(Photo: HWF)*

On both goblets the design shows a small pail standing beside a well. Curiously, the one on the old piece is square, whereas it is round on the reproduction. The colour on both goblets is a tip-off; the reproduction is whiter than white, while the genuine piece has a certain mellowness about it.

Another glass pattern that is often reproduced is the one called "Three Faces." When the copy and the original are placed side by side, the difference is obvious; the old one shows three detailed and very recognizable faces on the stem, while those on the new one are neither as clear nor as appealing.

The venerable Canadian Antique Dealers Association (CADA) landed itself in the centre of a controversy over a pair of thirty-nine-inch Sheraton-style maple beds that sold for two thousand dollars at CADA's 1976 annual spring show in Toronto.

The vendor claimed that they came from a home in Port Hope, Ontario, and were well over one hundred years old. However, prior to the show opening, the exhibiting dealers had questioned the authenticity of the beds, yet had not been taken seriously, and the beds were allowed to go to their new home.

Following the CADA show, many antique dealers and related trade papers paid much attention to the two beds, and several letters to editors stated that the beds were not genuine antiques. CADA never denied these allegations.

It appears a New Jersey man had made the beds in 1950 and sold them as new to an antique dealer. Subsequently, they were purchased by Sheldon Silverstein, a dealer from Lafayette, New Jersey, who sold them to a Massachusetts dealer in 1970. Eventually, R.A. O'Neil, now of Toronto, bought them for $250. They were then acquired as reproductions by another Ontario dealer and before long became the property of a founding member of CADA who sold them to a customer at the show. No one suggested that the CADA dealer who offered the beds knew the true story. It was a mistake, the kind people dealing in antiques can honestly make. The story is told here as another warning that good reproductions can lose their provenance and become vintage pieces. If this can happen to a founding member of the CADA and pass a vetting committee of "experts," it can happen to you.

Equally important are objects that began life long ago, but suffered partial minor or major alterations. Cupboards have been cut in half, the old top added to a new bottom and the old bottom attached to a fake top. The result: two antique pieces, worth double the money to the faker ... but a lot less to the collector. It is not unusual to find an early French-Canadian armoire without its proper doors or built up around two original doors. Any antique that has been "married," as this type of reconstruction is called, is worth little on the open market.

Another kind of fraudulent practise is overcarving, adding decorative details to enhance the value of authentic pieces. It often is applied to seventeenth- and eighteenth-century English walnut and oak pieces. Detection is difficult, yet the inclusion of a motif that does not fit the period often does give away the carver.

Reproductions, fakes and fraudulent materials turn up everywhere but are most prevalent at flea markets where items are sold by inexperienced vendors or at small country auctions that often serve as dumping grounds for larger deal-ers who want to get rid of bad purchases or clear out old stock. These places may be wonderful for experienced collectors but dangerous for novices. Stay clear of them. The bargains you pick up may turn out to be plain junk.

A Few Pointers

- Check museum catalogues and gift shops for the latest reproduction lines.
- Become familiar with various styles so that when you see a piece you'll at least have an approximate idea when it was made and whether it follows established patterns. Consult good books on your subjects of interest and visit museums that collect and display them.
- Learn how certain objects were made in the past. By understanding the materials used and knowing about techniques, finishes, mold marks, colours, etc., it is less likely that you will be taken in.
- Consider testing with an ultraviolet lamp. It will help you detect repairs on china, pottery, glass or on painted surfaces as well as spot new materials that may have been used. To an experienced eye, an ultraviolet light shows up surface repainting and repatination. Sometimes x-rays reveal the underlying structure on an original painting on the canvas.
- Subscribe to at least three major magazines/journals that specialize in your area of interest. Join relevant societies and collector organizations. These sources will keep you abreast of latest news concerning fakes and reproductions. Of special note, however, is *The International Foundation for Art Research* (Appendix 1, page 219) which publishes information, advice, notices, and news regarding all manner of recently discovered fakes, reproduction and frauds.

- Learn to differentiate between scratches caused through normal use and those that may have been artificially created. Furniture will show a lot of wear around the feet and in places where hands have pulled open drawers or cupboard doors. On chests, examine drawer runners; there should be evidence of thousands of openings and closings. Look at armrests and fronts of chairs; check bottom rungs where shoes and feet have rested for decades. Porcelain and glass will show wear around rims and bases. Consider how a person would have held such an object; look for marks to indicate usage.
- Learn some of the "antique" terms and understand what they mean. The word "patina" is especially appropriate when discussing objects made of wood. As it ages, the surface takes on a rich, almost mellow appearance that cannot be obtained from any other finish or polish. Learn to recognize and look for that warm glow on areas that have been exposed to air and light. The outside of a piece of furniture will be darker than the inside. Signs of patination also are helpful in determining whether the various parts of an object belong together. Woods exposed to the same light conditions will patinate in the same manner. A noticeable difference in colour indicates a problem. To check a table, turn it upside down. Have the top boards been replaced? The patina and colour of legs and table top should match. Check drawers to see if they are original or have been added later.
- Find out about saw marks. Early cabinet-makers used hand saws that left a clean pattern of straight lines at varying angles. Circular saw marks mean that a power driven buzz saw was used. (It did not make its appearance until the mid- to late nineteenth-century.)

- Early furniture was made with choice pieces of wood. A cabinet-maker rarely chose a knotted piece unless it was to become an integral part of the design.
- More likely than not, table tops were made from the widest possible boards. When you see two or more boards that have not undergone major repairs since the table was made, a large space or gap will appear between each board. The gap is a good indication that the piece is old because it was left there to allow for wood shrinkage. Aging wood shrinks *across* the grain rather than along the grain. Therefore, tables that were originally perfectly round should be slightly off kilter, and wood made originally on a lathe will in time lose its perfectly round, symmetrical shape.
- Early pieces made of wood will show undulations moving with the grain; they are caused by craftsmen working without machinery. Many primitive pieces will show marks along the inside left by the cabinet-maker's tools. Sometimes just feeling below the edges and around corners will yield this kind of information.
- When examining a cupboard, look at the base; that is the first place where major restorations could have occurred. Check the cornice. Is it original or has it been added at a later date? If the base, cornice or doors have been entirely replaced, the restoration is considered major, and the price you are asked to pay should reflect that condition.
- Hand-forged and square-headed nails were used prior to the late 1840s, they are still being made today and, therefore, cannot serve as sole proof of antiquity.
- Examine the screws. Blunt-ended and irregular screws were used before 1850. After that time, more modern types appeared.

Again, this isn't 100 per cent assurance, because old-type screws are still being made today. Also, over the years, old screws were often removed or got lost through normal wear and tear.

• Some pieces do not have metal hardware; they were put together with wooden pegs or dowels that may date a piece prior to the 1840s. The end of the peg should protrude slightly because of anticipated wood shrinkage. If the peg is perfectly flush with the wood, it probably is a recent addition. If dovetails, especially on drawers, are irregular and broad, the piece was made by hand, and probably before 1860. An evenly spaced, thinner dovetail could mean that it was machine-made. Again, there are exceptions.

• Consider the price. If it is far below the current retail market value, question it.

• Don't make a major purchase when you are thousands of miles away from home. Vacations are times when collectors become careless.

  If you discover while you are away what you believe to be "a great buy," take home the information, go to your local museum and/or specialist dealer to research the piece. If you still want it, transportation is easily arranged and a lot cheaper than buying a "mistake."

• Assume everything to be spurious; then set about proving it right.

5

Insurance and Appraisal

Insurance against theft, fire and natural breakage probably is the only way to lessen collectors' worries and fears of losing treasured possessions. Although some fatalistically disregard such potential hazards by dispensing with insurance altogether, most people who collect take out policies and look upon this expense as a necessary and unavoidable evil. Two options are open to them: they can either include their art treasures in a regular homeowner's policy or insure them separately under a special fine arts policy.

If they choose the first option, they must bear in mind that it normally covers the contents of a home for half the value of the house itself. It, therefore, must be high enough to include their antiques and other art objects as well as home appliances, fixtures and furnishings. Be sure to choose an " all risk" policy to cover all disasters (fire and theft), even if the cost is slightly higher. Avoid homeowner's policies that are so specialized that they stipulate either the one or the other.

Regarding silver objects, Canadian insurance companies have a clause in their homeowner's policies which limits replacement claims for such items to a maximum of five thousand dollars; above that amount they must be insured separately as part of a fine arts policy.

If your collection is of average value including it with your homeowner's insurance probably is the best route to follow. Before you sign any policy, be sure to:
- Itemize everything of value.
- Photograph and describe each item in detail, showing individual purchase prices, vendors' names and addresses, as well as histories and the approximate value of each piece at the time the list was drawn up.
- For easy reference and to establish proof of authenticity, attach auction catalogues, magazine articles or books describing similar pieces.
- Update your list at least every three years.
- File one copy together with photographs and reference material in a safe place in your home or with your insurance agent; a second copy, as well as duplicate photographs, should be kept in a safety deposit box.

Special fine arts insurance is essential for the peace of mind of anyone who owns a major collection. Such policies cover silver, jewelry, oil lamps, antiquarian books, furniture, textiles, porcelain, memorabilia, paintings, etc.

Again, collectors must itemize their pieces and provide a detailed descriptions, purchase dates and prices, vendors' names and addresses, histories and photographs. In addition, a fine arts policy must be accompanied by a formal appraisal executed by an accredited professional. But before incurring any expenses in this regard, discuss all appraisal matters with your insurance agent who will likely suggest names of appraisal firms but will only approve an appraiser you have chosen if he and his company are acceptable to him.

Copies of all documentation must be kept in at least two separate locations. Remember, the more proof of authenticity you can produce concerning insured items, the easier it will be to file a claim should the need arise.

It also might be worth noting that many insurance companies will reduce their premiums if a bona fide alarm system has been installed in your home. Although these devices are not failsafe, they have proved effective deterrents for many burglars.

Home Security

Collectors all over the world are concerned about home security. While some opt for expensive alarm systems, others devise simple yet effective gimmicks. For instance, one lady who dislikes dogs has placed large "Beware of Dog" signs on each side of her property and has draped dog chains (heavy ones) near each entrance.

There are all kinds of tricks and ploys that can be done, including the installation of a professional sonic sound system (recommended by the police department) rather than a heat sensitive unit, but if someone wants into your home badly enough there is nothing much to prevent it. However, there are, according to Sergeant Bill Cowie of the Metro Toronto police force, things that can be done to help locate the goods after they have been stolen.

Cowie advises that each piece be separately photographed in both black-and-white and colour so that art and antique magazines will be able to feature a good likeness of the stolen articles. In addition, everyone should carefully catalogue their collections, listing every item and its approximate retail value and all of its identifying features.

He suggests that collectors mark each piece in an obscure spot so that they will be able to identify it quickly should it be located. However, I would caution collectors that engraving or permanently marking any antique or piece of art would seriously diminish its value. Instead, try to pinpoint and note the location of particular wear marks and scratches. Some stationery shops sell an invisible marking pen which might just be the answer. At any rate, make a note of all the marks used and their exact location. If the marks are noticeable, thieves could remove them, but Cowie says that "there are certain tests we can perform to lift numbers that the thieves thought they took off." Furthermore, if the thieves erase marks, they will have to remove the patina or finish, providing a clue that an identifying mark was once there.

Cowie also suggested that crime prevention officers in the various divisions will lend engravers to people who wish to mark their artifacts. "They have a depth adjuster and will engrave most things including metal and wood." Again, I would advise antique owners to use this tool only after careful consideration.

Institutions and corporations should always make certain that their artwork is securely attached to the walls so that would-be thieves will have difficulty removing the pieces quickly. As well, Cowie said that owners should "consider housing all their works in one area because they most likely could afford the security involved in looking after pieces in one room or hallway, instead of having them spread out all over different buildings or through a high-rise structure."

People in homes with large collections should consider having certain areas off limits when they have a large party. And he stressed that everyone should make periodic checks and inspections. "A fellow in Toronto phoned us that he was missing a valuable piece of art. You know he did not know when it was taken because he had so much stuff. It could have been stolen months ago when he had a party, or yesterday."

Most collectors are always happy to have their antiques and art included in a major book or exhibition. However, many are afraid to have their names appear as owners of the artifacts, fearing that thieves will steal from them later. Cowie tended to downgrade that idea saying that in his experience, at least in the Toronto area, thieves don't know about art and antiques and are basically uneducated. "I don't think they ever read antique or art books. They just are not that sophisticated."

What should you do if you are at an auction preview, antique show or shop and spot something stolen from your home? "Call the police," stressed Cowie, "before telling the vendor. If you did it the other way and told him first, he might secret the artifact away or 'sell' it quickly."

What's It Worth?

The answer to the above question depends on who you ask — a dealer, a collector or a friend.

The dealer buys as cheaply as possible in order to make a profit. Therefore, to him, your treasure might be "worth" only a minimal amount of money. By the same token, if he were to own it and were to try to sell to you, it would be "worth" much more.

A collector, on the other hand, may be willing to pay a higher price. Your treasure might be worth more to him simply because he needs that specific item to fill out his collection.

A friend may think your antique is worth a fortune, but until he actually offers to purchase it from you, his evaluation doesn't mean much, flattering though it may be. In short, the old adage that a thing is worth only as much as someone is prepared to pay for it still holds true.

One way to find out the real value of a piece is to put it up for auction. If it is sold, you will have an accurate answer to your question but, obviously, will no longer own it. To retain a piece in your possession and know its worth you must consult a professional appraiser who will want to know why you want to know. Is it because you wish to:
- insure the object?
- buy or sell it?
- donate it to a museum or other institution?

Appraising Jewelry

Jewelry evaluations should be done only by certified gemologists who are knowledgeable about gems and precious metals and familiar with market fluctuations. Before you engage an appraiser, shop around. Take one piece to several appraisers until you find one you think you can trust. Check his credentials and make sure his work will be acceptable to your insurance company.

Not all professional gemologists necessarily agree on the value of a particular piece, according to one collector who recently received two very different appraisals for the same piece — a handcrafted gold pendant with a small diamond in the centre. One gemologist handed her a brief statement describing the item as "a ladies' diamond necklace in white gold with a 10-point

Victorian cut diamond. Value: $250." The second appraiser delivered a comprehensive report accompanied by a colour photograph plus a formal certificate in duplicate evaluating the piece at $349.80 including provincial sales tax. Both gemologists charged $15 for their services.

A bona fide jewelry appraisal should be typed on formal letterhead, describing the item in detail, stating its estimated value including sales tax, as well as at least one photograph. The appraisal price usually reflects current market values, the amount you probably would have to pay if you wanted to replace the piece within a three year period. It is not the amount you would receive if you wanted to sell it. The rule of thumb is that you will probably obtain less than one half of the appraised value at the retail level and one half of that again if you sell to a dealer.

A properly executed jewelry appraisal also serves as proof of ownership for customs purposes. This means that you can take valuable pieces out of the country when you travel and will not be asked to pay duty when you re-enter. Always carry a copy of your appraisal when you cross international boundaries.

Jim Hergal of JHEMZ, Toronto, is an experienced gemologist whose rates probably compare well with those charged by other experts in the field. To evaluate for insurance purposes a piece of jewelry that is brought to his office, he will charge $20 for the first appraisal and $15 each one after that. His certificates come with a 1:1 ratio photograph.

Most gemologists recommend that insurance appraisals be updated regularly at least every four years, although two may be the ideal time span.

Fine Art and Antique Appraisals

In Canada it is difficult to find competent fine art appraisers. We only have PADAC — the Professional Art Dealers Association of Canada — which specializes in contemporary and ethnographical art. Nor does this country have specific laws to regulate the art business (licensing, certification, etc.), other than those designed to protect the consumer.

Anyone looking for a professional fine art and antique appraiser should first contact organizations in the United States, as some Canadian appraisers are members of these societies.

In general, North American museums or art galleries under federal or provincial (state) jurisdiction are at liberty to advise you about the origin of a piece and tell you whether or not it is a fake; but they cannot attempt to evaluate it for you. Some antique shop owners are qualified to do appraisal work but their judgement may be biased. Nor can auction company appraisers whose fees generally are based on a percentage of the total appraised value be totally impartial in their evaluations. Appraisal companies charging a "flat fee" are probably the most reliable, as demonstrated by the code of ethics set forth in the statutes of the American Society of Appraisers:

> The Society takes the position that it is unprofessional and unethical for an appraiser to contract to do work for a fixed percentage of the amount of value, or of the estimated cost (as the case may be) which he determines at the conclusion of his work.

To illustrate what can happen when appraisals are mismanaged I would like to relate an event which in 1981 led to a $6 million lawsuit against Sotheby Parke Bernet Inc., New York.

The story began in 1967 when Dr. Joseph Sataloff, a Philadelphia ear, nose and throat specialist, bought a houseful of antiques for

$10,000. Among them was a floor lamp that at one time he had offered to sell to a local dealer for $250. It stood in the doctor's living room for many years until it was spotted by a visitor, an expert on Russian enamels and the curator of the Hillwood Museum in Washington, DC. He told Dr. Sataloff that it was a rare eighteenth-century Russian silver candlestick and offered to purchase it for this museum, which at that time was part of the Smithsonian Institution.

Both the United States Internal Revenue Service and the museum requested a proper appraisal, and in 1974 Robert Woolley, then Sotheby's expert on Russian art, was called in to evaluate the piece. He described it as an Imperial Russian repousse silver candlestick, five feet in height, which had been presented to a church in Moscow in 1726 by Catherine I, widow of Czar Peter the Great. Woolley appraised the piece at $130,000, and the museum subsequently acquired it.

Dr. Sataloff was allowed the appropriate income tax deductions. However, two years later, the IRS Art Advisory Panel reviewed the case and came up with a new value for the candlestick of between $15,000 and $18,000. As a result, they requested Dr. Sataloff to pay $86,789.33 in back taxes plus accrued interest.

Obviously distressed, the doctor consulted Borislaw N. Dvorsky, head of the Russian Department at Christie's, who advised him that the candlestick was silver plate, not silver at all and worth between $2,000 and $3,000. He determined its provenance sometime in the nineteenth century, disagreeing with Robert Woolley's original interpretation of the inscription. He maintained that many similar candlesticks had been used in churches throughout Imperial Russia and that they had no connection with Catherine I.

Dr. Sataloff subsequently launched a lawsuit against Sotheby's, demanding they pay the back taxes for which he had been assessed, all accountants' and lawyers' fees, $5 million in punitive damages and $1 million in compensation. He also claimed to have suffered extreme agitation and distress and was unable to continue practicing surgery in consideration for the welfare of his patients. In short, he blamed Sotheby's for handling the appraisal "recklessly and negligently."

The company laid a countersuit, demanding $1 million because "the resulting worldwide publicity greatly damaged the professional repu-

The Russian Candlestick. (*Photo:* The Maine Antique Digest)

tation, good will and standing of Sotheby Parke Bernet, Inc." They defended Woolley's appraisal of $60,000 to $70,000 which had resulted in a selling price of $130,000 to a charitable foundation, claiming it to have been fair because Dr. Sataloff had proposed an alternative appraisal for insurance purposes which, according to the custom of the trade, would generally double the fair market value."

The lawsuit was settled out of court, only minutes before the trial was supposed to begin. Regrettably, the terms of the agreement will never be made public, according to Sotheby's lawyer. A lot of questions regarding appraisals and methods by which artifacts are donated to government institutions, therefore, will have to remain unanswered.

Conclusion

Before you engage an appraiser spend time (checking with various associations, asking for references and verifying qualifications.)

Insist on a formal written estimate stating costs involved, especially if you have a large collection that may require several days' work. Ask for a breakdown on how values were obtained, a time estimate and a statement regarding the life of the appraisal.

The evaluation should include the appraiser's professional qualifications as well as a list of organizations he belongs to. Make sure the appraisal is in duplicate and includes at least semi-professional photographs.

The appraisal must state whether it was designed for insurance, probate, tax, or divorce purposes. It must contain concise descriptions of all goods, measurements, colour and materials used. If individual items are very valuable, additional appraisals should be obtained.

It is advisable to periodically take snapshots of different areas of the home where collectibles are displayed in case additional proof ownership for non-listed items is ever required.

Sources of Information

Appraisal Societies

The American Society of Appraisers, (ASA),
PO Box 17265
Washington, DC 20041
Founded in 1936. Potential members must furnish six references and pass an examination before being admitted.

Appraisals Association of America Inc.
60 East 42nd Street
New York, NY 10165

Art Dealers Association of America (ADAA),
575 Madison Avenue
New York, NY 10165
Write for information.

The International Society of Appraisers
PO Box 726
Hoffman Estates, IL
Founded in 1980. Potential members must furnish five references and must pass three examinations. Graduates can us CAPP after their names.

International Society of Fine Arts Appraisals
PO Box 280
River Forest, IL 60305
Founded in 1978; Elizabeth Carr, president.

6

Antiques and the Government

The Cultural Property Export and Import Act proclaimed by the Canadian government September 6, 1977 is designed "to preserve in Canada the best examples of Canadian heritage in movable cultural property." It makes the removal from Canada without government permit of certain classes of antiques and art punishable by a fine of up to $25,000 and/or a maximum sentence of five years' imprisonment.

Falling under the control list are objects that were made in the territory that is now Canada; that are not less than fifty years old but usually more than one hundred years, and "made by a natural person who is no longer living." As well, the controlled objects — which include ethnographic art; military objects; decorative art; fine art; scientific or technological objects; books, records, documents, photographic positives and negatives and sound recordings; textual material; cartography; photography; iconography; audio material, etc; — are those that have resided in this country more than thirty-five years. Each of the categories set out above have their own particular set of regulations. While we can't examine each in detail here, let's look at the section called *Objects of Decorative Art.*

Glassware, ceramics, textiles, woodenware and works in base metals that have a fair market value in Canada of more than one thousand dollars; and furniture, sculptured works in wood,

works in precious metals and other objects of decorative art that have a fair market value in Canada of more than four thousand dollars come under this heading. Subsection 2 breaks this list down even further.

Items described in the above paragraph include:

- utensils, tools, earthenware and such other household articles
- costumes, embroidery, lace and such other objects related to dress
- personal weapons
- objects of folk art

This list is broken down again:

Without restricting the generality of paragraph (1) (b) (as set out above) objects of decorative art described in that sub-item include: articles made of silver; jewellery; religious carvings; decorative sculpture; architectural features; furnishings; and objects of folk art ....

An object of decorative art that was made within or out of the territory that is now Canada by a person who at any time normally resided in the territory; and has a fair market value in Canada of more than six thousand dollars.

There is more on this subsection but we won't explore it further here. It is sufficient to point out that the current Canadian Cultural Property Export Control List, amended effective March 1986, is complicated. Before attempting to export anything, please send for a copy. Write to 300 Slater Street, Room 500, Ottawa, ON K1A OC8 or phone (613) 990-4161.

Any resident of Canada wishing to export protected artifacts must apply for an export license. (Forms are available from customs offices.) If the object being exported is subject to export control, the application is referred to an expert examiner (a museum curator knowledgeable about the type of object being exported or certain selected antique dealers) who then has the legal responsibility to either refuse the export permit or grant it. If it is granted, the permit is issued without further delay. If they recommend that it be refused, then the applicant has 30 days to appeal this decision to the Canadian Cultural Property Export Review Board. The Review Board will then hear the appeal, and may grant the permit or impose a delay period of between two and six months during which the object may not leave the country. While the delay period is in force, the Secretariat actively works to find an institution in Canada to purchase the object, and a grant is available from the Department of Communications to assist with this purchase. If no Canadian institution purchases it within the delay period the permit is granted and the object may be exported. If the applicant decides not to appeal the decision of the expert examiner they cannot reapply for an export permit for two years.

The Cultural Property Export and Import Act can also allocate a certain amount of money for repatriation purposes so that artifacts of national importance, offered on the international market, can be purchased and brought home. The amount of money available is determined by an annual Parliamentary appropriation and is cur-

rently set at $1.6 million.

Some dealers have commented, after having one or more important treasures turned down by museums because funds were not available, that had they quietly exported the artifact and then applied to bring it into this country, money would miraculously be made available from the repatriation fund. Of course, there are penalties, including fine and imprisonment for such infractions and I am not recommending this tactic, but the point is that the law seems to be too unwieldy and too difficult to monitor.

Initially, Canadian collectors were delighted with the new Act as many had watched thousands of pieces of Canadiana disappear into the United States only to assume a false provenance and history. However, when it became apparent that it was almost impossible to enforce the Act, they began to question its necessity.

Based on the theory that outstanding Canadian artifacts are of interest to Canadian collectors and that mediocre ones are not distinguishable from run-of-the-mill American and British pieces, it is believed that genuine antiques can take care of themselves and that the new Act merely constitutes another form of government interference.

Two incidents confirm this thesis and are discussed here at length because they are crutial for understanding of the history of the Act. The Breitman Antiques case is not dated, as some people working within the Cultural Property Export Review Board would like us to believe. It *is* important since there has not been any subsequent prosecution involving antiques.

The first situation involved the Montreal firm of Breitman Antiques, a company whose owner, Sonny Booth, decided, in 1979, to move his business to Dallas, Texas, subsequently renaming it Booth Galleries. After advising Ian Clark, founding chairman of the Canadian Cultural

Property Export Review Board, of his intention, he contacted important Canadian museums and private collectors with whom his firm had dealt during his fifty years in business. He placed advertisements in most Canadian antique publications and asked Jean Palardy, noted authority on early Quebec artifacts and author of *The Early Furniture of French Canada,* to list the items that should under the law remain in Canada. Fifteen pieces were considered to be of museum quality and on May 4, 1979, Booth applied for the necessary export licenses. When permission was denied, all fifteen pieces were subsequently acquired by various Canadian museums, including the Royal Ontario Museum, Toronto, the Confederation Art Gallery and Museum, Charlottetown, and the musée d'art of Joliette.

Disappointed by the lack of interest in the remainder of his collection, Sonny Booth left Canada but not before obtaining correct customs papers and clearances from United States authorities. He had, however, failed to apply for the export permits required under the new Act.

It was not until an anonymous complaint reached the RCMP that charges were laid against Booth. After due investigation it was found that he had illegally exported about eighty thousand dollars' worth of culturally important pieces of furniture. A delegation of RCMP investigators and Canadian antique experts, among them CADA members John Russel and R.G. Perkins, were sent to Dallas to view the Booth collection. When asked about the quality of the merchandise, Perkins remarked that he had not seen a single object that a Canadian museum would have wanted to acquire, although he was sad to see so many good pieces leave Canada.

Because the United States is not a signatory to the UNESCO Convention governing the illicit Import-Export and Transfer of Ownership of Cultural Property, Sonny Booth could not be forced to return to Canada to face trial nor could his stock be seized and shipped back. However, he did return of his own accord, bringing back twenty-one pieces. He pleaded guilty in June 1981. Nine of the artifacts were placed in museums; he was allowed to keep two as part of his personal collection; and one was judged to be of American origin. For the remaining nine he applied for and was granted export permits. "They made me bring those damn pieces all the way back here again," said Booth. "Shipping cost me about $2,000; legal fees, $5,000; and there was a

Canada's wedding gift to Prince Charles and Lady Diana included six pieces of furniture.

fine of $5,000." For the pieces placed in museums, the Canadian government paid about 95 per cent of the cost, according to Booth.

The unwieldiness of the Cultural Property Export and Import Act was brought home even more dramatically when in July 1981 the federal government became involved in the illegal export of part of Canada's wedding gift to Prince Charles and Lady Diana. It included one four-poster bed, one toilet mirror, one chest of drawers, one desk, two candlestands and a selection of Canadian books. These items were quietly shipped out of the country on July 7, 1981, without export permits. In a telephone interview on July 8, 1981, Sharon Van Raalt, program administrator of Movable Cultural Property advised me that three applications arrived at her office after the goods had been shipped and Jean-Paul Roy, chief of state protocol, reluc-

Along with the gifts, the Canadian government gave the Royal Couple a selection of vintage and contemporary books. This cartoon, featured in *The Toronto Star*, capsulizes the whole story. Collection: Hyla Wults Fox.

tantly admitted that these papers should have been filed sooner. Christine Grant, curator of history at the Museum of Man in Ottawa and expert examiner for the government, then hurriedly granted the missing permits because, in her opinion, their quality did not warrant keeping them in Canada.

The other problem concerns the wedding gifts' provenance; John Russel, proprietor of Beaver Hall Antiques in Gananoque, Ontario, had sold five of the six pieces to the federal government. He said in a tape-recorded interview that the bed was American in origin and the other pieces had "no great background." Several specialist dealers who had examined photographs of the furni-ture agreed that the provenance of at least half of the pieces was questionable, although Huguette LaBell, under secretary of state, had informed me earlier that the government had asked for "typically Canadian" furniture from the eighteenth and nineteenth centuries. John Russel, defending his position, told one reporter that no one had insisted that the pieces be Canadian. Rather than putting any of the blame on Russel, a man with decades of experience in the antique business, it would be safe to assume that the government gave him little in the way of information. Most likely he did not know why the pieces were being purchased or where they were to be used.

How were the wedding gifts selected? Madeline D'Aurey, the Government House press representative, knew that Colonel George Bernier, director of state ceremonial, had headed a selection committee made up of Esmond Butler, secretary to the governor general; Huguette LaBell, under secretary of state; one representative from the Prime Minister's Office; and another one from the Canada Council. Jean-Paul Roy, chief of state protocol, confirmed that five of the pieces were purchased from Beaver Hall Antiques and that the sixth — a drop-front desk — came from Harry Porter's Antiques in Martin's River, Nova Scotia, having been selected by Mr. and Mrs. Esmond Butler who, according to Mr. Roy, "are very fond of antiques."

It is difficult to determine how much was spent on the wedding gifts as the Prime Minister's Office refused to reveal the price tag "as a matter of etiquette." The minimum estimate is $6,000 — the base amount required for the export permits, covering the desk, the chest of drawers and the fourposter bed. Not included are the two candlestands and the toilet mirror, assessed at below the $2,000 limit. When Waddington's former Canadiana specialist David Tyrer was asked at the time how much the six pieces would fetch at auction, he estimated they might bring around $4,000.

Following the "Royal Gift Incident," some of Canada's most prestigious collectors, dealers and museum personnel formed an organization, in an attempt to forestall similar government "mistakes." Calling themselves the Canadian Heritage Antique Society (CHAS), the executive committee issued the following statement:

> Based on our experience as a group of dealers, collectors and cultural historians we resent the use of this furniture to represent our Canadian heritage. Three of these six pieces are probably American. All of this furniture is run-of-the-mill and aesthetically inferior. We ask the federal government to recall these inappropriate pieces and to find, instead, authentic Canadian furniture as a gift to the Royal Couple.

Not surprisingly the government did nothing. Sonny Booth's comments, however, still echo in collectors' minds: "Don't you know? There is one law for us and one law for them. They proved it."

Importing Antiques & Art Into Canada

According to the most recent (C1990) Customs Tariff brochure, articles, other than spirits or wines, produced more than 100 years prior to the date of accounting under such regulations, may be imported free into this country if they have proof of age. This includes photographic or photomechanical representations, numbered and signed by the artist or numbered and otherwise authenticated by or on behalf of the artist; original engravings, prints and lithographs produced directly in black and white or in colour of one or of several plates wholly executed by hand by the artist, but not including such articles produced by any mechanical or photo-mechanical process; original sculptures and statuary in any material; paintings, drawings and pastels — all the foregoing when produced by an artist and valued at not less than twenty dollars each; and antiques of an age exceeding one hundred years, furniture was specifically mentioned.

To avoid problems, collectors bringing antiques into Canada should have a full bill of sale bearing a complete description of the goods purchased as well as showing a vendor's statement pertaining to the age of the individual items and, if possible, the approximate date of creation. The importer also should submit magazine articles, books or other proof of provenance relevant to the imported objects to satisfy Canadian customs officials.

For further details and information write to the Tariff Division, Finance Canada, 140 O'Connor Street, 14th floor, L'Esplanade Laurier, Ottawa, ON K1A OG5. Collectors can also contact regional customs offices in or near the closest port of entry.

Region	Address/Telephone
Atlantic	Customs Office 6169 Quinpool Rd., Box 3080 Halifax, NS B3J 3G6 (902) 426-2911
Quebec	Customs Office 130 Dalhousie St., Box 2267 Quebec, PQ G1K 7P6 (418) 648-4445
Montreal	Customs Office 6th Floor, 400 Youville Square Montreal, PQ H2Y 2C2 (514) 283-9900
Ottawa	Customs Office 360 Coventry Road Ottawa, ON K1K 2C6 (613) 993-0534/998-3326
Toronto	Customs Office Box 10, Station A 2nd floor, 1 Front St. W. Toronto, ON M5W 1A3 Weekdays: 8:00 a.m.–4:30 p.m. (416) 973-8022 Sat., Sun. and holidays (416) 676-3643
Hamilton	Customs Office, 10 John St. S., Box 2989 Hamilton, ON L8N 3V8 (416) 572-2891 Evenings and weekends (416) 679-6202
Windsor	Customs Office 1st Floor, 420 Devonshire Road Windsor, ON N8Y 4T6 (519) 973-8500
Winnipeg	Customs Office Federal Building 269 Main Street Winnipeg, MB R3C 1B3 (204) 983-4507
Alberta	Customs Office Box 2910, Station M Room 720, 220 Fourth Ave. SE Calgary, AB T2P 2M7 (403) 292-4666
Pacific	Customs Office 1001 West Pender Street Vancouver, BC V6E 2M8 (604) 666-1545

Great Britain also has laws governing the export and import of works of art. Anyone contemplating an "antique" visit to that country should obtain a brochure from the reviewing committee on the Export of Works of Art, Office of Arts and Libraries, Horse Guards Road, London, SWIP 3AL.

Donating to Museums

"Not everything belongs in museums and public institutions," according to Larry Ryan, executive secretary of the Gifts and Bequests Section of the Ontario Heritage Foundation. "It is artificial and unnatural to have to go to a museum to see anything of the past," says Mr. Ryan. "A great many things should be recirculated, auctioned off and passed down to children and grandchildren." He believes that only national treasures that need protection because of their historical importance belong in museums.

Besides artifacts that have landed in museums are forever removed from auction houses, dealers and collectors; they can no longer circulate in the open market, nor financially benefit the people who would normally handle them. In fact, by removing them from the private sector they are being taken away from those who love, care about, and appreciate them.

Since the majority of public institutions cannot afford to mount large exhibitions or produce well illustrated catalogues, many collections languish in museum storerooms, rarely to be seen by the general public. Even if catalogues are published, they seldom are on display in museum bookstores and unless collectors attend specific exhibitions, in person, they usually are not even aware of their existence.

Ideally, collectors should have access to museum artifacts almost at will, but in many instances the opposite is true. Curators tend to look upon museum holdings as their own private domain. As a result, private collectors and legitimate researchers are hampered when they wish to investigate and examine certain pieces. Frequently they are denied access to the goods. In documented cases, curators would not allow material and photographs to be used for future publications because they themselves may wish to publish them one day. Many museums charge permission fees for photographs to be reproduced in books and magazines, and in some instances questionable fees for curatorial time have been levied on bona fide researchers. For instance, I was examining the textile collection of a major Canadian museum several years ago while the curator remained in her office and spent the time talking on the phone. A week later, after I returned home, I was billed thirty-five dollars per curatorial hour for two hours.

Two unrelated events that occurred in the fall of 1982 raise some serious questions about the manner in which museums dispose of artifacts, be it for reasons of duplication, lack of storage space or changes in collecting policies. Because neither the provincial nor the federal govern-

ments ever established firm policies or standard procedures in deaccessioning, some unusual situations developed, the most recent involving the decision by the Ontario Agricultural Museum to auction some two thousand items. They were a small portion of the Matthews Collection purchased in 1967 by the Ontario government for the Ontario Science Centre and then passed on to the museum in Milton, who retained what they could use, offered some to other institutions on loan and put the balance in storage where it remained for years.

Robert Carbert, general manager of the Agricultural Museum subsequently advised the museum community that he intended to dispose of the merchandise in storage by holding an auction sale. He wanted to use the proceeds to acquire necessary new pieces. Although he had placed an advertisement in the *Museum Quarterly* more than a year before the event, he received little or no response.

After the sale that incidentally netted the museum twelve thousand dollars, some members of the museum community felt that the auctioned artifacts should have gone to various institutions instead. Others claimed they had not been told about the dispersal, and a few admitted that they would have wanted some of the items for their museums but ethically could not have bought them at auction with taxpayers' money because the collection had originally been paid for by the Ontario government. As one curator explained: "How can I justify spending the taxpayers' money again to buy things that they have paid for once already."

About a month after the Milton auction furor had died down, a Toronto collector-researcher bought a rare specimen of a student's lamp at the Harbourfront Antique Market. Catherine Thuro, author of *Oil Lamps: The Kerosene Era in North America,* the new owner, questioned the vendor about its provenance and was told that he had bought it *with a museum acquisition number* on its base from a man who re-wires fixtures. The vendor admitted stripping off the nickel-plated finish to reveal the brass underneath because he thought he could not sell the lamp in its original state. Some patent dates revealed the manufacturer's name and country of origin. According to Mrs. Thuro, the lamp was uniquely constructed; in fact, it was the only instance she had ever found "where the fuel reservoir was lower than the font." Unfortunately, one of the patent numerals as well as the museum accession number had been stripped off.

Hoping to obtain the missing numbers, Mrs. Thuro again questioned the vendor who told her the student lamp had come from the Grange collection of the Art Gallery of Ontario. When she contacted the Grange, she was told they had no record of the particular item nor of other things recently disposed.

An archivist at the Ontario Art Gallery confirmed that she had telephoned "a nice man who has done a lot of work for us" and asked him to come and look at "a lot of stuff" and take what he wanted. "Unfortunately, he sold this article to somebody and made mention that it belonged to the Grange ... that was the one and only piece in the whole bunch of junk that could have had any merit ... they were all just bits and pieces."

Mrs. Thuro subsequently bought from that same "bunch of junk" a unique copper penholder with an attached burner for melting scaling wax. Apparently, some other rare burners had been part of the Grange lot which had sold, but she could not track them down.

The foregoing also bears a direct relationship to the way in which museums acquire collections. Not only is it important to understand this as a collector but is equally valuable information for people who intend to donate to museums.

Some artifacts are purchased outright. However, in light of today's sagging economy and serious budget cuts, museums encourage donations, rewarding donors with substantial tax deductions. Unfortunately, many administrators will take anything that is given to them and then store excess material at some expense or dispose of it as they see fit.

David L. Newlands, former assistant professor and coordinator of the Museum Studies Programme at the University of Toronto believes museums have to be stopped from accepting things they don't really want, with the idea that they later can sell them "out the backdoor." He thinks some problems could be eliminated by having all donations go through heritage foundations that are agencies of the Crown. Donors would also benefit because by giving to a foundation they receive a 100 per cent tax deduction and often can name the museum of their choice, whereas for direct donations to museums the tax benefits are much smaller. In turn, the foundations could "funnel" these donations to the appropriate institution. Conversely, museums could pass on their excess material to these foundations who, in turn, would have to find a way to dispose of them. The result would be a central clearing house where museums could select artifacts and where they could be sold after a certain period of time, perhaps at an auction once every three or four years.

According to Professor Newlands, most museums must submit their collecting policies to the Ministry of Citizenship and Community, and donors should "ask curators for a copy of these documents." Donors should check whether or not the goods will ever be sold or passed on to another institution. If the donor approves the sale of an artifact and a new item is purchased with the proceeds, it should be attributed to him so that the idea of the gift will be carried on.

The unique copper pen holder with attached burner for melting wax. Collection: Catherine Al.V. Thuro. *(Photo: HWF)*

Income Tax Exemptions For Collectors

By providing tax exemptions for cultural objects, the Income Tax Act and the Cultural Property Export and Import Act encourages private owners to donate or sell their property to museums, art galleries and other institutions. Since only category A institutions are permitted to grant the exemptions, collectors are advised to obtain a current list from the Movable Cultural Properties Department in Ottawa. (Their full address is noted at the beginning of this chapter.)

Under the Income Tax Act, a taxpayer who has made a gift may be entitled to deduct the value of the gift when calculating his taxable income for that year. Charitable deductions are limited to a total of 20 per cent of net income in each year. If the total value of a donation made in a single year exceeds 20 per cent of the donor's net income, the excess may be deducted within the next five years, and in the case of de-

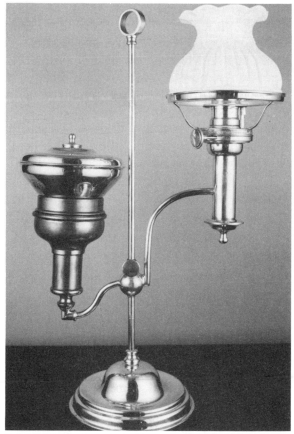

This was the lamp included in "that whole bunch of junk" which the Grange gave away. Collection: Catherine M.V. Thuro. *(Photo: HWF)*

ceased persons, the excess could be carried back one tax year. Also it should be noted that capital gains tax applies against the amount which the property has increased in value since the owner acquired it and is payable in the year the owner disposes of the property.

Revenue Canada also allows a capital cost allowance for art-prints, drawings, etchings, paintings, sculpture, etc. — costing more than $200 if the artist was a Canadian when the piece was made and if the artwork was purchased after the November 12, 1981, budget. However, no capital cost allowance is allowed for engravings, etchings, lithographs or woodcuts made before 1900 and acquired after November 12, 1981.

To complicate matters further, potential donors should know that the Cultural Property Export and Import Act was designed to give major tax incentives to people who donate property of outstanding significance to category A Canadian institutions. According to the Act, the donor may deduct the fair market value of this kind of gift up to 100 per cent of his net income for the year of the gift. As well, the Cultural Property Act also exempts the donor from paying capital gains on tax on the gift. The sale of a gift, therefore, is tax free. In the fiscal year 1989-1990, the latest year for which statistics are available — Canadians sold or donated cultural property valued at $60 million to Canadian institutions.

After the donor and the museum send application forms and two appraisals from reputable dealers to the government review board, they may receive a cultural property tax certificate. When the donor files his tax return he must submit both the certificate and an official receipt from the museum. However, Revenue Canada has the authority to examine all appraisals and indeed question the whole transaction.

In addition to donating and selling such artifacts to designated institutions through the government's certification procedure for tax purposes, collectors can also make their own arrangements with most heritage foundations that operate in various Canadian provinces. (Contact the appropriate foundation for precise details.)

Names and addresses of provincial heritage foundations that will assist individuals and/or corporations to dispose of historically important material are listed under Sources of Information. Details regarding donations, how they are accepted and how donors can benefit are usually outlined in pamphlets published by the relevant ministries.

Sources of Information
Provincial Heritage Trusts and Foundations
Alberta Historic Resources Foundation, Provincial Office, 121-8th Avenue, Calgary, AB T2D 1B4.
British Columbia Heritage Trust, Parliament Buildings, Victoria, BC V8V 1X4.
Direction du Patrimoine de Québec et de Chaundière-Appalaches Centre des dossiers, 225, Grand Allée Est, Bloc C, Road C, PQ G1R 5G5.
Heritage Trust of Nova Scotia, Suite 522, Roy Building, 1657, Barrington Street, Halifax, NS B3J 2A1.
Historic Resources Branch, Tourism, Recreation, Cultural Affairs, 200 Vaughan Street, Winnipeg, MB.
New Brunswick Heritage Foundation, Mr. Allan Magee, President. Box 484, St. Andrews, NB.
Newfoundland Historic Trust, PO Box 5549, St. John's, NF A1C 5W4.
Ontario Heritage Foundation, 77 Bloor Street West, 2nd Floor, Toronto, ON M7A 2R9.
Planning & Development, Government of Yukon, Box 2703, Whitehorse, YK Y1A 2C6.
Prince Edward Island Heritage Foundation, 2 Kent Street, Charlottetown, PEI C1A 1M6.

In the United States a Gifts of Heritage program was recently inaugurated. Information can be obtained from Dwight L. Young Director, The National Trust for Historic Preservation, 1785 Massachusetts Ave. N.W., Washington, DC 20036, (202) 673-4000.

7

Antique Furniture

Furniture is an indispensable component of civilized life. That it has become an art form is a tribute to the ingenuity of man. Although scholars and historians have clearly defined the various periods, styles often carry over from one to the next, with a time lapse existing between furniture for the nobility and that made by and for the "ordinary folk." In addition, provincial joiners, turners and carpenters frequently copied the fine pieces, long after the rich had discarded a particular style. All of which makes it difficult for the novice to accurately date furniture and place it in its correct time period.

Comparatively few pieces made before 1700 have survived, and those that have are in museums and not available to collectors. However, to fully appreciate antique furniture, knowing something of its evolution is necessary. Because most of the pieces found in Canada today originated either in Canada, or were imported from England, I have included data on French and Italian styles if they, in some way, influenced English and Canadian styles. As well, it should be remembered that this chapter is only a brief survey.

Ancient Furniture

Ancient furniture can be found in a few of the world's great museums. It is rarely offered on the open market, but it is important to note that its designs depicting sphinxes, lions, acanthus leaves, gods, etc., handed down to us on Greek pottery fragments and carvings, did inspire the work of later European craftsmen.

The largest collection of Egyptian furniture, dating back to about 1350 B.C., was found by archaeologists in the tomb of Tutankhamun. They unearthed thrones, folding beds and stools, chests and a variety of small tables, some gilded and inlaid with stones, others made of plain carved wood.

Greek furniture featured inlaid woods, ivory, marble, precious stones and metals, such as bronze, iron and silver. The Greeks as well as the Egyptians ate at small low tables, reclining on couches that were barely above floor level. They also are credited with inventing the *Klismos,* a small portable chair, which consisted of a seat on inward curved legs. Its back was made of two uprights fitted to a curved board which reached to shoulder height.

Roman furniture closely followed the Greek design, adding elaborate decorations to pieces made of rare woods.

The Middle Ages

Although little has survived from this period, much design evidence comes from illustrations on mosaics and old manuscripts. Basic pieces — chairs, trestle tables and coffers, which were often used for beds, as well as luggage containers — were small. While the wealthy had several homes, they owned little furniture, and what they did possess they carried with them whenever they travelled. At first, most of the furniture was owned by the churches, but when people, even the wealthy, began to acquire pieces for their homes, they became status symbols.

By the time the Byzantine era arrived, the art of turning had been mastered. Extant pieces show Gothic — pointed arches and tracery — stained glass windows. Carved grotesque heads and linen folds appeared on furniture as well as on other woodwork.

In England, oak was the preferred wood and remained the favourite for several centuries because of its resistance to woodworm and the natural elements. The era until about 1500 was known as the "Age of Oak."

Although heavily carved coffers were the most popular items, chairs began to appear more often. In the fourteenth and fifteenth centuries they were mostly folding stools with frames that formed the letter "X;" later, construction was rigid, and they were equipped with high backs. During the early part of the sixteenth century, three main seating facilities existed: the lidded chest or stool; the cushioned settee with armrests and a straight high back; and chairs with shoulder high backs, the seat supported by two turned front legs and two plain legs at the rear. Stretchers were barely two inches off the floor.

Early Italian Furniture

Except for beds and roughly made tables, wealthy Italians had little or no interest in furniture until the eleventh and twelfth centuries when they began to paint the few pieces they owned. By the fifteenth century, chests were the most important items in the home. Properly called *cassone,* they were first used to hold and transport a bride's dowry and, as such, became a symbol of wealth and status. Backs and arms were added to the cassone by the early 1600s to complement the heavily carved and sculpted tables, beds and chairs that wealthy Italians had acquired to decorate their homes. Richly carved with scrolls, foliage and shells, made from softwood and gilded, this new style, which was born in Rome, came to be known as Baroque.

In the seventeenth century the key words were opulence and splendour, boldly expressed

Sotheby's, London, offered a c. 1620 James I oak panel-back armchair in their October 1982 auction. Estimated to fetch between £2,000 and £2,500, it went under the hammer for £3,630. *(Photo: Sotheby Parke Bernet, London, England)*

in architecture and furniture design. As the *cassone* lost favour, heavily decorated chests of drawers, tables and massive bookcases, primarily in walnut and fruitwood, came into vogue.

French Furniture

Furniture in France, especially during the Middle Ages, was simple in construction. Artisans relied on the mortise and tenon (groove and tongue or dovetailing) method, with oak being the preferred wood. Most surviving pieces from that era are carved, rather than painted.

When Charles VIII went to war with Italy in the late 1400s, the richness of the country's life made an indelible impression on him, and he arranged for Italian craftsmen to come to France so that they could teach their techniques and ideas to his subjects. Their influence was strong during the fifteenth and sixteenth centuries.

The French nobility could now enjoy many new domestic comforts. While chests were still important, buffets with carvings appeared by 1550; armoires and rectangular-carved tables were first seen by 1600. Most chairs were chests, but they soon sported arms and were either portable and lightweight or massive and throne-like. Oak was preferred; however, walnut became more prevalent, especially at the turn of the century.

The furniture of Louis XIII's reign featured elaborately turned legs, sometimes spiral, beaded or baluster in shape and small chairs with tables in sets. The most important advance occurred when the art of veneering came to France from Germany early in the seventeenth century. The technique of gluing a thin sheet of figured wood, which had been cut and sawn by hand, over a solid base proved a good way of utilizing rare materials and helped counteract warping, cracking and splitting. Soon, marquetry also appeared on furniture, a technique for making designs by inlaying one veneer next to another.

When Louis XIV ascended the throne in 1661, he set up a Ministry for the Arts and appointed the painter Charles Le Brun (1619-1690) as its head. By combining Flemish and Italian craftsmanship with that of the French, Le Brun created new experts in tapestry, weaving and cabinetmaking. The style of furniture made, although known as Louis XIV, was a modification of Italian Baroque and earlier Classical elements. It was opulent but at the same time Classical and symmetrical. When Le Brun died in 1690, he was succeeded by thirty-year-old Andre Boulle, considered to be the best cabinetmaker in Paris. Under his direction, Louis XIV pieces still featured decorative motifs taken from antiquity, but they were soon replaced by the king's own symbol of the two interlaced "L's," a fleur-de-lis and a sunburst motif. Boulle also perfected the use of metals — brass, silver, and pewter — as well as tortoise shell, horn, ivory and mother-of-pearl inlays on wood. He is credited with developing the commode or fine chest of drawers and its later bombé form. Because his work was so innovative, French furniture soon acquired international repute.

The Tudor Period in England

The ascension of Queen Elizabeth I to the throne in 1558 coincided with England's rise to power as a trading nation. Architectural and furniture designs were imported from Holland, Germany and Italy to provide an incentive for English furniture-makers. Most of the pieces, still mainly oak, were constructed by the panel and frame technique whereby a board was held in place by a framework of grooved rails and stiles, the panel fitting snugly into the grooves.

Three ornamental features appeared on most English furniture of that time — bulbs on table legs and bedposts, inlay and strapwork as well as intricate ornamentation consisting of flat bands interlaced with foliage and flower patterns.

The trestle table was replaced by the draw table with extending top. Simple dressers became more ornate and larger cupboards appeared in bedchambers and dining rooms. Also popular for the display of silver and ceramic pieces were the court cupboards — open three-tiered structures about four feet in height.

The Jacobean Period in England

By the 1640s the English middle classes had become a dominant force, demanding furniture for their smaller houses. Many of the current styles were adapted to meet their needs. The plainer and more functional gate-leg tables with rectangular, round or oval tops were suitable pieces when space was at a premium. One or two legs could be opened, and the table extended when necessary. Although wood turning had improved, the heavy Gothic-looking, ornately carved pieces became less popular, especially after the civil war when luxury and pomp were frowned upon.

When Charles II came to the throne in 1660 he introduced many new ideas he had picked up during his exile from England. Some historians feel that this was the time when English furniture-making really began. As imported walnut replaced oak, pieces became more delicate with

Top left: Phillips, London, sold this William and Mary japanned lacquer cabinet in the fall of 1982 for £1,700. *(Photo: Phillips, London)*

Left: This Queen Anne walnut wing armchair with a stuffover back and outswept scroll arm supports on cabriole legs sold for £1,900 in a fall auction in 1982. *(Photo: Phillips, London)*

finer carving and more precise turning. People favoured the "new" furniture, the chests of drawers, writing tables, cane chairs, daybeds and winged armchairs. Upholstered winged settees and mirrors became fashionable, especially among the nobility. Upholstered chairs had been seen infrequently before the 1700s because they had been so costly. When they did appear, it was the upholstery that represented the greater portion of the value of the chair. Today we admire the wood, craftsmanship and the lines of a piece, but in the past, it was the upholstery and other fabrics in the room that attracted the greatest attention.

Lacquered screens imported from Japan and China also became the rage, and the English soon invented a technique they called "japanning," which allowed them to decorate almost anything in that manner.

Basically, the English followed French styles, adapting them to their own more subdued way of life. The furniture of the wealthy boasted a great deal of marquetry work, another technique taken over from the French. It was liberally applied to tables, chests, cabinets, clocks, mirrors and picture frames.

William and Mary Furniture

The style named after the English king and queen who ruled between 1689 and 1702 had elegant, mildly Baroque lines with elaborately turned legs, usually in scroll or spiral forms. The period also is remembered for its high-back and single upholstered chairs which had become the rage among the wealthy. The magnificent needlework on furniture done not only by women but also by skilled men is dearly coveted by collectors today. Also connected with the era are daybeds, double chests (tallboys) and cabinets, ideal for showing off precious porcelain pieces. The long-case clock or Grandfather clock, as it is known today, became an important addition to the wealthy home. Among the Huguenots who

In November 1982, Christie's, New York, sold this Louis XVI ormolu mounted marquetry and ebony bookcase for $209,000 plus 10% buyer's premium. *(Photo: Christie's, New York)*

One of a pair of c. 1725 George I parcel-gilt walnut side-chairs sold for $70,000 plus 10% buyer's premium at a Christie's, New York, auction in October 1982. *(Photo: Christie's, New York)*

had arrived from France as refugees during William and Mary's reign were some excellent craftsmen; it was they who promoted the use of marquetry and veneering.

The cabriole or S-form leg, significant in early eighteenth-century furniture, is thought to have originated in that period as well, although it did not achieve great popularity until well after Queen Anne ascended the English throne.

The Queen Anne Style

Although Queen Anne's reign did not begin until 1702, her name has been associated with a furniture style that was in vogue from the late 1600s until about 1750 in Europe, and until almost 1800 in North America. It was innovative in that it rendered furniture more functional, more comfortable and at the same time displaying a refinement and an elegance not previously experienced in English furniture design.

The delicate, elongated, S-shaped and curved cabriole leg, thought to have originated in the William and Mary period, was used on chairs, tables and case furniture. Walnut was the preferred wood, while oak was only used for lining the inside of drawers.

Whereas, previously, chairs had been square and tall, their new, more rounded shapes made them better suited to the human figure. The backs blended with the curves resulting in a flowing line, while bottom stretchers disappeared almost entirely. At first, chair knees were plain but soon carvings and other elegant-looking decorations were added. Later, the legs ended in a simple club foot or in the more elaborate claw-and-ball design. The famous "Windsor" chair, as well as the English bureau — a set of drawers topped with a fall-front which, when lowered, became a writing surface — made their first appearance. By that time, marquetry and veneer furniture seemed to have fallen from favour, although still being made.

Louis XV and Louis XVI Styles of France

The word Rococo is derived from the French *rocaille*, referring to the rock and shellwork surrounding the castle of Versailles. The style made its first appearance by the 1730s when Louis XV was on the throne of France. Unlike the masculine-looking Baroque, it was soft and feminine, emphasizing ornaments with landscape, rock, shell and even waterfall motifs; sometimes Chinese pagodas and Chinese figures were also included.

Commodes became even more fashionable, later equipped with doors and slender legs; console tables, beds and some chairs were decorated in the same manner. While much of the furniture was in plain wood, some was painted pale blue, lilac, sea-green or contrasted with gold and white, pink and green, yellow and silver paint.

By 1760 French furniture (known today as the Transitional or Louis XVI style, despite the fact that the monarch did not ascend the throne until 1774) was in the midst of yet another change. Some pieces were clearly Rococo, others Neoclassical and a few combined elements of both. Initially, Louis XVI furniture was conservative and elegant. However, under the influence of cabinetmaker Jean Henri Riesner (1734-1806), it gradually changed. Riesner had extensive experience with marquetry in light, contrasting colours and gold lacquer. He combined Oriental with ancient motifs, and his masterpieces included many small items which were especially designed for prominent women, such as Queen Marie Antoinette.

Fall-front desks and roll tops appeared around the 1760s. George Jacob (1739-1814), a prominent French manufacturer, introduced chairs with carved splats and motifs of wheat sheafs, wicker baskets and the lyre motif. His early chairs were painted and covered with gilt, but he later preferred to work in plain mahogany, an idea he had acquired in England.

The Georgian Period

George I began his reign in 1714, yet most of the eighteenth century is considered part of the

This Chippendale-period carved mahogany library chair fetched £2,800 at a Phillips, London, auction in the fall of 1982. *(Photo: Phillips, London)*

Georgian era. Furniture during the early years was curved and flowed in elongated S-lines. The cabriole-shaped leg was still preferred, although the carving was restricted to the knee of a chair or a table leg. It began to increase around the middle of the century, although English pieces were less ornate than the French and Italian. By 1750 Rococo was accepted and widely used by the rich. Mahogany was the favoured wood, and Chinese-inspired designs and patterns became important for furniture as well as for porcelain and silver. In addition, embroidered counterpanes (bedhangings), upholstery and tapestries in dazzling designs were produced by many talented men and women.

A Sheraton rosewood and satin birch cross-banded sofa table brought £1,300 in a Phillips, London, auction in late 1981. *(Photo: Phillips, London)*
Left: A set of eight Regency carved rosewood dining chairs sold in 1981 at a Phillips auction for £2,800. *(Photo: Phillips, London)*

Among the craftsmen who dominated the Georgian era were Chippendale, Hepplewhite, Sheraton and Adam. They gained wide acceptance, although their individual styles were not always clearly definable. Most of these men published furniture design books, and while they showed pieces and features popular at the time, they were not always unique and often plagiarized or copied from others. Few exact renderings were made of the actual published patterns and designs as most workers adapted them to suit their own personal tastes and skills and the wealth of their patrons. Exact duplicates most likely date from the nineteenth century or later. Although, for example, some

pieces of American Chippendale furniture have claw-and-ball feet, they only show up once in Chippendale's design book. Many so-called Chippendale pieces were not made by him at all, and no copies have been found that are positively attributable to him. His pattern book first published in 1754 under the title *The Gentleman's and Cabinet-Maker's Director* included examples derived from and incorporating the Rococo style, Gothic and Chinese motifs.

Basically, Chippendale's pieces were well proportioned. His carved and decorated knees on table and chair legs as well as his tables with delicate fretwork or piecrust rims were important features of his work. Most of his furniture was made in carved mahogany and, in a few instances, in gilt wood. Copies appeared throughout his lifetime and again starting in mid-Victorian times. Late in his career, he was known to have executed Rococo designs for architects Robert Adam and his brother James, who were regarded as *the* important Georgian designers.

Active from approximately 1770 to 1790 the Adam brothers created pieces to suit the buildings they were erecting. Nearly all the designs on their delicate-looking furniture was influenced by ancient Greek or Roman motifs — urns, garlands of foliage, berries, and Classical figures. Generally, Adam furniture was not made of mahogany but was painted or gilt wood, satinwood and other rich inlaid woods. The Adam sideboard was significant in that it tended to place new emphasis on the dining room.

There are no documented, surviving George Hepplewhite pieces, yet his book *The Cabinet-Maker and Upholsterer's Guide* published by his widow two years after his death in 1786 gave him immortality.

Known to have worked mostly with mahogany, sycamore, chestnut and occasionally satinwood, he was strongly influenced by the then fashionable Neoclassical elements.

Yet, he is best remembered for his chairs with shield-shaped backs, some showing wide ovals with spreading and pierced splats, others having finely spoked wheels emanating from the centre. His gracefully shaped chair legs usually were squared-off or tapered at the end.

During Hepplewhite's time, the secretary cabinet made its appearance. It had a chest of drawers as its base, the top-most drawer equipped with hinges that allowed it to be opened downward to form a desk or writing surface. Other typical Hepplewhite pieces were the small sideboards with bow fronts and the pembroke table with rectangular or semicircular flaps.

Thomas Sheraton's *The Cabinet-Maker and Upholsterer's Drawing Book* was first published in 1791 with subsequent editions until 1794. It is not known whether he actually had a furniture factory or whether he, himself, ever made pieces. He was, however, a designer who lent his name to a French-influenced style that relied on delicate, Classical motifs. His furniture was functional, often lightweight and portable, such as the small work tables and petite desks especially designed for upper-middle-class women. He probably is best known for his chairs with rectangular backs, divided by a centre splat with two smaller vertical splats on either side. Almost every piece featured this stylized elongated urn motif in one form or another. His chair legs tended to be reeded and sometimes vase-shaped as well. Solid mahogany and mahogany with inlaid coloured woods were his favourites, and he preferred brass ornamentation and paint to the japanned-look.

The Empire and Regency Periods

The excavations at Pompeii and Herculanum in the mid-1700s were partially responsible for the resurgence of Classical elements in French and English furniture design. Another contributing factor was the collection of ancient artifacts Napoleon had brought back from Egypt. As a result, English furniture still dominated by French taste during the early part of the 1800s, relied heavily on motifs such as sphinxes, leaf scrolls, masks, wings and gods; even the Klismos, the famous Greek chair, was being reproduced.

The only thing English furniture-makers did not imitate was Napoleon's own gilt emblems such as his initials, which graced most French pieces of the period.

In France the first quarter of the new century

was known as the Empire period while the same time span in England was referred to as the Regency era. In North America, the large heavy-looking pieces usually with an overhang and S-scrolls were generally considered as Empire style.

George IV as the Prince of Wales had extravagant tastes leaning toward the Oriental. His Brighton Pavilion reflected this interest and led to the popularity of Chinoiserie that was seen everywhere by the 1820s. Bamboo in its natural form and as a design pattern was exceedingly fashionable and repeatedly used on chair legs. By the 1830s with the advance of technology, elegance and the time-consuming handwork on furniture were on the wane.

The Victorian Era

When Queen Victoria came to the throne in 1837, furniture, for the most part, was made by hand. However, when her reign ended in 1901, most of the middle class were buying furniture produced by machine.

The invention of the steam engine launched the mass production era, and following Thomas Jordan's invention of the carving machine in the late 1840s, repetitive ornamental carvings no longer had to be made by hand. Furniture manufacturing became an industry that could satisfy everyone's tastes and pocket books, although some pieces were still fashioned by hand. They had no particular style or design but were influenced by many periods — ancient, Gothic,

John H. Belter made these laminated pierced armchairs in the "Fountain Elms" pattern. *(Photos: Richard and Eileen Dubrow)*

Elizabethan, Oriental and Sheraton themes, as well as those of the Art Nouveau movement.

Furniture, therefore, presents problems to inexperienced collectors. To date it is difficult, and it is hard to distinguish between original pieces and later copies. Noting the changes in screw-and-nail design and recognizing the differences between hand and steam-powered saw marks may help. However, some confusion is unavoidable.

For the first ten to fifteen years of Queen Victoria's reign, furniture was Neoclassical in design with Gothic and Oriental overtones. By the 1840s and 1850s the Grecian and "antique" style, as the Victorians liked to call it, had all but disappeared. Pieces tended to be heavier, although still exhibiting good workmanship. Mahogany and rosewood decorated with machine-made moldings and carvings were much favoured.

The Victorian Empire style emerged at the same time, employing rosewood, mahogany or mahogany veneer over pine. Furniture was massive, plain and curved and many pieces featured C- and S-scrollwork on legs. Feet were either bracket or bulbous, chair arms tended to be rolled rather than straightedged, and chair seats were heavily upholstered, usually in velvet.

Some time after the 1840s until about 1870, Victorian Baroque and Rococo appeared, obviously influenced by France's Louis XV style. Raised carvings depicting foliage, bunches of grapes and vine leaves were prevalent on the less costly mahogany and walnut items, while rosewood was reserved for more expensive pieces. (India ink was often used on walnut to imitate the desirable rosewood grain.) Sets of furniture, especially for bedrooms and dining rooms, became exceedingly popular; stuffed settees with matching chairs for ladies and gentlemen were also fashionable.

This Renaissance revival walnut and burl veneer bedroom set, made in the United States in the 1860s, sold at a Skinner auction in December 1982 for $2,500 plus 10%. *(Photo: Robert W. Skinner Inc., Boston)*

A c. 1909 Gustav Stickley chair made from white quarter-sawn oak with a leather spring seat and cushion. *(Photo: Jordan Volpe Gallery, New York, NY)*

A Queen Victoria press back chair. *Collection: Part-Time, Antiques, Unionville, Ontario. (Photo: HWF)*

- John Henry Belter who came to New York from Germany in the 1840s created a unique style of furniture, much in demand by today's American collectors. His favourite pieces were sofas, mirrors and tables, using ornately carved, pierced and laminated wood, sometimes with more than eight layers, in combination with scrolls and other ornaments. While, to my knowledge, no Belter furniture has surfaced in Canada, it is worth watching, as there is a highly developed market for good examples in the United States.

The Renaissance revival style frequently was used for sideboards, headboards and marble-topped sidetables. It featured heavy straight lines with machine-carved ornaments and applied raised moldings. Another style used carvings with swags of flowers and spiral twists. Machine-made spool turnings were seen on furni-ture such as Jenny Lind beds, chairs, tables and what-not shelves.

Victorian country and cottage furniture made between 1840 and 1900 is popular with today's collectors and decorators. Simple in design, using pine, walnut, chestnut, butternut and maple, it generally resembled other furniture made during this time, but because it was produced for the middle and lower classes it was less sophis-ticated.

The Victorians were noted for using all kinds of other material in furniture. Iron appeared as early as 1851 in plant stands, beds, hall racks, umbrella stands and garden furniture. By 1870 wicker and bamboo was popular and, in fact, is enjoying a revival at present, as collectors look for unpainted, natural tan-finished pieces.

The last portion of the Victorian era was dominated by cheaply made, mass-produced factory items, the kind offered in Canadian and American mail-order catalogues such as Eatons, Simpsons and Montgomery Ward. They were made mostly from ash and oak and other woods stained to look like oak. Sturdy round tables, desks, chairs, beds, dressers and other pieces, which some time ago could not even be given away by some antique and used-furniture dealers, are now fashionable collectors' items, and as yet available at comparatively low cost. It is, however, doubtful that they will ever attain the value or the importance of earlier hand-made pieces.

Charles Locke Eastlake was an English architect who wanted to see a return to the sturdy and simpler furniture of the past. In his first book *Hints on Household Taste* published in 1868 and in later works appearing in the 1890s, he featured rectangular, linear designs in natural wood without stain or paint. He used oak, cherry and pine for his less costly pieces but made his best items — Canadian and American — of walnut or a combination of cherrywood and ebony. Eastlake's innovative approach had a marked impact on furniture design, especially in North America, and helped fuel the Arts and Crafts movement. When American manufacturers began to copy his pieces they not only were in cheaper woods and of shoddy workmanship but incised carvings were added to his basically simple lines.

The Arts and Crafts Movement

Charles Locke Eastlake was a forerunner of the movement that began in England in the 1870s and was adopted by other British furniture designers such as William Morris and Charles Rennie Mackintosh who also rejected the currently popular, heavily carved, mass-produced commercial furniture of the Victorian era. The pieces they created had simple medieval lines — chairs and tables consisting of a series of flat vertical or horizontal boards, oak being the favoured wood.

Gustav Stickley (1857-1942) was the first documented American designer to revolt against Victorian fussiness. Following a trip to Europe, he began to make furniture in 1898, and when it was shown at the Grand Rapids Furniture Exposition in 1900, it became an instant success. Stickley's line, known as "Craftsman," was well constructed, using the old mortise and tenon joint method. Although it appeared massive, its rectangular planks, splats and boards in dark stained oak indicated a well-organized approach to life.

Others quickly copied Stickley's ideas, including his own brothers. The names of Elbert Hubbard and Charles Limbert frequently appear on similar types of furniture but there were many other imitators whose products were not as well made and, therefore, are less valuable collectors' items.

Stickley also was the first to encourage people to make furniture at home from his patterns. Many of the pieces found today are either these home-made examples or those factory-produced by numerous, less prominent makers. They have little value in today's market; however, any with labels of the famous exponents of the Arts and Crafts movement, especially Stickley, are worth considerably more.

As the twentieth century progressed and

machinery was developed, it became possible to make furniture more cheaply. The press back chair was typical of manufacturers' first experience with mass production, and it became the poor man's answer to carved furniture. These chairs are discussed here in some detail because so many have survived and are offered at different mall shows and flea markets.

To make a press back chair, the wood — ash, elm, maple or oak — had to be softened by steaming so that it could be put through a press. With better technology the imprints became clearer and deeper, resulting in bolder designs. The way to recognize an older chair is to examine its profile. If the back legs and the back appear as one continuous line, it is probable that the chair was made at the turn of the century.

Reproductions imported from Hong Kong and Taiwan are now flooding the market; some are made in Toronto and sold as new without any attempts to fool the public. The seats on them consist of several two-inch strips of unseasoned wood whereas the seats on old pieces are usually one thick plank. Braces on old chairs, because they had been steamed and then curved, rarely fall apart or crack, but most of the new pieces have laminated braces that do not stand up well, especially if the chair is in constant use. The backs on newer products are curved backward, at least ten degrees more than the older models. On the other hand, the pressed images on the newer chairs seem to stand out better.

Specialized dealers maintain that there is not that much interest in individual pieces but rather in the refinished, matching sets of six or more. No one is quite certain just how many patterns exist or who made them originally. The Burning Bush or Flame is especially popular; cameos, swans, North Wind, triple presses, lions and devils are well known, but the costliest and the most coveted are the commemorative chairs with images of Queen Victoria, Sir Wilfrid Laurier and other prominent people pressed into the middle of the chair backs.

Canadian Furniture

Canada was and still is a mosaic of different cultures. Those who came here — French, English, American, Scottish, German and Polish — brought with them their own individual traditions and customs which they nurtured and maintained. As a result, the pieces of furniture made here were direct copies of those they had seen and used in their homelands. This mix of styles makes Canadian antique furniture especially appealing.

When this country was settled in the early 1600s, only a handful of communities dotted the countryside. The French had established a small

This primitive chair was created from a whole section of a pine tree trunk, and the rockers were added at some later date. *(Photo: Black Creek Pioneer Village, Toronto, Ontario)*

settlement in Acadia (now Nova Scotia) and later proceeded west into New France (Quebec). Until 1760, all of Ontario was part of New France. When it fell to the British in that same year, the population increased and spread out. By the 1780s Canada was home to many different groups from various places. Change also was brought about by the American Revolution as thousands fled to Canada trying to remain loyal to the Crown. Known as the United Empire Loyalists, they settled in the Maritimes and in various parts of Ontario such as the St. Lawrence valley and Nagara. Among these people were Quakers and Mennonites and were joined, after 1812, by a new wave of immigrants from Britain and Ireland. They all left their mark on this country which is, of course, also reflected in the type of furniture they made and used.

Early Canadian furniture consisted of three basic types: primitive, imported and locally constructed fine pieces. The first included rustic items made from available materials and used by the "common folk," farmers and fishermen. Country furniture or "Canadians" made in rural areas tended to be more primitive than the pieces constructed in large centres such as Quebec City and Montreal. Furniture brought to Canada by immigrants, particularly the British officers and people from the United States and Europe, usually consisted of chests and a few family heirlooms. The fine pieces made here were copies of fashionable furniture used by the nobility at home. Formal and traditional in style they were used by the wealthier immigrants who normally settled in towns rather than in rural communities. Their furniture was well constructed and beautiful, although not quite as pure in design as the original pieces on which it was based. When expensive wood such as mahogany was not available, cabinetmakers had to substitute typical Canadian woods such as cherry, birch,

butternut, maple and even pine. The big difference between Canadian-made and imported furniture was that local products often were decades behind England's and Continental Europe's latest styles.

Until the 1840s Canadian furniture was custom-made and sold directly to the consumer. When the settlers began to prosper a little, they could afford to buy professionally made pieces from merchants who acted as the middlemen for the producers. At the same time, furniture-makers aided by new steam powered equipment started offering cheaper products, and by the 1870s carvings and mouldings could be mass-produced.

Nova Scotia

Acadia, which then included Nova Scotia, New Brunswick and parts of Maine, was settled by the French in 1604. In 1656, it was conquered by the British, returned to French rule in 1667 and won back by the British in 1713.

When 6,000 Acadians refused to swear allegiance to the British Crown, they were banished from Canada and had to flee to the United States where they remained for many years. To replenish the population the British government encouraged Americans to settle in Acadia, offering them free transportation from Connecticut, Massachusetts and Rhode Island. They came in droves, and by 1763 some of the exiles were allowed to return. The British also offered money to persons from Germany, Switzerland and France who were willing to settle here. By 1783 over 20,000 United Empire Loyalists arrived and with them came countless artisans and craftsmen, some capable of making furniture in the English, French, American, German, Swiss and Scottish traditions.

Because so many immigrants were French, much of the Acadian furniture exhibited French

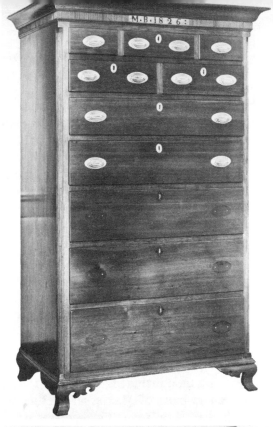

characteristics, although with much less carving. In general, the furniture from this region can be described as elegant and somewhat curved-looking, although there were many exceptions.

Fine English-style furniture was built for British officers, government officials and the wealthy, while rustic pieces such as blanket boxes, dressers, tables and chairs made from pine, bird's-eye and curly maple, birch, butternut and ash were for the less affluent.

New Brunswick

By the year 1784, parts of Acadia became New Brunswick. A lot of furniture was made there at that time, yet little has survived; most extant pieces date from 1795 onward.

Some of the craftsmen were Acadians, although most belonged to other groups. Their furniture differed from the Acadians' in that it tended to be straighter-looking.

New Brunswick antique scholars suggest that 1812 was the turning point in local furniture-making. The British soldiers who had returned to England encouraged many of their compatriots to seek their fortunes in the New World — many came, among them some fine artisans who settled in Saint John and Fredericton. One of them was Thomas Nisbet who arrived in Saint John in 1813. He soon became the country's finest furniture-maker. His earliest

Top left: This impressive Waterloo County chest of drawers in the Chippendale style was made of walnut and white pine. The initials M.B. refer to Mary Bricker, whose father, a Mennonite, arrived in Waterloo County in 1802. *Collection: Private. (Photo: Angus C.M Buchanan from* A Provincial Elegance *by Barbara and Henry Dobson)*

Left: A Niagara Peninsula linen cabinet signed on the base section with the name Jacob G. Culp. Collection: Private. *(Photo: Angus C.M. Buchanan from* A Provincial Elegance *by Barbara and Henry Dobson)*

pieces featured sideboards with ornamentations, four-poster beds, chairs and tables with spiral-twisted legs. From the 1820s onward, his furniture was influenced by the Neoclassical, featuring acanthus leaves and elaborate scrolls. Most of it was mahogany, while some smaller pieces were made of bird's-eye maple. A lot of Nisbet's work was marked with paper labels, and although some were lost or even removed, the examples, many actually of museum quality, that retained them are greatly coveted by collectors.

Ontario

Upper Canada, created in 1791, included land north of Lakes Ontario and Erie and the upper St. Lawrence River. In 1841 it was known as Canada West and in 1867 became the province of Ontario. This information may be incidental to the novice collector but is important for the identification of some furniture as well as of artifacts such as crocks, textiles and photographs. Some of these items were signed or marked with initials, such as U.C. (Upper Canada), C.W. (Canada West), which not only identify the places where they originated but also provide some sort of time reference.

Many of the earliest Ontario pieces showed formal British styling, although some were adaptations of Jacobean, William and Mary and Queen Anne designs. Extant pieces from that era are few and far between so that conclusions only can be based on contemporary writings, sketches and drawings.

Particularly influential on furniture design were the United Empire Loyalists who brought with them such well-developed American styles as the Windsor chair. (Sometimes known in Canada as the arrowback or the rodback.) Many were in plain or stained wood, but the choicest

examples boast the original paint and decorations.

In several parts of Ontario, individualized styles were created which are much coveted by today's collectors. They include furniture of the Niagara Peninsula and Waterloo County, both influenced by the Pennsylvania Germans, as well as the pieces made by Polish settlers in Wilno, Ontario.

Many of the Germans originally were from the Palatinate, an area around the Rhine River in Germany. They had come to Ontario via the Mohawk Valley in New York State and settled in the Niagara Peninsula, Cornwall, the Bay of

A Quebec birch chair with shaped apron dates from the mid-18th century. *Collection: William and Jane Siegel. (Photo: Angus C.M. Buchanan from* A Provincial Elegance *by Barbara and Henry Dobson)*

Quinte, and York and Waterloo counties. Their furniture was decorated with stylistic designs, beautifully carved and painted in contrasting colours. A lot of the pieces had heart motifs and inlay work, and the painting, sometimes made to look like woodgraining, is descriptively called finger painting or feathering.

Polish immigration to Ontario did not begin until 1858, yet the furniture made in the little village of Wilno until the early 1900s not only has become synonymous with the people who settled in this tiny part of northeast Renfrew County but also is very collectible. Having survived in surprisingly large numbers, the pieces brought from the Polish homeland and those made in Ontario were clearly related to a Baroque style. They featured scrollwork and arches, as well as painted decorations of flowers in baskets, bouquets and single blooms. Their glazed dish-dressers (cupboards with glass-paned doors on the upper half), boxes and tables are popular collector's items.

Jacques & Hay

Jacques & Hay was a prolific organization producing high quality furniture from the mid 1830s until 1922. For almost a century they furnished the best houses, hotels, offices and political residences. In fact, in 1866, the *Globe* newspaper business section wrote that their furniture "is distributed through the length and breadth of the

Top left: A c. 1750 two-tier Quebec buffet with wooden pegged construction throughout and early rat-tail hinges. *Collection: Dr. Herbert Schwarz. (Photo: Angus C.M. Buchanan from* A Provincial Elegance *by Barbara and Henry Dobson)*
Left: The early 20th-century Doukhobor table from Verigen, Saskatchewan, held a small cabinet on the bottom plank. It is red with dark red and green decorations. *(Photo: Michael Bird)*

land so completely that there is scarcely a house in the whole of Canada which has not some article the product of their workshops ... Messrs. Jacques & Hay make weekly from 2,000 to 2,500 chairs and 200 bed-steads."

According to Ruth Cathcart, the author of the only book on this company, John Jacques, an Englishman and Robert Hay, a Scot, established The Jacques & Hay Co. in 1835 at King and Bay Streets in downtown Toronto with a measley $800. So successful were they that five years later they opened a separate factory near Lake Ontario and in 1843 moved their showroom to another corner of King and Bay Streets. By 1853 they had expanded moving again to a large five-story brick building at Front and Bay Streets, all in Toronto's downtown core.

After enduring two major fires which destroyed their stock they bought land and a mill site about 60 miles north of Toronto in a village known as New Lowell. Robert Hay put his brother-in-law, Peter Paton, in charge of the new division.

Not only did the New Lowell division manufacture and produce stuffing for mattresses, chairs etc, but they also made various parts for furniture such as bed posts, rails, chair backs, and exported them to Glasgow and of course, the Toronto operation. Their lumber was sold to various manufacturers in Upper New York State.

As well, they built all kinds smaller items such as boxes, crates, railroad ties, ladders, clothes-pins and some low level furniture which is often referred to as 'cottage furniture', made mostly for "new settlers in Canada. This furniture was marked with an ink stencil "H & P NL" (Hay & Patton, New Lowell.)

John Jacques retired in 1870 and Robert Hay acquired controlling interest changing the company name to R. Hay & Co. Then, in 1885, Ro-

A small painted brown pine Mennonite corner cupboard from the Rosthern Mennonite Reserve in Saskatchewan. *Collection: Rosthern College Mennonite Museum. (Photo: Michael Bird)*

bert Hay retired and a long standing employee, Charles Rogers took the reigns changing the name to Charles Rogers & Sons Co. He died in 1891 but the company survived until 1922. (See the bibliography at the end of the chapter for more information about Cathcart's book.)

French-Canadian Furniture

New France, or Quebec as it is now known, was settled in the early 1600s by the French who came to the region via Acadia. If they brought any furniture with them at all, it would have been chests to hold their precious bedding and clothing. What they made after they settled in New France and in various parts of Ontario and

Acadia closely resembled the pieces they had used in their homeland, although they were simpler and larger yet just as sturdy. The best were made before 1825, while later examples were influenced by the tastes of American and English immigrants. Pieces made between 1650 and 1750 were typical of the Louis XIII style with straight lines, turnings, pediments and large surfaces. After the 1750s the Rococo style appeared, lasting well into the next century. As in many other parts of Canada, the craftsmen of New France leaned toward pine, yellow birch and butternut woods, maple becoming an additional favourite in the early 1800s.

Rather than bearing painted motifs, most of the furniture was stained and by the 1750s many pieces were painted in either red, blue, dark green or an iron oxide. Chests and buffets were common; however, the armoire was a distinctly early French-Canadian piece of furniture. It had two doors, the more elegant ones with carved panels often referred to as "lozenges." This motif was later replaced with carved diamond-points. By the 1870s, scrollwork, shaped doors, rosettes and even shells began to appear on armoires, and at the turn of the century they exhibited Louis XVI styling. Armoires in mint condition which have never been stripped of their original paint and still are equipped with original hardware are difficult to find.

Early French-Canadian chairs also were distinctive. One type known as the Ile d'Orléans with turned legs, H-stretchers of birch, pine-board seats and open-frame backs was deceptively flimsy-looking. Around the 1850s came armchairs in the Louis XIII manner with curved armrests, heavily turned legs and stretchers, high backs and upholstery. The capucine chair, a variation of yet another armchair, had straw or rush seats, shaped-back rails, plain legs, stretchers and arm supports.

Ethnic Furniture of Western Canada

Although collectors of furniture from Eastern Canada have benefited from the scholarship and documented research of people such as Jean Palardy, Philip Shakleton and Howard Pain, Western furniture has been virtually ignored and undocumented. The reasons may be that the West was settled so much later and that the bulk of the furniture, if it did survive, was either imported or Victorian. The only exceptions may be pieces now called Western Canadiana or Prairie folk art furniture, but because they date from the period later than 1880, they are frowned upon by many collectors. Also, the brightly coloured painted and carved pieces, may not appeal to everybody's taste.

Prairie folk art furniture is perhaps the last frontier for collectors, dealers and antique enthusiasts. Prices are low in comparison to those for pieces from other areas, and selection is still good. If any "bargains" exist, this type of Canadian furniture certainly qualifies, as first-class examples are obtainable for under one thousand dollars.

Furniture made by the Mennonites, Hutterites, Ukrainian and Russian Doukhobors, who settled in various parts of Saskatchewan and Manitoba, is remarkable for its workmanship, colouring and folk art qualities. The Doukhobors constructed cupboards with raised linen-fold panels, as well as wall shelves and spinning wheels with turned styles. Their tables are most appealing as they all were made with mortise and tenon joints, turned legs and box stretchers with shaped, molded and carved skirts. Birch, pine and/or spruce were the most favoured woods.

Ukrainian pieces boast an array of chests, tables, benches and wardrobes in bright colours or with overpaint. If the paint has been stripped, the value of the piece is completely lost.

The Canadian Market

From about the 1920s to the mid-1960s Canadian collectors ignored country furniture and as a result a lot of it was shipped south of the border where it took on American provenance.

Although things changed about 1967, the year of Canada's centennial, country Canadiana has become the domain of a select group of collectors, numbering fewer than three thousand. Auction prices for prime examples are still relatively low compared with those realized for similar pieces in the United States.

Also, by the time specialty dealers and literature began to appear in the early 1970s, many collectors had stripped the pieces of their original paint and finish, preferring that "honey-pine" look. Unfortunately, that stripping removed all the charm and patina which separate antique from new furniture. Those who want natural pine pieces would do better to buy modern reproductions. On the other hand, some of the furniture that is still in its original state is too dilapidated to appeal to many people. If expert artisans could restore it — I deliberately avoid the use of the word "refinish" — it could become acceptable, although pieces with original paint and decorations would be more valuable.

There is one serious drawback to buying Canadian country furniture. Regrettably, it has no market outside this country, and anyone just beginning a collection should carefully consider this problem.

Tips on Buying Country Canadiana

When most of the country furniture was being made, the trees, when felled and processed, could produce planks measuring between twenty to thirty inches in width. Tabletops of one or two boards were the rule, not the exception. And the sides of cupboards generally would have been made with one or two planks, not several pieces of wood. If the furniture you have selected has too many boards, be suspicious.

Occasionally boards from barns or pine floors were substituted for the original wood. Check whether all woods in the piece match in colour. Wood or furniture exposed to the same environmental conditions acquires an even patina. Look for knots in the wood. The early artisans had plenty of perfect lumber to choose from and would have avoided using knotted examples, unless the knots or swirls could have been worked into the design. Check the wood by gently running or skimming your hand over the surface. Planks planed by hand are not smooth, and light undulations will be noticeable. Circular saw marks made with an old hand-held saw are different from the smooth surface left by an electric saw or tool.

Wooden pegs usually indicate a pre-1860 manufacturing date, although collectors should remember that such pegs can be faked or added at a later time. Old wooden pegs tend to be of various sizes, rarely match and hardly ever are flush with the wood, as they either were slightly too large or would have expanded over time.

Check the inside of drawers and the sides where the front was attached. Sometimes they were joined by dovetailing. Authentic antique furniture would rarely have even or symmetrical dovetailing, and one side would rarely match the other precisely, although there were certain similarities. Pre-1840 screws are blunt, modern screw bits are tapered and sharp. The heads of old nails are irregular, heavy-looking and appear hammered. Their shafts are never uniform in size or thickness and generally are tapered on four sides instead of being rounded. From the 1830s and 1840s until approximately the turn of the century, nails were square-tapered on two sides; after that time, they were machine-made.

Nails can be reproduced by contemporary artisans, and some collectors or dealers have been known to use old nails to "jazz" up a questionable antique. I'd rather see new tools and new hardware used so that future owners will know exactly how the furniture was repaired. (See pp. 70-71 for more information.)

Bibliography

Blackie and Sons. *The Victorian Cabinet-Maker's Assistant.* London: Dover Publications, 1970. (First published in 1853.)

Blundell, Peter S. *The Marketplace Guide to Oak Furniture, Styles & Values.* Toronto: Thorncliffe House, 1980.

Blundell, Peter S. and Phil T. Dunning. *The Marketplace Guide to Victorian Furniture, Styles and Values.* Toronto: Thorncliffe House, 1981.

Chippendale, Thomas. *The Gentleman and Cabinet-Maker's Director.* London: Dover Publications, 1966. (Reprint)

Clarks, Robert Judson, ed. *The Arts and Crafts Movement in America.* Princeton University Press, 1972.

Dubrow, Eileen and Richard. *Made in America 1875-1905.* Schiffer Publishing Ltd., 1982.

Friedman-Weiss, Jeffrey and Herbert H. Wise. *Made With Oak.* Links Books, 1975.

Hayward, Charles H. *Antique Furniture Designs.* Evans Brothers Ltd., 1979.

Hayward, Charles H. *English Period Furniture Designs.* Arco Publishing Co., 1978.

Hill, Conover. *Antique Oak Furniture, an Illustrated Value Guide.* Collector Books, 1976.

Hepplewhite, George. *The Cabinet-Maker and Upholsterer's Guide.* Dover Publications Inc., 1969.

Jervis, Simon and the Victoria and Albert Museum. *Victorian Furniture.* Ward Lock and Co. Ltd., 1968.

Joy, Edward. *Antique English Furniture.* London: Ward Lock and Co. Ltd, 1981.

Kenworthy-Browne, John. *Chippendale and His Contemporaries*. London, England: Orbis Publishing, 1971.

Kirk, John T. *The Impecunious Collector's Guide to American Antiques*. New York: Alfred A. Knopff, 1976.

Longlin, David. *The Case of Major Fanshawe's Chairs*. Universe Books, 1978.

Marsh, Moreton. *The Easy Expert in American Antiques*. J.B. Lippincott Co., 1978.

Riley, Noel, ed. *World Furniture*. London, England: Octopus Books Ltd.

Rodd, John. *Repairing and Restoring Antique Furniture*. Van Nostrand Reinhold Co., 1976.

Rubin, Jerome and Cynthia. *Mission Furniture*. San Francisco: Chronicle Books, 1980.

Sack, Albert. *Early American: Fine Points of Furniture*. Crown Publishers Inc., 1950.

Schwartz, Marvin D. and Edward J. Stanek and Douglas K. True. *The Furniture of John Henry Belter and the Rococo Revival*, 1981.

Sheraton, Thomas. *The Cabinet-Maker and Upholsterer's Drawing Book*. London: Dover Publications, 1972. (Reprint)

Smith, Nancy A. *Old Furniture, Understanding the Craftsman's Art*. New York: Bobbs-Merrill, 1975.

Canadiana

Barbeau, Marius. *I Have Seen Quebec*. Macmillan Co. of Canada Ltd., 1957.

Cathcart, Ruth. *Jacques and Hay: 19th Century Toronto Furniture Makers*. Boston Mills Press, 1986.

Dobson, Henry and Barbara. *A Provincial Elegance*. Kitchener-Waterloo Art Gallery Exhibition, published and sponsored by Electrohome Ltd., Canada, 1982.

Dobson, Henry and Barbara. *The Early Furniture of Ontario and the Atlantic Provinces*. M.F. Feheley Publishing Co., 1974.

Ingolfsrud, Elizabeth. *All About Ontario Beds, All About Ontario Chests, All About Ontario Tables, All About Ontario Chairs*. The House of Grant, Toronto (Canada), Ltd., 1973,'74,'75,'76.

Pain, Howard. *The Heritage of Upper Canadian Furniture*. Van Nostrand Reinhold Ltd., 1978.

Palardy, Jean. *The Early Furniture of French Canada*. Macmillan of Canada, 1963.

Ryder, Huia G. *Antique Furniture by New Brunswick Craftsmen*. Ryerson, 1965.

Shackleton, Philip. *The Furniture of Old Ontario*. Toronto: Macmillan of Canada, 1973.

Webster, Donald Blake, ed. *The Book of Antiques*. McGraw Hill Ryerson, 1974.

Webster, Donald Blake. *English-Canadian Furniture of the Georgian Period*. McGraw-Hill Ryerson, 1979.

8

Antique Jewelry

Jewelry reflects the tastes, the fashions and the artistic directions of its time. By glancing at pieces from a particular era much can be learned about the people who created and wore them.

This historical connection is only one reason why collecting antique jewelry is so appealing. Unlike paintings that hang on walls or coins and textiles that have to be kept in fixed locations, jewelry can be worn. Storage is not a big problem because most pieces fit into safety deposit boxes or small spaces. Many people collect because they like to wear something unique which is not readily available to everyone.

There are more people who randomly buy two or three pieces of antique jewelry than almost any other kind of antique. Curiously, it is the one field about which most buyers know very little. They rely on their eye and sense of design when, in fact, they should accumulate some knowledge. Not so much because it is easy to be 'taken' by unscrupulous dealers but rather to help them make a better choice.

To bring antique jewelry from its lofty heights to a more accessible level, let us first examine some of the more popular metals. Gold, silver and platinum are known as precious metals, while most others come under the heading of base metals. Gold, silver and rhodium are also used to cover or plate an object made from a base metal. When this is done the object is considered to be plated.

Gold filled jewelry has an exterior of gold alloy and a core of base metal, usually copper. Gold filled merchandise is made from sheets of base metal to which the outer covering of alloyed gold has been applied *before* the object is shaped. (Much like a sandwich). Gold plating takes place after all of the manufacturing is completed. By industry standard the gold content should be at least one-twentieth of the total content of the object. Some pieces done in this manner are marked or stamped with the letters G.F.

Gold-filled jewelry can be detected with a magnifying glass or a jeweler's loupe. If the gold has rubbed off to reveal the base metal in any one spot, the piece is gold-filled, not pure solid gold. Obviously, gold-filled items and those made of solid gold are more valuable than those that have been gold-plated.

In North America the quality of gold is measured in karats which simply indicate the number of parts of pure gold. Twenty-four karats (24K) is pure gold; 14K, fourteen parts pure gold to ten parts of another metal; and 10K, ten parts pure gold to fourteen parts of another metal. Jewelry is seldom made from 24K gold. Jewelers prefer working in lower Karats such as

14K since it is stronger and does not damage as easily.

Europeans use the decimal system to measure their gold, .584 is equivalent to 14K, .750 to 18K, and .417 to 10K. For interest sake, English use the spelling carat (ct). Karat (with a K) is the American spelling.

Karats (North America)	Fineness (in grams) (Continental)
24 – 100.00% gold	1.000
22 – 91.65% gold	.916
18 – 75.00% gold	.750
15 – 62.50% gold	.625
14 – 58.33% gold	.584
10 – 41.67% gold	.416
9 – 37.50% gold	.375

To guarantee genuineness and high quality, gold and silver usually are hallmarked, a practise that began in the Orient and came into effect in London, England, in 1238. By 1300, a statute passed all over England regulated measurement of these two metals by having them tested and approved by select members of the Goldsmiths' Guild in London who would mark them with a leopard's head. Items which failed to meet their standards had to be turned over to the reigning monarch.

Generally, English hallmarks were four tiny punches aligned in a row, denoting the maker's and the standard mark, as well as the assay office's mark and the date stamp. Early makers used symbols but later stamped products with their initials, the assay-office's mark and the date stamp. The assay-office marks signified the location (or office) responsible for the marking; the standard mark was proof of the metal's quality and a letter of the alphabet indicated when it

was made. Karat punches help in determining the age of antique jewelry. In England, before 1854, the word 'gold' meant 18ct or better; after that time, 15ct, 12ct, and 9ct became legal; and in 1932, 12ct, and 15ct gold were replaced with 14ct.

A good reference book on English hallmarks and other markings is essential for the addicted antique jewelry collector. *English Goldsmiths and their Marks* by Sir Charles J. Jackson is the one most often used by dealers and collectors. Originally published in 1921 it has since been reprinted by Dover Press.

Not all hallmarks are reliable, according to James Snider, a Toronto gemologist-appraiser. With some exceptions, markings may be dubious in certain Central and South American countries as well as in Asia. Hallmarks from Hong Kong and Mexico are often misleading too. Usually, Russian, British, South African and Canadian hallmarks can be trusted, but Mr. Snider warns that anything purchased in 'touristy' parts of the world should be treated with caution. "There is a definite business in improperly marking goods," says Snider, "and even in countries that are otherwise reliable, marks can be applied incorrectly. (See page 59, Fakes and Reproduction chapter for more information on a gold and silver forger.) The only real guarantee can come from an accredited gemologist and appraiser or a trustworthy dealer."

Silver is less complex than gold. In its natural state it is too soft to be made into jewelry and, therefore, is alloyed with a harder metal, usually copper. Its hallmark indicates the number of parts of pure silver per thousand of weight in decimals; .800 is 800 parts pure silver to 200 parts copper; sterling, is .925; Britannia Standard, .959; and coin silver, .800.

In Britain, where marks have been used since 1300, a lion's face is the London sterling mark, also used as proof of assay in most English provincial offices. A lion passant (walking sideways) is the London standard mark, also used in most English provincial centres; this is replaced by a thistle in Edinburgh, a lion rampant in Glasgow or a harp in Dublin. Ornate capital letters with a crown or fluer-de-lis often indicate that a piece is French, and a spread eagle is often sign of German origin although it was sometimes a symbol used by Russians. Because the variety of marks is so diverse and complicated, collectors should use either a good reference book or consult an expert.

Antique jewelry can be divided into two categories: primary and secondary. Primary pieces are valued for their design rather than their precious metal contents. Most of them were made to complement current fashions, and because many were so elaborate they could only be worn at gala functions. Few from this category have survived, since they often were redesigned to match current fashions.

Secondary pieces were meant to be worn daily, and because their initial cost was not as high as that of primary pieces, they are available to collectors in greater numbers. Jewelry can be grouped according to the periods in which it was made and worn. The time spans below are approximate, as styles and fashions frequently carried over from one era into the next.

Ancient	Egyptian, Roman Byzantine Eras
Medieval	1100–1500
Renaissance	1400–1600
Georgian	1714–1830
Regency	1811–1820
Victorian	1835–1915
Edwardian	1902–1910
Art Deco	1920–1940
Collectible	1940–1960
Contemporary	1960–

Ancient

Jewelry from the Egyptian, Roman and Byzantine eras usually was made of pure gold and, therefore, has survived in surprisingly large numbers. Also, since wealthy people were buried wearing their finest clothes and jewels, many pieces were and still are being retrieved from ancient tombs and burial sites.

Noel Mele, proprietor of a gallery devoted to ancient art in New York City, believes that the reason why these pieces have universal appeal is the fact that "the ancients only used twenty-four karat gold and that the gold itself takes on an orange-coloured patina as it ages. It looks brighter and gives off an almost mystical aura; it becomes golder than gold."

Because of these qualities there is a brisk market in stolen goods of this type, as well as high interest in faking and copying them. It, therefore, is imperative to buy only from specialized dealers after visiting museums, such as the Metropolitan in New York the Walters Art Gallery in Baltimore, the Brooklyn Museum, the Cleveland Museum of Art, the Museum of Fine Art in Boston, the Art Museum, Princeton University and the Museum of Fine Art in Richmond, Virginia. At all these institutions, ancient jewelry forms part of their collections.

Medieval

During the Medieval period, jewelry was a definite sign of status and wealth. Not only worn for adornment, it was also used to signify mourning, for sealing documents, for religious purposes and many other reasons. Rings worn on all fingers, on the upper as well as the lower joints and on the thumb were special favourites with both men and women. Bishops and lower members of the clergy wore them as part of their regalia. Members of occult sects and those practicing witchcraft wore rings that often bore intricate initials and secret inscriptions.

Renaissance

The rebirth of the arts and sciences during the Renaissance was dramatically reflected in its jewelry. Only the nobility could afford it, favouring ornate brooches, massive pendants and heavy gold chains of various lengths worn in layers. Tiaras and long dangling earrings were popular, but bracelets were considered less fashionable. This becomes apparent when we study portraits of the period which also reveal that many ladies liked to adorn themselves with enamelled pieces.

The pocket watch was invented in the 1600s. Rose-cut gem stones were first developed at this time meaning that diamonds, emeralds, rubies and sapphires could be cut with greater brilliance than before. The gems rather than the precious metals that encased them became the more important part of jewelry. Unfortunately, few pieces from that era have survived as most were eventually reset or melted down.

Georgian

The eighteenth century ushered in an exuberant and elegant time. Dress and jewelry fashions, dominated by French taste, were soon adopted in England and elsewhere in Europe. To complement the gowns of heavy silk and brocade, the nobility wore bracelets, broaches, earrings and rings studded with clusters of stones, especially diamonds. The less wealthy, in an attempt to emulate the rich adorned themselves with artificial stones and pieces fashioned from man-made substances that resembled gold.

Some of these imitations deserve special mention. Paste, for instance, was coloured glass cut to look like real gems. Although Egyptian, Medieval and Renaissance craftsmen had made paste jewelry in their time, it really came into its own when talented Georgian artisans found a way to add more life to the "stone" by placing foil behind the glass to reflect light. But paste pieces, although often beautifully set in silver, gold or gilt metal, were meant to be worn by candlelight, not in daylight which exposed their many flaws. However, to people, even the very wealthy, who followed the latest fashion trends, paste was as precious as real gems.

Telling the difference between paste and the real thing is relatively simple. Genuine stones possess more sparkle and feel colder than paste when held against the cheek. Although much of the workmanship of these imitations was exquisite, they are considered "junk" by many of today's collectors. Paste, therefore, may be a worthwhile area for the novice to consider, especially as so many pieces date back to the Georgian era.

Marcasites are natural iron pyrite stones which are most brilliant when cut small. Dating back to the 1750s they enjoyed great popularity in Georgian times when they were set in beautifully rubbed-silver mounts, just like precious gems. Cut-steel jewelry, originally designed to imitate the sparkle of diamonds, is often confused with marcasite. While the reverse side of marcasites is smooth, the earliest cut-steel pieces used studs that were riveted onto a background, making the reverse side appear uneven.

Although vintage marcasite pieces are obtainable today, the market is being flooded with reproductions. These new pieces generally use larger stones than the vintage pieces. Obviously, the original pieces will have a lasting value and are a much better buy.

Another imitation popular in the Georgian period was Pinchbeck, a man-made substance that looks and feels like gold. It was first produced by the English clockmaker Christopher Pinchbeck (1670-1732), who fused 17 per cent zinc with 83 per cent copper. No one has been able to imitate his exact formula, although it certainly could be duplicated with today's modern chemical analysis methods. Pinchbeck's two sons inherited the secret after his death but refused to pass it on to their descendants.

Pinchbeck was used for jewelry, snuff boxes, watches and buckles. It often is mistaken for gold fill, although Agnes Gillespie, a noted Toronto antique jewelry dealer, maintains it is easily recognizable because no matter how old it is, it never shows wear marks and does not change colour. On the other hand, Gary Wine, a Toronto dealer, formerly of Dublin, Ireland, believes Pinchbeck does not have a distinct colour, look and feel to it. "Only a gemologist's test can provide the answer," says Wine, "and even that is not one hundred per cent reliable." If knowledgeable and experienced professionals cannot agree, what can the novice collector do? When purchasing a piece that is sold as gold, make sure the vendor marks the karat and other details on your invoice so that you have someone to return to should you, at a later date, find out that it is Pinchbeck.

The Georgians were sentimentalists who wore miniatures as pendants and brooches. These tiny portraits were painted in oils or watercolours or enamelled on ivory, porcelain or parchment backgrounds. Round or oval and framed in gold, they came in various sizes but were never larger than something that could be held in the palm of the hand. Some miniatures showed the picture of one eye, and many modern scholars feel that symbolized "the mirror of the soul" and would bring a lover's image closer to the wearer; others believe that as an amulet it offered protection against injury and evil spirits.

Some miniatures were signed by the artist, usually in the lower right-hand corner, but most found in Canada today bear no signature. New collectors should watch out for pieces that had the original painted portraits, replaced with old hand-coloured photographs. Some dealers claim that miniatures with portraits of people are less appealing to collectors than those showing landscapes.

Regency

During this time intricate and beautifully executed goldwork made its appearance as direct copies of ancient jewelry. At the same time, pearls, turquoises and other semiprecious stones became fashionable.

Victorian

Queen Victoria strongly influenced the jewelry fashions of her time by wearing extravagant, primary pieces for evening gala functions but plainer, secondary pieces, especially those with sentimental value, during daytime. These gold and silver chains, rings, pendants, lavaliers, earrings for pierced ears set with onyx, garnets, amethysts, corals, jet, ivory, seed pearls, and enamelled pieces are collected with passion today. They seem to go well with current fashions and are available at relatively low prices.

When Queen Victoria wore a black jet necklace to her cousin's funeral in 1850 she began a trend that carried over into the twentieth century, although the practice of wearing mourning jewelry — *memento mori* — started much earlier. Members of the upper classes would make provisions in their wills to have pieces distributed to special friends and relatives after the funeral. In some cases, a person would have already purchased such tokens before his/

her death, and the beneficiaries would then have them engraved with the name or initials of the deceased, as well as the dates of birth and death. Pieces that carried such inscriptions are most coveted by collectors today.

The custom of wearing mourning jewelry soon spread to North America, but not until after George Washington's death in 1799 did it really come into its own as an art form. Black enamel and onyx were often used as backgrounds to images of weeping willows, sobbing women, Grecian urns or a lock of hair.

Hair played an important role in mourning jewelry and was used to make actual pieces. With a fine crochet hook mourners would plait and work the hair into bracelets, brooches, necklaces and earrings and then dip it into a fixative. Pieces found today used dark brown or black hair, although blond is a colour much in demand by collectors. (Curiously, no one has ever seen memorial jewelry fashioned with red hair.)

Pieces made from jet (a black coal-like substance), sometimes described as fossilized wood which is found only in England, can be classified as *memento mori*. It can be polished to a high gloss or given a dull finish. In contrast to black glass which many countries used instead, jet is full of static electricity and much lighter in weight. Nor could the beautiful carvings on the most exquisite pieces ever be duplicated on glass. Bog oak, a wood substance found preserved in Irish peat bogs, could be carved into various shapes, including cameos, and used for memorial brooches and necklaces.

Cameos were also popular in the Victorian era. They either were made of stone (amethyst, coral, turquoise, onyx), shell or lava. Stone cameos are the most valuable but shell cameos are found in antique stores today. Lava cameos are still made today, mostly for the souvenir

A miniature portrait of Andrew Jackson by Ralph E.W. Earle sold for $2,000 in a Phillips, New York, auction in January 1980. The reverse side contains elaborately worked hair. *(Photos: Phillips, New York)*

market. Workmanship tends to be mediocre because the material is brittle and chips easily. Also, since they only come in one colour, clear distinction of shadings is difficult to achieve.

The quality of a cameo is based on strong colour contrasts between background and image, as well as on depth of cut and overall workmanship. The subject matter is important and will influence the price; a woman's head, for example, is not nearly as costly as a well-executed landscape.

When choosing a cameo, novice collectors should reject those with the image pasted onto a background and not carved out of one piece of stone. (That is, unless it is inexpensive and falls into the costume jewelry category.)

Love Tokens

Like so many other celebrations or holidays, St. Valentine's Day has become a tribute to the development of our hurry-up, lackadaisical, commercially oriented society. Flowers, chocolates, or store-bought, mass-produced cards are all that remain of a once imaginative, free-spirited, romantic day.

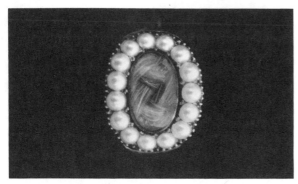

Hair ring, inscribed "Mr. Jethr. Hunter died April 1797, aged 53." Collection: Agnes Gillespie Antiques. *(Photo: HWF)*

When our ancestors wanted to say "I love you," they made something special. It is these love tokens, as they have come to be called, that are collected by folk art and jewelry enthusiasts all over the world.

Some collectors specialize in carved wooden objects but others, perhaps because they are easier and cheaper to find, collect love token jewelry created out of defaced or mutilated coins. These are easily recognized as one side of the coin was filed smooth so that it could be engraved with a message, a name, or initials.

Although the earliest known love token is a 1707 British half-crown of Queen Anne, with three initials and a sword, the custom did not begin in earnest until around 1750. Then, British sailors would scratch a girlfriend's name or an important date into the coin. The custom soon spread to the New World.

Initially, love tokens were simply bent or broken coins which were associated with separated lovers. Divided into two pieces, each lover kept one half. A play, written by John Gay, performed at Drury Lane in London in 1715, explained this custom clearly. He wrote:

Yet justice permit us ere we part,
To break this ninepence as you've
broke our heart.
As this divides, thus are we torn in twain,
And as this meets, thus may we meet
again.

While the making and wearing of love tokens originated in England, they became popular in the United States shortly after the Civil War. At approximately the same time the craze spread into Canada, and peaked at the turn of the century. It all ended, however, in 1909, when the American government decreed that defacing coins was illegal.

Some tokens were professionally engraved at country fairs or by regular jewelry engravers but the most coveted were done by hand. "My love token collection," says a collector who prefers to remain anonymous, "does not include one machine-made engraving. I only buy those that are obviously done by hand; that are unusual."

One of hers, a dime, boasts the initials OWS placed beside a lighthouse on top of a hill, near a building. Birds are flying in the sky. Another has the initials ODB and the date 7/5/01. A third has a donkey pulling a little cart — hardly romantic. But the most curious token has to be a hand-drawn skull and bones. What could have prompted that?

A natural extension of the romantic love token was done to denote filial love, with the words Mother, Father, Mama or Papa engraved onto the surfaces. One particularly fine Canadian bracelet includes the whole Paradis family. In other instances, the coins are devoted not to love but to music, politics, groups or societies and include special dates such as births, weddings and even deaths. Some have fancy enameling and precious stones. Occasionally gold was inlaid on top of the silver.

Most collected of all are those with the word "love" or hearts, bows and arrows, birds, cupids and so on. Multiple pieces are desirable. Brace-

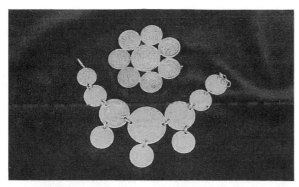

A fine example of a multiple-piece love token necklace. Obviously it is connected to the Bertrand/Paradis family and includes one fifty-cent piece, two quarters and seven dimes. *(Photo : HWF)*

lets, necklaces, pins, belt buckles, watch fobs, cufflinks, earrings are always in demand. Collectors prefer those that have names, not just initials.

Love tokens of American origin are relatively easy to date as the coins were usually minted with dates on both sides. But it should be understood that just because a coin bears an early date, it does not necessarily indicate that it was made into a love token, in that year. Unfortunately, in most cases, dates on Canadian coins were on one side only, and were obliterated when the coin was milled to make the surface ready for engraving.

Almost every coin series has been used for these tokens. Dimes were the most common as they were the cheapest silver coins available. While there were many American love token coins made on gold coins, not one has ever surfaced on a Canadian one. Large cents were rarely used. Numismatically, these defaced coins have no value but, for some reason, the largest collectors of love tokens are coin dealers, which may explain why it is so difficult to find examples in coin shops. Antique dealers' junk boxes and sometimes antique jewelry dealers are the best sources. Prices range from $10 for single, simple coins to more than $150 for multiple pieces.

For those who are intrigued by the subject, The Love Token Society (see page 237) is open for membership. At the time this book was being re-written (the summer, 1990) the Society was in the last stages of preparing a hard cover book on the subject. For more details regarding prices etc. write to the Society directly.

Art Nouveau

The movement originated in France and soon spread to other European countries, as well as to North America. It expressed itself not only in jewelry design but also in various other fields of applied art, including furniture and fabrics. In contrast to the Victorian era's morose fascination with death, the movement celebrated the joys of living. But it also was a time when people revolted against industrial dependence, emphasizing romanticism and the sensuality of the female form. Art Nouveau fashions and other art forms accentuated gently flowing lines, subtle warm colours and stylized plant, flower and insect motifs.

In France, René Jules Lalique (1860-1945), best known for his moulded glass designs, was the originator of this change in taste. Other exponents of the modern style were the Czech painter Alfons Mucha (who had settled in Paris and was designing jewelry for artisan George Fouquet), Louis Aucoc and the enamelist Eugene Feuillatre.

In the United States Louis Comfort Tiffany (1848-1933) became the most important promoter of Art Nouveau, whereas in England, Arthur Lazenby Liberty, founder of the London department store Liberty and Company in 1875, was the first to recognize the potential of the new trend. He commissioned artist Archibald Knox to create a line of jewelry consisting of hammered silver, gold and enamelled pieces, especially in shades of blue and green.

Edwardian

Most jewelry in this category was made just before, during and for some time after World War I. Unlike Art Nouveau and the later Art Deco it was extremely stylistic and delicate, incorporating fine and lacy filigree work and rose-cut diamonds. Early examples frequently were mounted on top in platinum or white gold with yellow gold on the back. For later pieces one kind of metal was used throughout. Much in demand today are rings and bar pins in elongated, narrow settings.

Art Deco

Although a great deal of Art Deco jewelry — the term Art Deco is derived from *L'Exposition Internationale des Arts Decoratifs et Industriels Modernes*, held in Paris in 1925 — was made with precious stones set in gold and silver most featured aluminum, steel and plastic, in contrasting primary colours. Smooth in texture, many pieces had simple, geometric or bold linear motifs of red, yellow, green or orange imposed on black, white or silver backgrounds.

Costume Jewelry

It has been called many names over the years: costume jewelry, fashion jewelry, popular jewelry, junk jewelry, vintage jewelry and even glitz. In this case, however, names don't matter. Whatever it is called, collectors all know what they are referring to, hunting for and buying with a passion. Without doubt, this must be one

Unfortunately, the workmanship and beauty of this c. 1940 earring, brooch and necklace set — all bearing the 'Miriam Haskall' signature — cannot be fully stated in a black and white photograph. The vibrant emerald green of the stones, contrasted against the patinated soft gold finish and the small pearls and rhinestones make this a fine addition to any vintage jewelry collection. Collection: Giancola. *(Photo: HWF)*

of the fastest growing collecting areas of the 1980s and from the looks of it, the 1990s. Department stores are selling it, right along with contemporary modern examples. Articles are being written and books about the subject are being published at a surprisingly rapid rate. (Just look at the list at the end of this chapter.)

The reasons are obvious. With some exceptions the pieces are unique, the workmanship outstanding. They give wearers a special, anti-off-the-rack look. It has become a status symbol equal to the collecting of art. The major difference is that this is wearable; you don't have to leave it at home. Price is a major consideration too. Not only is it cheaper than most equivalent contemporary examples but it's not a major expense to carry. Most collectors rarely bother having their pieces appraised, let alone insured. And unlike most contemporary jewelry, its value doesn't evaporate the minute the price tag is removed. Since the outlay is minimal, the maintenance low, the insurance nil, the look en-

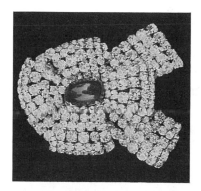 

 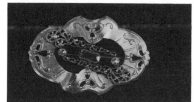

Found in a job lot at a Toronto area flea market in 1989, this brooch, which boasts handset rhinestones, and an oval, prong-set greenstone, is signed "Christian Dior, made in Germany, 1963." The owner, involved on a daily basis in the fashion-retail business, consulted with executives at Dior who advised that it was a one-of-a-kind piece, not represented in their archives and worth a great deal more money than the owner, an astute collector, could have imagined. Collection: Giancola. *(Photo: HWF)*

This collection of c.1900-1910 brass jewelry, including one bracelet with amber-coloured glass stones and two sash pins, one having a large, apple-green stone and the other, several small dark blue coloured stones, are very appealing. Although these pieces are not signed, it is very likely they were all made in Bohemia (present day Czechoslovakia) and exported throughout North America, Europe, and Britain. Previously neglected by collectors, they have now become desirable items and coveted fashion accessories. Private collection. *(Photo: HWF)*

chanting, is it any wonder that it is enjoying such a revival?

Several factors spurned the birth and then the development of costume jewelry in the 1920s, 30s and 40s. The first, of course, was the new free-looking dress styles, but the two most important contributing factors were the great depression and the Second World War. Women had very little money to spend on themselves especially for glitz and glamour yet were tired of the darkness and the feel of poverty. So they turned to rhinestones and inexpensive, dime-store jewelry as a pick-me-up, as a way of looking attractive and glamorous.

As well, history has credited Coco Chanel, the talented French dress designer with helping to launch the costume jewelry industry. While she certainly did not invent it, she gave it credibility; she allowed and encouraged women to wear fakes. In the mid 1920s, sensing the times, Chanel started adding little touches to brighten up her dresses. Chains, rhinestones on the clothes, an assortment of bobbles such as brooches made out of plastic and rhinestones and yards of fake pearls. It didn't take long for jewelry designers and manufacturers to notice that one of the reasons her clothes sold so well, was the inexpensive, yet unusual touches she added. Soon French, European and American jewelry designers were copying the trinkets that made her 'costumes' so special.

Talented jewelry designers, Americans and newly arrived Americans — such as Hobé, Trifari, and Eisenberg — saw the vacuum and jumped right in. Jewelry done by these names have survived and have formed the nucleus of many of the best collections. But perhaps the best known name, and the most collected of all 20th century costume jewelry, has to be Miriam Haskell. She felt her clients were used to wearing real jewelry and therefore would appreciate delicate, as opposed to strong, bold designs.

That theme characterizes her pieces which are known for their intricate seed pearls, hand wiring and gold filigree work.

Not too much is known about Haskell except that she was born in Indiana in 1899 and started her New York City jewelry business in the mid 1920s. Apparently she was a personality in her own right, was friends with Coco Chanel and the Rockefellers and travelled extensively.

Unfortunately, her early pieces were not marked but those made during her most prolific period, from the 1930s, 40s and 50s usually were, as they are now. She sold the business in the early 1950s, to her brother Joseph Haskell, who in turn sold it to Morris Kinzeler and later, Sanford Moss, who worked with the firm for many years. He is still the president of Haskell Jewels, Ltd. Miriam Haskall died in 1981 in Kentucky but her jewelry lives on to the delight of the thousands who collect it.

Bakelite

Initially, most people have difficulty spending 'real' money on plastic jewelry but somehow the vibrant colours, dramatic designs and geometric stylings win them over and they become enchanted with the look.

At first, these plastic trinkets were made to imitate the late Victorian and Edwardian styles. Pieces were designed to look like amber, ivory, horn, mother-of-pearl and tortoiseshell. Soon however, the jewelry began to have a life of its own. Stylized abstract and geometrical forms appeared taking on a very streamlined, sleek look. For the most part, buyers consisted of less wealthy women, however, after Coco Chanel introduced the idea of costume jewelry in 1925, the wealthy, fashion conscious women started buying and wearing it.

During the depression, women couldn't afford to spend grand sums on jewelry. Instead, they turned to inexpensive, colourful, plastic pieces. These are the artifacts that we are hoarding now, but they are no longer cheap. Five years ago we could buy the best examples, for a few dollars, but now we are looking at prices that are climbing almost daily. It would not be out of line to spot a good pin with rhinestones for $75, a bracelet with chrome for $125 or a necklace with dangling bits, for $150.

Most coveted today are examples that are in mint condition and are complete. The best exhibit great style, depth and intricate carving. Metal additions are also highly valued. Multi-coloured examples are more desirable than single coloured pieces and are harder to find. Often the hanging parts were damaged or broken.

Plastic has been around for over one hundred years, in simpler forms, but it didn't take on its current look, consistency or ability to hold colours, until about 1907 when New York City resident, Dr. Leo Baekeland invented the first wholly synthetic plastic. He patented his resin in 1909 and called it Bakelite. Initially, Bakelite was used for electrical insulation. Later it was shaped into handles, buttons, game pieces like poker chips, laminated plastic like formica, radio cases, which are the rage now and all types of jewelry. Bakelite had hundreds of uses because it was rock hard and could tolerate machine fabrication. As well, it could be tumble-polished to give a rich, high luster.

Jewelry pieces were formed generally by using Bakelite blanks which were sliced from special tubes or sheets of plastic, carved with lathes, and often hand finished by a specially trained worker. It was then buffed or tumbled, sometimes decorated with rhinestones, inlay work of contrasting Bakelite trim, or even chrome and aluminum accents.

Many companies, in Europe and the United

States were manufacturing bakelite jewelry but one of the most prolific was George F. Berkander of Providence, Rhode Island. He began with barrettes and fancy hair combs (which retailed at $1 a piece) because he noticed, in the late 1920s, that women were starting to let their hair grow long again. They caught on quickly and were wholesaled out all over the United States and probably Canada too. Other companies copied his ideas and soon no one was certain which pieces were created in his factory. Unfortunately for today's collectors, very few bakelite pieces were marked or stamped.

Vintage Wristwatches: 1920's–1950's

People who wear vintage wristwatches are not concerned with the time of day. They have their own reasons for turning their backs on the quartz revolution. Some purchase these timepieces because they are classic and look just as good with Ralph Lauren-type clothes as with faded jeans. Others are attracted because of their nostalgic and sentimental appeal.

Nancy Waite, an avid Toronto collector, says that vintage wristwatches give her a sense of continuity. "The fact that they have been worn by other people fascinates me. It is like having a little bit of history on my arm."

Collectors like Waite are described by those in the trade, as fashion buyers; concerned solely with the look, the size and the design of the watch. Others, who make up about 60% of the watch collecting community, are the purists. While these die-hard enthusiasts have to be taken with the beauty of the piece they mainly buy examples that are technically excellent.

Wholesale and retail dealer, Steve Oltuski says that the connoiseurs, the second group, are after the complicated watches — the ones that do more than tell time — such as those with calendars which must be set at the end of every month or perpetual calendars, which self-adjust to the leap years. Among the most desirable complicated examples are the moon phase watches which show the phases of the moon by a revolving image in a window on the dial.

According to Oltuski, sophisticated collectors want examples made by the status watchmakers such as Switzerland's Patek Phillippe. They are one of the few companies who support the vintage watch market by buying back choice examples, from their earlier years. Not only are their timepieces precision-made but "all their watches and case mounts are numbered and each piece belongs with the correct part. A collector can contact the company and they'll authenticate the watch, advising if the parts belong together."

Dealers very often determine price by the manufacturer. Patek Phillipe as discussed earlier, Vacherone & Constantin, Audemars Piguet, Cartier, Piaget, Universal Genève, Rolex and Baume Mercier are the most expensive. After that, rarity and condition are taken into account, followed by design and form. Fashion conscious collectors, on the other hand, reverse the list, putting design and form on top.

They would be thrilled to have the stylish 1930s Bulova, the Longines or the curvex Gruen with its curved case and works. They are also hot after the art deco designs with enameled motifs and precious stones. Other coveted timepieces bear the names of manufacturers such as Rolex, Elgin, Waltham. While there are lots of vintage women's wrist watches available, current fashion buyers are attracted to the large or over sized men's timepieces. All in all, most of the gold filled pieces can be acquired from $100 up to $300, while the solid gold examples start at $400 and have been known to go as high as $100,000.

Purist collectors prefer not to have any personal engraving on the watch because it detracts from the original condition. Others, like Nancy Waite, feel it enhances the value. "Not too long ago I was admiring a 1930s gold man's watch in a dealer's showcase. When I turned it over and saw my initials on the back of the case, I was stunned. It was as if the watch was waiting there for me."

Although the vintage wrist watch market has been active for many years, it has heated up significantly in the last few. Auction results, especially by large firms such as Sotheby's, New York, have always been used to gauge current market trends. Vintage wrist watches are not an exception. In 1980 for example, they held a sale in which six antique wristwatches fetched $16,000. Seven years later one auction brought in more than a million dollars.

Highlighted at that sale was a gold, 1946 wristwatch by Patek Phillippe, complete with perpetual calendar and moon phase. It sold at Sotheby's 1980 auction for $7,000. That same watch went under the hammer in February 1987 for $66,000 (American). Also offered and sold was a duo-dial, stainless steel, Rolex Prince which fetched the astronomical price, for this particular model, of $9,900. Apparently the artifact went much over the $2,000-$3,000 estimate because it was from an important Italian collection.

Toronto's Ron Dupuis, the head of his own jewelry auction firm attributes the wristwatch's rise in popularity to the fact that the market is hot and heavy in Europe and New York. "This interest has spread here. Watches, especially from the 20's and 30's are getting hard to find and when choice examples surface, the prices reflect the rarity."

In another respect, vintage watches just might be a better buy than new ones. Oltuski notes that one reason the market has jumped so

dramatically in the last little while is that "a new Patek Phillipe can cost about $5,000 U.S., but a good dealer could probably get you a fine, vintage example between $2,000 and $3,000."

It is also interesting that the market is highly developed in gold watches, not silver. According to dealer John Dryden, silver wrist watches are not strong sellers, in fact there weren't that many status companies who used silver at all. "Collectors would rather put their money into gold, than silver," he says, adding that "gold watches always are worth a lot more money than silver." On the other hand, fashion buyers who fall into the 'winter' category and who tend to wear silver rather than gold, might be able to find some wonderful, art deco buys under $100.

No one is sure how or when the wristwatch was invented. Legend has it that a European woman was suckling her child on a bench in a public park. To keep track of the time she pinned a pocket watch onto her arm. An inventor who happened on the scene, expanded the idea by soldering a strap to a lady's watch. Shortly thereafter Parisian women began wearing expandable bracelets and it wasn't too much longer that someone attached small watches to the jewelry. Wristwatches were available for consumers by World War I, which is generally considered to be the time span when these artifacts were really invented.

Buying vintage watches can be tricky especially since there are so many reproductions on the market. The only way to prevent being taken is to buy from reputable dealers or auction houses; get bills and receipts properly documented and of course, the best advice is to do your homework by reading all the available research material.

After that, take care of your watch. Vintage examples are more fragile than contemporary quartz models. A knock or fall might cause serious damage. Repairs can be expensive and in some cases, parts might be difficult if not impossible to locate. Beyond that, vintage watches are not nearly as accurate as the modern examples. Count on loosing five or ten minutes each day. Handle them carefully.

Contemporary

To accurately assess jewelry trends of the 1970s and 1980s will likely take another twenty years or so. It might, however, be fair to conclude that these two decades will be remembered primarily as the era of the imported, mass-produced gold chains.

The Market

Traditionally, gemologists, appraisers and people who handle new jewelry believe that the real value of a piece is determined by the wholesale price of raw stones and precious metals. Antique jewelry experts reject this notion, maintaining that there is more to a piece of jewelry than its melt-down value. The workmanship and quality of design of some Georgian examples, jewelry with granulation (a lost art today) and Edwardian filigree work — all done by hand — cannot be compared with today's mass-produced items.

The major advantage to buying jewelry is its marketability. When a collector tires of a good piece of antique jewelry, it is quite easy to sell. He will likely get most if not all of the original price back. However, it is extremely difficult to sell a piece of contemporary jewelry. In most instances the owner will be forced into accepting much less than half his initial cost.

Useful Tips and Hints

- Look at a lot of jewelry before deciding which styles or eras you would like to collect. Define your tastes. Read and learn as much as possible about your chosen area.
- Don't look at appraised values when initially considering a piece. Make sure you like it, regardless of price. Then look at the price and compare it with the appraisal if one is available. Check appraisals carefully, remember that some may be unrealistically high, especially if they were done for insurance purposes rather than for resale.
- If you intend to purchase from a dealer with an in-house gemmologist or appraiser, always get a second, independent and unbiased appraisal from someone else, removing sales tags and invoices before submitting it to him.
- Ask yourself if the piece is wearable. Will it go with many different fashions or styles?
- Is it in good condition or will you need to spend money to have it repaired?
- Make sure your invoice shows complete details regarding the karat of the metal, the size and type of the stone, the provenance of the piece and how much you paid for it so that you have recourse should some of the information prove incorrect at a later date.
- Acquire and use your own loupe. Those employed by dealers usually only magnify five times. To properly examine a stone or a hallmark, tenfold magnification is required.
- To determine the quality of a coloured stone, watch for intensity of colour, brilliancy, transparency and the number of inclusions visible to the naked eye or under a loupe. Modern diamonds flash and blaze better than old cuts; make sure you know the difference between the two. Understandably, old ones are worth less than modern examples. Never

place a new diamond in an antique setting — it will not look right. For more information consult *Diamonds*, second edition, Eric Bruton; F.G.A.; N.A.G. Press Limited, London, 1978.

- When buying a ring, make sure the setting is not too large or too small for your hand. Settings also determine the value of gems; those mounted in poorly designed and cheap metal are either worth less, fake, or made of glass. Don't worry about sizing. This is inexpensive.

- Generally speaking, antique jewelry does not go out of style. If you see a piece you love, even if it does not match your current wardrobe, buy it and put it away until later.

- Never sell jewelry when you are in need. To get the best price, take it to a reliable dealer when you don't require money instantly. Ask him to sell it for you within a reasonable time span, at a mutually agreed price, less 25 per cent commission.

Storage and Maintenance

- Don't store all your jewelry in one container; keep each item separately, preferably in its own box. If an antique piece has its original box, keep it; it will add to the total value should you wish to sell it.

- If you store your jewelry at home, avoid the master bedroom as this is the first place where thieves are likely to look. Find an alternate, safe spot but stay away from your freezer.

  A story is told about a lady who, before leaving on vacation, wrapped all her jewelry in freezer foil, marking the package "T-bone steak." During her absence, a friend, looking after the house, discovered that the power had been off for several days and being a caring person she disposed of all the "rotten food" in the freezer before the lady of the house returned.

- Make sure your jewelry is fully insured.

- Acids and skin oils can be damaging to porous stones such as opals and turquoise, as well as to pearls. Avoid direct contact with perfume, hair spray and cosmetics.

  Opals should not be exposed to heat, cold or water. Wash turquoise from time to time in mild soap and water, rinse and dry it quickly. Pearls must be allowed to "breathe" and should be worn periodically. Do not store them in airtight containers or in a vault for any length of time. Have pearls restrung when the ropes get soiled or loose. Wash them in mild soap, not detergent. Foiled jewelry must never get wet. The stone will become dull and lifeless if moisture penetrates to the layer behind it.

- Have your jewelry serviced at least once a year to check prongs and clasps. Some delicate pieces may have to be looked at every six months.

- Here is a simple recipe for a polish recommended for cleaning diamonds, gold, silver, platinum and other clear stones. It must not be used on porous stones (opals, turquoises), opaque stones such as jade, pearls and pieces that have been painted or glued. Nor must you ever dunk a watch in it.

  Mix one tablespoon Ajax liquid cleanser with one tablespoon ammonia and eight tablespoons water. Soak the piece in the solution for five to ten minutes. Brush with a soft toothbrush, and rinse in tepid water. When the solution looks dirty, throw it out.

  Keep out of reach of children.

(Reprinted by permission of James Snider, Emile James Limited, Toronto, Ontario.)

Repairing Antique & Vintage Jewelry

Novice collectors very often are frightened to buy jewelry that needs repair. To eleviate some of these concerns, two Toronto gemologists were surveyed for an idea of their basic rates. While every gemologist will have different specialities and price structure — depending on overhead costs and experience — these figures will give the novice some idea of the going rates. Outside of Toronto, consult friends and experienced dealers for referrals.

Laura Beard of Beardsley Enterprises, specializes in antique jewelry repairs, custom design and fine handcrafted jewelry. She is an expert in working with costume jewelry and does a quality job with the repair of marcasite pieces. She does not do formal, written appraisals but is comfortable with giving verbal opinions.

A quick survey of her rates includes the following:

- Restoration of a piece of jewelry depends on the condition and the new materials needed to do the repair. Roughly she charges $40 an hour, however a complete quote is given after inspection and before the job is tackled.
- Pearl and bead restringing with knots, $20 and up; without knots, $10 and up.
- Replacing marcasites $2.50 per stone, and up; replacing natural seed pearls $4.50 and up.
- As well Ms. Beard does sizing; saftey chains; earring conversions; ring reclawing; brooch parts; soldering of chains, etc.

Although Jim Hergle of Jhemz Jewellers & Gemologists works with all manner of precious materials he is equally good with costume jewelry, something many gemologists shy away from. As well he does an excellent job with written appraisals necessary for insurance purposes. He charges $20 on the first item and $15 on each item thereafter. If you phone for an appointment the appraisal can be done while you wait. (Actually, it's a good rule of thumb not to leave your jewelry with anyone while it is being appraised.)

His pricing schedule includes the following: sizing of gold rings, down, varies from $9 to $12; sizing of rings, up, varies on width of gold band and colour of gold, from $10 up to $42 Sizing of silver rings up or down: $10 to $13; sizing of platinum from $24 to $100.

He also does expansion or reduction of wedding bands; soldering of chains; hand made settings in gold and/or silver; wax model carving; plating; watch and clock repairs; replacing of marcasites; engraving, etc.

Bibliography

Balls, Joanne Dubbs. *Costume Jewelers: the Golden Age of Design*. Schiffer Publishing Ltd., 1990.

Baker, L. *Fifty Years of Collecting Fashion Jewellery, 19250–1975*. Collector Books, 1986.

Baker, V. *Fabulous Fakes: The History of Fantasy & Fashion Jewelry*. London and Toronto: Grafton, a Division of Collins Books, 1988.

Becker, Vivienne. *Antique and Twentieth-Century Jewellery*. New York: Van Nostrand Reinhold, 1982.

Bell, J. *Answers to Questions About Old Jewellery, 1840 to 1950*. Crown Publishers, 1982.

Black, J. Anderson. *A History of Jewelry: Five Thousand Years*. Published in the United States as *The Story of Jewelry*, Park Lane; distributed by Crown Publishers, Inc., New York, 1974.

Branson, Oscar T. *What You Need to Know about Your Gold and Silver*. Agincourt, Ontario: Dominie Press Ltd., 1981.

Curran, Mona. *Collecting Antique Jewellery*. New York: Emerson Books, Inc., 1970.

Darling, Ada W. *The Jeweled Trail, Collecting Antique Jewelry*. Wallace Homestead Book Company, 1971.

Dolan, Maryanne. *Collecting Rhinestone Jewelry*. Books Americana, 1984.

Ettinger, Roseann. *Popular Jewelry, 1840-1940*. Schiffer Publishing Co. Ltd., 1990.

Flower, Margaret. *Victorian Jewellery*. A.S. Barnes & Co., Inc., 1951, 1967.

Foskett, Daphne. *A Dictionary of British Miniature Painters, Vol. 1 & 2*. Praeger Publishers, 1972.

Gere, Charlotte. *American and European Jewelry, 1830-1914*. New York: Crown Publishers, Inc., 1975.

Greek Gold; Jewelry from the Age of Alexander. Brooklyn, NY: Brooklyn Museum, 1965.

Gregorietti, Guido. *Jewelry, History and Technique from the Egyptians to the Present*. New Jersey: Chartwell Books Inc., 1978.

Hallmarks and Date Letters on Gold and Silver. London: N.A.G. Press Ltd., 1944, 1970, 1973.

Hickl-Szabo, H. *Portrait Miniatures in the Royal Ontario Museum*. Royal Ontario Museum, 1981.

Hughes, Bernard and Therle. *Collecting Miniature Antiques*. William Heineman Ltd., 1973.

Hughes, Graham. *A Pictorial History of Gems and Jewellery*. Phaidon Press Ltd., 1978.

Kelley, Lyngerdan and Nancy Schiffer. *Costume Jewelry: the Great Pretenders*, Schiffer Publishing Co. Ltd., 1987.

Lynnlee, W.L. *All That Glitters*. Schiffer Publications Ltd., 1986.

Poynder, Michael. *The Price Guide to Jewellery, 3,000 B.C. to 1950 A.D*. Woodbridge, Suffolk, U.K.: Antique Collectors Club.

Rainwater, Dorothy. *American Jewelry Manufacturers*. Schiffer Publishing Co. Ltd., 1988.

Sataroff, Joseph. *Art Nouveau Jewelry*. Dorrance & Co. Inc, 1984.

Scarishrick, Dianna. *Jewelry*. London: B.J. Batsord Ltd., 1984.

Schumann, W. *Gemstones of the World*. New York: Sterling Publishing Co. Inc., 1977, 1979.

Sheilds, Jody and Max Vadukul. *All That Glitters: the Glory of Costume Jewelry*. New York: Rizzoli, 1987.

Shiffer, Nancy. *Costume Jewelry; the Fun of Collecting*. Shiffer Publications Co. Ltd., 1988.

Ward, A. and J. Cherry, C. Gere, B. Cartlidge. *Rings Through the Ages*. Rizzoli International Publications Inc., 1981.

9

Ceramics

The term ceramics is derived from the Greek word *keramos* meaning potter's clay — a firm, plastic, fine-grained earth produced by the deposit of fine rock particles in water. Ceramics include all things made from clay. Within that category are two distinct groups: porcelain, commonly known as china, and pottery.

Porcelain, often referred to as "china," was initially discovered by the Chinese sometime between the sixth and thirteenth centuries A.D. It is a hard white translucent substance (the degree of translucency may vary) which fractures with a clean break. Although each factory's formula was different, porcelain is divided into two parts: hard and soft paste. Hard paste is a mixture of moistened clay and the mineral feldspar. After firing at high heat it becomes impervious to scratches and cannot be cut with the edge of a file. The finished product should "ring" when gently tapped with a finger nail or a hard object.

Soft paste, a combination of clay and silica (ground glass), was developed in France as early as 1690. The English used it almost exclusively for their china, replacing the silica with bone ash; hence the term bone china. Less heat is required to fuse soft paste and the finished product can be scratched or cut with the edge of a file. Pieces made from soft paste must be glazed before firing.

Pottery is an opaque clay substance which can be divided into earthenware, and stoneware. Earthenware, because of its porosity, must be glazed after being kiln-baked at medium-high heat. Stoneware which is nonporous and water-resistant hardens after being fired at high heat. Glazing is done to give the appearance of smoothness.

When in doubt as to whether a piece of china is porcelain or pottery, hold it over a strong electric light bulb. If no light shines through, it is pottery; if it is translucent, it is porcelain. Porcelain, if broken, will chip with small shell-like breaks, while pottery cracks on a line. Porcelain is light, thin, more durable and more expensive than pottery.

If you are tempted to buy a piece of pottery or porcelain, look at each one carefully for damage. Even a tiny blemish will reduce the value and you should draw it to the vendor's attention in case it's just a fresh wound that isn't reflected in the price. After that you should check the bottom of the piece for marks. If the name of the country of origin is on the bottom the dish was likely made after 1891 for that is the year that the American import laws made such marks compulsory. The words "Made in England" or some other country, indicate the piece was made after 1914.

Antique porcelain tablewares and ornamental pieces, except those of Chinese origin, usually bear the mark of the pottery or factory where they were made. Complicated looking trademarks were used during the last half of the nineteenth century. And, if the actual word 'trademark' appears it usually indicates that the piece was made in England after 1855, and the pieces with the letters 'LTD' indicate a post 1880 manufacturing date.

Each pattern of English china was registered with the government patent office after 1885. Diamond shaped marks which contained coded information on the patent date and manufacturer were used from 1883. Many books, explaining these markings and those done in other countries have been published, over the last decades, and are fairly easy to understand. Knowing how to break the codes will give the collector a great deal of information about the pieces they own.

When considering the subject of ceramic collecting, the generic term "china collector" seems to disparage those who indulge in the pastime, possibly because it still conjures up visions of little old ladies stuffing bow-front cabinets and Victorian "what-nots" with ubiquitous cups and saucers and prosaic salt and pepper shakers. Today's enthusiasts are a more discerning lot. They specialize in such things as transfer-printed earthenware, willow ware, quimper and historical china pieces. This is a hobby that means more than the aquisition of a few pretty dishes.

Transfer Ware

Henry Comor, a former Toronto collector and antique dealer, believes that when transferred earthenware first came on the market it heralded dramatic social change. The factories that produced these blue-and-white dishes during the first half of the nineteenth century sparked the creation of the trade union movement in Great Britain, especially at the Staffordshire potteries where the workers had banded together, threatening to go on strike as a means of forcing the owners to pay them higher wages. These early attempts by an organized labour group did not succeed because the government stepped in and quickly shipped the militant leaders to Tasmania where many were forced to remain to the end of their days.

The first industrial accident occurred at Josiah Spode's pottery in Staffordshire after he had installed machinery in the early 1820s to mechanize his clay-mixing process. One day his hat got caught in one of the engines and when he tried to retrieve it, his hand was cut off.

During that time, merchandising techniques also changed drastically as companies such as Spode, Minton, Davenport and Wedgwood had to think up new ways to compete in a comparatively small market. Some opened retail outlets throughout England to sell their products directly to consumers, and china manufacturers were the first to tailor their wares to suit the export market.

Surviving examples of blue-and-white transfer ware indicate that the first ones were made in the early 1780s by Thomas Turner of Caughley in Shropshire. His technique and that of other potters was to apply cobalt-blue ink to an artist's copper-plate engraving, press a tissue over it, rub the tissue, with a cloth soaked in soapy water and then carefully peel it off the copper plate. These "transfers" were then cut into sections to fit the earthenware piece. Traditionally, the foregoing steps were performed only by young females, whereas the application of the cut sections usually was done by older women. On most transfer-printed earthenware produced prior to the 1830s, tiny separations are clearly visible between the engraving patches or strips;

after that date when machinery and new methods were employed, a smoother and tighter match was achieved.

The next step was to dip the pieces into a blue-green glaze, a type used before 1830 when the hand-mixed clay was quite gray in colour; adding the blue tinge made the finished product appear whiter. If a particular transfer-ware piece was hand-made, the bits of glaze clinging to the reverse side, particularly around the rim, will confirm that it predates the machine age.

Following the glazing, the pieces were stacked in an oven, each supported by three small sticks known as stilts or spurs which always left a mark on the back of early pieces. Sometimes the marks appear as a set of three small dots, as single dots or as short lines.

Collectors frequently ask why only cobalt blue was used in this early transfer process. Apparently, it was the only colour (mostly imported from Germany) that could withstand the high oven heat to which these pieces had to be subjected. Later, additional colours such as brown, pink and green were introduced; however, the blue pieces are still the most coveted, despite the fact that the other colours are much rarer.

Thomas Turner's transfers were based on line engravings mostly of Chinese-type designs and patterns so fashionable in the 1780s. A few decades later when his original techniques were combined with stipple (dots), the designs changed from Oriental motifs to views of India, the United States, Portugal and Italy, showing rural scenes, historical houses and grandiose castles and usually embellished with ornate and intricate borders.

Transfer-printed earthenware made between 1780 and 1830 is the most coveted, since later examples obviously are not as rare nor as costly to acquire. Yet collectors can choose from a wide variety of pieces; some may specialize in a particular manufacturer such as Spode or Wedgwood, while others may only be interested in pre-1830 examples or unusually shaped serving dishes of a later period.

Before buying any transfer-printed earthenware, consult *Blue and White Transfer Ware, 1780-1840* and *Blue-Printed Earthenware, 1800-1850*. (See Sources of Information for complete references and information on Friends of Blue.)

Blue-and-White Willow Ware

The exact beginnings of the willow pattern, identifiable by its blue Chinese pagodas, birds, bridges, people and willow trees on white background, are obscure. In the past, it was believed that the original design was inspired by an ancient Chinese love story. However, more recent findings tend to indicate that the pattern did not originate in China at all but in England where prior to 1780 the Oriental motif was familiar to the public, since most dinnerware had come to Europe from the Far East. At the turn of the nineteenth century at least two hundred companies in the Staffordshire region were producing willow pattern dishes. Unfortunately, many were unmarked, and it is almost impossible today to identify the individual potters. As the popularity of the pattern spread to other countries — Holland, France, Germany — local manufacturers began to make their own willow transfers, and at the beginning of the twentieth century many American companies started to copy the traditional design.

Quimper

It was pottery that put the small French town of Quimper in Brittany on the map. The popular tableware, distinguishable by its brightly painted

A Quimper platter. Collection: Betty Knowles. *(Photo: HWF)*

figures and motifs on a white or cream-coloured background, has been manufactured there since the late seventeenth-century. As the local craft became industrialized in the late nineteenth century, people all over the world began to love and admire the Breton ware. It is still being made today, but antique collectors are naturally more interested in earlier pieces.

From its very beginning, Quimper (pronounced campair) faience, a porous earthenware, appealed to the masses because its designs depicted scenes from everyday peasant life. Decorated with profiles of men and women, hand-drawn geometric patterns and pictures of roosters, pheasants or swans, it never was as expensive as other French-made pottery or porcelain.

Originally, there were three potteries in Quimper; the first was established in 1685 by Jean-Baptiste Bousquet and his son Pierre after the family had moved to Brittany from the south of France. The business remained under their control until 1915 when the last family member Guy de la Hubaudiere was killed in World War I. The factory which still exists today was sold twice; the last time in 1968 when it was merged with Maison Henriot.

The second Quimper pottery was started in the late 1700s by Francois Eloury. When his daughter married Charles Porquier in 1809 its name was legally changed to Eloury-Porquier. The business was sold several times until Alfred Beau acquired it. He was responsible for making some of the most beautiful Quimper pieces.

Jules Henriot owned the third factory and purchased the Eloury-Porquier business in 1904, including Alfred Beau's molds, patterns and the "PB" trademark.

Historical China

Almost all the earthenware and porcelain tableware used in nineteenth-century Canada were imported from Great Britain. Immigrants could purchase a variety of goods either in local shops or through mail-order advertisements in city newspapers. But the tableware that present-day collectors know best and most actively search for is, the kind now referred to as "historical china, earthenware decorated with transfer prints depicting early Canadian views. Although these pieces do well in the marketplace today, they were not so popular among the people for whom they were originally created. According to Elizabeth Collard, doyenne of Canadian ceramic scholars, china merchants were reluctant to advertise them because no matter now much they tried to market them they never sold well in Canada. Expressly made for the North American market, these pieces were available in the United States and sold in Canada to visiting Americans.

Enoch Wood and Sons of Burslem in England manufactured the earliest of these wares between 1818 and 1846. They made almost sixty different landscape views but only three showed Canadian scenes: Quebec City, Montmorency Falls near Quebec City and Niagara Table Rock. All were printed in dark blue with a shell-type border. On the reverse appeared an impressed eagle with shield and the words "E. Wood and Sons."

Podmore, Walker and Company were in business in Staffordshire from the early 1840s to approximately 1959. They manufactured sets of multi-scene views, one image appearing on plates and another on platters, as well as auxiliary pieces. Executed in light blue, brown or black, each showed a different view of Canada including scenes from what are now Ontario, Quebec, New Brunswick and Nova Scotia. The series known as "British America" exclusively used W.H. Bartlett's Canadian scenery drawings. To adapt these Bartlett engravings was not unusual. Francis Morley and Company did so with the multi-scene patterns known as "Lake," and Taylor Ashworth who joined Morley's in 1862 used them as well. Another potter was Thomas Godwin who worked for Enoch Wood and Sons in Burslem from 1840 to 1859.

Images of beavers and maple leaves were widely used on plates from the 1850s onward. Perhaps the most interesting pieces were produced by Edward Walley, a Staffordshire potter, who in about 1856 combined the two emblems with the Latin motto *"Labor Omnia Vincit"* and the French slogan *"Nos Institutions, Notre Langue et Nos Lois."* Thomas Furnival and Sons also utilized the two emblems, placing the beaver in the central portion of the piece and making the maple leaves part of the border design. This type of tableware was still being offered in Quebec shops before the turn of the century.

Scottish potteries also did big business in Canada. In the 1880s Marshall and Company produced a series of patterns called "Canadian Sports" which depicted snowshoeing, lacrosse playing and skating-activities popular in this country at the time. According to Elizabeth Collard, all the scenes were related to a series of Christmas and New Year's cards published by Bennet and Company of Montreal at the beginning of the 1880s. Another Scottish firm, Robert Cochran's Britannia Pottery of Glasgow, sent pieces to be sold by Francis Thomas, a prominent Quebec City merchant who had opened a china business in about 1874. Showing views of Quebec, they were decorated with a border of beavers, leaves or Scottish motifs such as the thistle and the rose; they were marked on the reverse side with the importer's instead of the manufacturer's name.

Although there were many more types of

This unmarked water jug was made to commemorate some event. It says: "Robert Simpson, New Market, C.W." Collection: Private. *(Photo: HWF)*

historical china, the ones listed here are those that now are very popular with Canadian collectors. They still can be found in Canada, but they are becoming scarcer every year. Novice collectors should not try to put together an entire dinner set of "Canadian Views" but to pick up odd pieces wherever and whenever they surface. The most difficult patterns to locate today are Podmore, Walker's British American multi-scene series, followed closely by Enoch Wood and Sons' three Canadian scenes. Of those, Niagara Table Rock is the rarest, currently selling for around $600 a plate. The Montmorency Falls pattern is more common and about $150 cheaper. Although this series is of an earlier vintage than "Canadian Sports," it seems that the latter fetches still higher prices. Recently a

"Canadian Sports" series teapot, in perfect condition, sold for two thousand dollars.

In general, hollow ware such as sugar bowls or gravy boats are more expensive than plates because fewer numbers have survived. Naturally, goods that are cracked, discoloured or chipped will fetch lower prices than perfect pieces.

Moorcroft Pottery

William Moorcroft was born in Burslem, England, in 1872. He studied art in England and France, receiving the Art Master's Certificate in 1897. The same year he was hired by James Macintyre of Burslem as head of his new art pottery department where for many years he designed and produced a variety of high quality ceramics. Florianware was the first to be launched under his direction. Made of fine white clay it was freely shaped on the wheel, then painted in a fine slip to produce a relief effect. The colour was super-imposed before the pieces were glazed and fired at 1100°C.

Much of Moorcroft's early work already showed his interest in floral and plant motifs, so typical of his later designs. His colouring was subdued, although some pieces boasted elaborate gold decor or gilding.

In 1902, he brought out the Hazledene pattern, recognizable by its stylistically drawn trees in subtle shades of blue and green. It is much sought after today, commanding prices in the $1,000 range. Later, Moorcroft switched to brighter colours, using white and cream as backgrounds. By 1911 his designs, too, were much bolder, and he concentrated on deep purples and blues. Some of his most popular patterns featured fish and toadstools, while Oriental motifs graced his Flaminian ware — pottery decorated with bluish roundels on a light-green base.

A Pansy pattern: 1913 bowl and 1922 vase made by William Moorcroft. Collection: Audrey Hayes. *(Photo: HWF)*

In 1913, shortly after Macintyre's art pottery department permanently closed, William Moorcroft established his own firm in Cobridge where he continued to make some of the Macintyre pieces as well as starting his new line. Son Walter and brother John carried on after his death in 1945. They are still in business, although the Moorcroft vases, pots and lamps manufactured today bear little resemblance to the original designer's pieces.

One way of determining the age of Moorcroft's vintage pottery is to look at the colour of his signature; up to 1920 he signed his pieces in green, after that in blue, either in full or with his initials W.M.; the exceptions were those signed in red or brown.

One of the leading Moorcroft pottery dealers in Canada is Audrey Hayes who has four hundred pieces in her own collection, including a striking-looking vase from Moorcroft's Florian period. Similar pieces are hard to find these days and any that might be available retail from $800 to $1,000 depending on size and condition. Mrs. Hayes maintains that at present a lot of material is available to collectors in Canada, more so than in England in fact because between 1915 and 1945 Moorcroft pieces were one of the most popular wedding gifts. "The market is strong and prices have gone sky high in the last few years," she said, "as the pottery has been rediscovered in England and collectors are coming to Canada to buy and ship them back home." Fewer pieces are available in the United States but there is little demand for them there.

China-Matching Service

Despite meticulous care to protect porcelain

pieces from breakage, accidents do happen. Until recently, replacing a missing saucer, the lid of a sugar bowl or a teapot was virtually impossible, especially when manufacturers discontinued a particular line or pattern.

Mrs. Elsie Smith of Chilliwack, British Columbia, managed to turn this frustrating situation into a full-time business. It started in 1957 when she wanted to add certain pieces to a vintage dinner service but discovered to her dismay that her pattern was no longer available. She scoured want ads, visited auctions, antique shops and secondhand stores until she was able to complete her set. Her friends soon asked her to perform the same service for them and what had started as a hobby developed into a unique kind of enterprise, unassumingly named "Match your Chinaware."

Most of Mrs, Smith's requests come from people who want to replace a broken item. Some may send her shards for identification, and others even call at her home with their treasured fragments wrapped in towels and blankets.

Collector Plates and Limited Editions

To bona fide collectors the mere mention of the words "collector plates" and "limited editions" provokes shudders and grunts of contempt. And yet, an estimated one-quarter to half a million people collect these porcelain goodies in Canada alone, and there are at least six full-time dealers who make their living selling them.

Collector plates and limited editions certainly do not hold their value, and when they are offered at auction they either fail to sell at all or obtain low prices. Experts tend to think this is because everyone who wanted an example in the first place ordered when it initially appeared on the market. According to Sheldon Parks, formerly of Phillips Ward–Price, a few high-quality

items by Royal Worcester, Hummel, Royal Copenhagen and Wedgwood may be better buys than Franklin Mint's which do not seem to have a resale market. The reason for this is obvious. The success of Franklin Mint is entirely based on clever marketing techniques. Their products are never sold on the open market. They send letters to known plate collectors announcing their latest edition. Production is limited to the number of orders received.

Although collector plates have been around for almost one hundred years, it was not until 1969 that they became popular in North America. How they became intertwined with antiques is a mystery because they certainly do not belong.

Radioactivity in China, Glass and Pottery

In the spring of 1981 a professor at the University of Waterloo discovered that Fiestaware dishes, bright orange dinnerware made in the United States and sold in Canada between 1930 and 1971, were emitting radioactivity. Alberta's Glenbow Museum asked the Atomic Energy Control Board to check their three-hundred-piece collection of Medalta and Medicine Hat pottery. Radioactive levels were found ranging from one to six millirems per hour, on contact, whereas the acceptable or "safe" limits are less than .25 millirems. The Medalta orange (not yellow) wares with the swirl pattern (identified by the company's own stamp on the bottom) are the main culprits. Radioactivity also was found in the ridged and swirled Matina ware, produced by the Medicine Hat Pottery Company between 1936 and 1966. An Indian head stamp identifies their pieces, although many are unmarked. In addition to place settings many auxiliary pieces were produced including cream pitchers, sugar bowls, egg cups and salt and pepper shakers.

Ron Getty, curator of the Glenbow Museum's Cultural History Department advises collectors not to be unduly concerned about radioactivity, as it is absorbed by glass and wood if the pottery is stored in a corner or on top of a cupboard. "It's a factor of distance," he said, "the further away you are from the items, the less radiation you are likely to receive. The real problem develops when people eat off the pieces because the glaze made up of uranium salts is soluble in mild acids even vinegar, and if it is scraped with a knife or any other utensil, actually you could be ingesting minute radioactive particles."

Dr. David Greyson, associate professor of Radiology at the University of Toronto and director of the Department of Nuclear Medicine at St. Michael's Hospital in Toronto explains that "every person has radioactive elements within their bodies. Apart from the naturally occurring radioactivity in the environment which is increased even more if the individual lives above sea level, works in a highrise building and frequently flies in an airplane, you'll get more that way than by sleeping on one of these plates." He too cautions not to place acidic foods on the dishes as some of the uranium might leach from the glaze.

To check possible radioactivity in depression glass, I took a few samples to Dr. Ron Hancock, senior researcher for the Slowpoke Reactor at the University of Toronto. After testing them he found that the clear cobalt blue and pink glass was totally free of radioactivity. Yet, the late Henry Faul, professor of Geophysics at the University of Pennsylvania (also known as Moreton Marsh, antique writer and scholar), maintained that green and yellow depression glass did emit some radioactivity because the manufacturers had used radioactive substances to produce these particular shades. Shortly thereafter Catherine Thuro noticed some light-green oil lamps fluorescing "like crazy" under ordinary household fluorescent tube lighting.

To colour some glass, uranium was added. But the required amounts were so minute that the level of radiation is not that dangerous, according to Jane Shadel Spillman, curator of American Glass at the Corning Museum of Glass. Apparently, the first to be coloured with uranium was vaseline glass, yellowish-green in appearance, which made its debut in the second half of the nineteenth century in North America as well as in Europe.

If you are at all suspicious of any of your old pottery or glass, contact the Atomic Energy Control Depots in Mississauga, Oshawa and Elliot Lake, Ontario. Some major hospitals and universities also are equipped to test such pieces.

It might be worth noting that today's amateur potters can easily obtain small quantities of uranium dioxide as a glaze additive but are under no obligation to notify their customers of the fact. Nor do they require permission or a license to use it unless they handle more than ten kilograms of uranium dioxide a year.

Bibliography

Bondhus, Sandra V. *Quimper Pottery: A French Folk Art Faience.* P.O. Box 203, Waterdown, Connecticut 06795. The book, a must for anyone interested in Quimper, is obtainable from the author at a price of $45 U.S. plus $3 U.S. handling charges.

Collard, Elizabeth. *Nineteenth-Century Pottery and Porcelain in Canada.* Montreal: McGill University Press, 1967; second edition, 1984.

Collard, Elizabeth. *The Potters' View of Canada.* Montreal: McGill-Queen's University Press, 1983.

Coysh, A.W. *Blue-Printed Earthenware, 1800-1850.* London: David and Charles, Newton Abbot.

Coysh, A.W. *Blue and White Transfer Ware, 1780-1840.* London: David and Charles.

Godden, Geoffrey A. *British Pottery, An Illustrated Guide.* London: Barrie and Jenkins, 1974.

Webster, Donald Blake, ed. *The Book of Canadian Antiques.* Toronto: McGraw-Hill Ryerson, 1974.

Services: China-Matching

Old China Patterns Ltd, 1560 Brimley Road, Scarborough, ON M1P 3G9.

Mrs. Elsie Smith, 8780 Vicars Street, Chilliwack, BC V2P 6V8; enclose a stamped, self-addressed envelope. She requires a description of the piece, noting colour and dimensions, a snapshot and a photocopy or sketch of the hallmark.

Echo's is another matching service. (1433 Lonsdale Avenue, Lonsdale Court, #121, North Vancouver, BC V7M 2H9. (toll free in Canada 604-981-8011, or 604-985-4825.) They buy and sell crystal, miscellaneous china, silver plate and sterling hollow ware, etc.

10

Glass

We know little about the Canadian glass industry prior to the 1880s. Few if any catalogues, advertising pamphlets or other factory records survived. This means that scholars had to rely for their research material on secondary sources such as oral histories and books. Although there were a few exceptions, the bulk of the Canadian glassmaking industry during the first three-quarters of the nineteenth century produced basic bottles such as druggist containers and unmarked preserving jars.

Mallorytown, Ontario, was the site of the first known and documented Canadian glass manufacturing company. All that is certain is that it operated for just one year from 1839 to 1840, and it is thought to have produced free-blown pitchers, tumblers and covered sugar bowls in a common aquamarine colour. Five years later the first company to make and sell window glass in Canada began to operate in St. Johns, Quebec. It existed for merely two years and was replaced by several other companies in Ontario and Quebec. The first one to make pressed-glass tableware in Canada was the St. Lawrence Glass Company of Montreal (1867-1874) and the Burlington Glass Works, established in Hamilton, Ontario, in 1874. They advertised that they manufactured oil lamps as well as chimneys and shades. William Beach,

Burlington's manager, set up the Nova Scotia Glass Company in New Glasgow, specializing in lamps, chimneys and, later, tablewares.

The glass industry in Canada was slow to develop because of poor economic conditions, small population and lack of experienced craftspeople. Consumer distribution was difficult until rail and shipping services were expanded between 1860 and 1870. When Sir John A. Macdonald's government imposed a 30 per cent import tax on glass in 1879, some of the smaller companies merged and soon began to flourish all over Canada including the West. Sydenham Glass Company of Wallaceburg, Ontario, probably was the largest, shipping their Gem and Doolittle fruit jars as far as British Columbia and to New York State. They operated between 1894 and 1913 when they were purchased by the Jefferson Glass Company of Toronto, a subsidiary of Dominion Glass. They manufactured goblets, covered sugar bowls, creamers and other pressed glassware, especially pieces in the famous rayed heart pattern. The company remained in business until 1925. Others came and went, among them the Toronto Glass Company (1893-1920) and the Manitoba Glass Company of Beausejour, Manitoba (1906-1918).

Glassmaking

A high quality, small grained white sand was needed to produce glass. Known as silica, it sometimes was locally available but often had to be imported from the United States and France. To fuse silica it had to be heated to above 2,000°F for about twenty-four hours. Potash, soda or lead oxide were added to the heated batch to assist the melting process. Chalk or limestone stabilized the mixture; cullet (broken pieces of glass) also aided the melting, while carbon hardened the substance. With this basic formula the glass produced was greenish in colour, due to the natural impurities in the sand. To obtain clear glass, manganese dioxide had to be added not to remove the impurities but to mask them. Various oxides were used to create other colours; for instance, gold, to make ruby or cranberry red; cobalt for blue; and iron and manganese to produce amber coloured glass.

Basically, there were three different ways to shape glass — free-blowing, mould-blowing or pressing. For the first, a glass blower would dip his blowpipe — a hollow iron rod three to six feet long — into the glass pot through a hole in the side of the furnace. The glob of glass, called a "gather," adhering to the rod was then blown and shaped by the worker. He then applied a pontil rod to the bottom of the object and using a small bit of molten glass removed the piece from the blowpipe. The glass then was reheated and worked into its final shape. To gradually reduce the temperature, the object was placed in an annealing oven (also known as a "cooking down" oven).

Mould-blown glass was simpler to produce. The glassmaker would put molten glass into a metal mould and blow it to impress a design onto the outside of the piece. He then removed it from the mould, further expanded it and then tooled it into its final shape.

When the glass-pressing machine was invented in the United States in the mid-1820s, identical, multiple copies of one particular pattern could be produced with ease.

The machine was introduced to Canada in

This pressed glass colourless breakfast set, known as the rayed heart pattern, was made by the Jefferson Glass Company (Dominion Glass) of Toronto and is especially popular with collectors. *(Photo: Waddington's)*

1867 when the St. Lawrence Glass Company became the first to use it for the manufacture of pressed-glass objects.

Flint Glass

Over the years, some types of glass confused collectors because of changes in names and meanings. Flint glass is a prime example. When clear glass was first introduced in England in the late seventeenth century, ground flint instead of sand was used in the manufacturing process. Later, even though sand and lead had replaced the flint, the name "flint glass" was retained to describe any type of glass that was clear. In the second half of the nineteenth century a soda lime formula was introduced to make clear glass, and again the name flint was adopted. To further confuse the issue, the United States glass-blowers union who has jurisdiction over the manufacture of all types of clear glass (today made without flint, of course) is still known as the American Flint Glass Workers Union.

Crystal

Crystal also has gone through several name changes. In the fifteenth century precious, decorative dishes and comports were carved out of a rock or quartz substance. When the Europeans later found a way to make clear glass by adding soda to the mixture they named it crystal because it resembled the original rock. Lead was added to English glass in the latter part of the seventeenth century and also became known as crystal, because it was clearer, thicker and could reflect light better than before. At that time it was also discovered that lead crystal could be cut. Today, it is a clear cut glass with lead added in various proportions depending on the quality of the object to be made. The term generally in-

dicates a hand-blown good quality glass as apposed to a commercial, mass-produced mould-blown product.

Cut Glass

Most cut glass made by Canadians and now found in Canada originated between 1905 and 1930. George Phillips Company of Montreal manufactured it from 1900 to 1916, but since their objects were marked with paper labels they cannot be identified today. Another company that started in Toronto in 1905 operated as the Clapperton Cut Glass Company from 1920 until 1973. In 1976 it was revived as the Clapperton Kingston Company of Kingston, Ontario. It folded only recently. Roden Brothers of Toronto remained in business from 1905 until 1922. Their mark was an old English "R" with a lion on either side of the letter. A glasscutting and bottle-making company operated in Winnipeg from about 1907 to 1912.

Sandwich Glass

This is another term frequently misused by collectors. Deming Jarves of Sandwich, Massachusetts, founded two companies, Boston and Sandwich Glass Company in the 1820s and the Cape Cod Works in 1859. The first was reputed to make only high quality products — coloured pieces with attractive designs and lacy patterns — while the Cape Cod Works, which only stayed in business for about ten years, produced a top line as well as less costly items. Many pieces claimed to have originated in Sandwich were made elsewhere.

Mary Gregory Glass

While most collectors easily recognize a piece

Examples of Mary Gregory glass.
(Photo: HWF)

of Mary Gregory glassware — Victorian glass that has been decorated with opaque, white enamelled figures which generally feature children and fern vegetation in the background — very few actually know anything about it and what little they do is usually based on outdated research.

Many collectors insist that Mary Gregory was employed by the Sandwich Glass Company in the United States in the 1870s and that she not only created this method of decorating glass, but also painted every piece herself. Some also believe that pieces with flesh-coloured faces are the only legitimate pieces of Mary Gregory glass and all the white-only pieces are fakes.

These stories are false, although there was a Mary Gregory who did work for the Sandwich Glass Company. According to the Historical Society at the Sandwich Glass Museum, Mary Gregory was born in Rhode Island in 1856 and was employed by the company between 1886 and 1888. But the society is not certain what she did at the factory, saying she either worked in the bookkeeping department or as a "liner," a person who paints lines on articles after they have been decorated.

She did not invent this method of decorating glass and, according to the society, there is no documentary evidence that Sandwich produced this glassware at all. Even after doing extensive excavations of the glass site, they have not uncovered one fragment of Mary Gregory glass, nor have they ever come across any catalogues, photographs, letters, advertisements or other proof that the company manufactured this kind of glass.

Research indicates that this type of decoration was first used in Bohemia (now Czechoslovakia) during the second half of the 19th century (about the time that the real Mary Gregory was born) and was later copied by English glass manufacturers. The glass decoration was brought to the United States in the 1870s, where it was copied at several glass factories in New England. The problem that frustrates glass scholars is that no one can explain why the glass is called Mary Gregory. Until more research is done in Europe to determine what the glass was called originally, collectors will only be able to speculate.

Mary Gregory type decoration was done on clear and coloured glass, such as cobalt blue, green, amber, amethyst and red, but the cranberry colour is the most coveted and hence the most expensive. For the most part vases, bowls, pitchers, perfume bottles and other simple shapes were used.

There are two basic styles to the Mary Gregory type decoration made in England. Some of it was very finely worked, showing a great deal of detail, much like the Bohemian examples, while other pieces were clumsy and blotchy, giving a great deal of flesh colour to faces and hands.

Although adults are occassionally pictured, Mary Gregory glass is characteristically decorated with silhouetted children and whispy fern bushes or trees. The children are often depicted fishing, holding hoops, blowing bubbles, flying kites, holding birds or examining flowers. As well, the enamel work itself varies in quality. The best examples have a translucency and create astonishing effects of light and dark by varying the thickness of the white enamel.

Unfortunately, the market has been flooded with fakes and reproductions. Someone is even taking vintage glass and creating new Mary Gregory type decoration over it. To tell the difference, examine a great many pieces of Mary Gregory glass to become familiar with the characteristic patterns.

New pieces don't exhibit the fine workmanship that the vintage pieces do. Look at details such as the waves in the children's hair and their clothing. Compare one piece to another. Many of the fakes use a very thin enamel and appear to be painted in a slap-happy fashion, so that the shading is either non-existant or poorly done. Prices for vintage pieces vary according to the workmanship, detailing and rarity, but generally good examples can be bought for around $200.

Art Glass

In the last quarter of the nineteenth century many American glassmakers, among them Tiffany, Carder and Lutz, produced a kind of hand-blown and hand-decorated glass we now call "art glass." It was never made in Canada and any that is found here today must be presumed to be of American or English origin.

Depression Glass

The name refers to a type of machine-made tableware marketed between the late 1920s and the early 1940s. Gas stations and movie theaters gave away pieces singly as premiums or they could be exchanged for cereal box tops. A complete twenty-piece dinner set could be purchased for as little as $1.99 at local five-and-dime stores.

Contributing to the initial popularity of depression glass was the fact that the industry had been automated just prior to the Depression years and could mass-produce low-cost items for the first time, although clever marketing techniques were responsible for making glass dinnerware acceptable.

Until the mid-1920s most inexpensive glassware was available only in clear white. When coloured pieces could be manufactured in sizeable quantities, depression glass became an affordable novelty that seemed to appeal to a large segment of the population in times of severe economic stress. Consumers could buy dinner sets in at least one hundred different patterns and designs and had a choice of amber, pink, light and dark green, blue, yellow, ruby, purple, opaque, transparent and translucent glass.

Depression glass has enjoyed a revival in recent years and has become yet another "hot" collectible. Only a small portion made during those early years has survived intact because the glass was of inferior quality to start with; pieces that did — bowls with matching lids or decanters with stoppers — sell for a lot more than specialty items without secondary parts. They are difficult to find because they never were as popular or as reasonably priced as standard tableware. According to some depression glass dealers, the patterns most popular among collectors are American Sweetheart, Cherry Blossom, Madrid and Mayfair. New collectors, therefore, would be well advised to select a pattern that is in less demand.

Only six major glass companies produced this type of tableware in North America — Federal Glass and Hocking Glass, Ohio; Macbeth-Evans Glass and Jeanette Glass, Pennsylvania; Hazel Atlas Glass and Indiana Glass, both of West Virginia. In Canada, Dominion Glass Company of Montreal and Toronto made it in limited quantities but ceased production around 1942. Their pieces were plain in design and came in clear bottle green and in a few pastel shades. Not many have survived, and because they never were too attractive are of little interest to collectors.

Many of the moulds for the one hundred or so American patterns were destroyed after the mid-1940s. Iris, one of the few in use today, was still being made as late as 1969, while others, in an effort to cash in on the collecting craze, have been deliberately faked. Spotting reproductions is not difficult, according to depression glass specialist Vi Brennan of Ancaster, Ontario, "because the new glass is of poor quality and not as clear. The colours are different, and the molds are not as good either."

In the 1940s and 1950s when the first depression glass craze was over, most people either got rid of their few remaining pieces and replaced them with china dinnerware or used them at the cottage. Many resort areas, therefore, are good hunting grounds for depression glass.

See reference list of books at the end of this chapter, as well as the magazine listings in Appendix 1 for information.

Oil Lamps (1860-1920)

Oil lamps command handsome prices, which are increasing rapidly. Joyce Burne, Canada's foremost kerosene oil lamp dealer, who resides in Orangeville, Ontario says that in 1979 a blue Eaton lamp, sometimes called an Onion, sold for $1,200 (U.S.) at a big American auction. "An astounding price for the time," she recalls. Then, in late 1985, a blue Eaton went under the hammer, at the same auction house, for $6,000 (U.S.) and a lavender example fetched $7,500 (U.S.) Today, those same two lamps would be more than $10,000 each (U.S.)

Interestingly, oil lamps haven't been around all that long. They began appearing in the late 1850s around the time of the first commercial oil-well drilling, once kerosene was discovered to be a useful by-product. Before that, illumination was exclusively provided by burning candles, lard, whale oil or a highly volatile mixture of redistilled turpentine and alcohol in an earlier form of glass or metal lamp.

In 1846 Abraham Gesner, a physician and geologist from Nova Scotia, demonstrated the benefits of coal oil in Charlottetown, Prince Edward Island, but did not patent his discovery until 1854, by which time a British man had scooped him by two years. However, it was

Gesner who first invented and coined the name 'kerosene.'

North Americans quickly took to the new fuel because it was cleaner, safer and burned brighter than anything they had used before. By 1860, dozens of lamp manufacturers had sprung up in the Ohio River Valley area, New England and eastern Canada, producing a variety of table lamps, hanging lamps, banquet lamps — even small hand lamps.

The appearance and makeup of the lamps changed periodically, helping to date them. According to Catherine Thuro, the North American oil lamp authority, the styles, colours and techniques of the 1860s and 1870s were quite different from those manufactured later. "Bases and fonts (the font is the part used to hold the oil), often sold separately, could have been put together by wholesaler, retailer or by the customer. A broken part may also have been replaced with one having a different color or design. These factors may explain why some rather strange combinations occur and relatively few identical combinations are found today."

The earliest kerosene lamp catalogues illustrate examples made with glass fonts, brass or glass stems and marble bases. These were generally produced between 1857 and 1870 and, according to Joyce Burne, demonstrate more artistry than later examples: "As lamps became more popular, the skill and workmanship decreased. Dealers needed large quantities at cheap prices to keep up with the public demand."

Burne feels that handling a lot of lamps and careful study will teach collectors how to tell the difference between earlier and later examples. And she says that certain shapes are a giveaway. For example, "You only see the turnip-shaped fonts in the 1860s. Rarely later." Another clue is the connector, a metal piece of hardware used to connect the stem and the font. "The early lamps in almost every instance had a connector."

Some highly sought-after lamps of the 1860-70 period were made from a cased or overlay glass. A spectacular effect was achieved by grinding designs through the outer surfaces of two or more layers of glass. Wide-angle lenses that focus on the interior of the lamp were thus created, giving a many-mirrored effect. During the late 1880s and 1890s lamps became even fancier. Bases often featured opalescent, opaque or alabaster glass, which was translucent with flecks or a granular appearance. Gradually from that point into this century, lamps and shades were often made with white opalescent accents and patterns, particularly spots and stripes.

All-glass lamps, made with mold-blown fonts fused to a pressed-glass base, were the most common. Thousands of early all-glass lamp patterns have been recorded. Most were colourless, or "clear," and varied in quality. Today these are the least expensive, ranging in price from $35 to $200 each. Coloured lamps are the ones that advanced collectors covet. "Green, lemony, yellow, blue and cranberry colors (in that order) made during the 1860-70 period are the rarest and the ones that command the most money," says Burne, selling between $20,000 and $30,000 each. In fact the highest price at the the November 1989 American auction, which saw some of the Catherine and Carl Thuro collection dispersed, was for a small, cranberry to clear lamp. It brought $19,000 (U.S.).

"Lamps from the 1880s that are prized are the opalescent ones, the cranberry, the blue or some combination of those," says Burne. But you can get a green example of a bull's eye, a type of patterned lamp made by the Dominion Glass Co. of Montreal, for about $225.

The use of fully automated glassmaking machines and the threat that electric lights would make kerosene lamps obsolete contributed to the

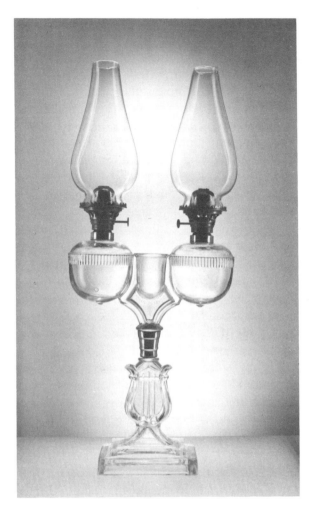

rapid deterioration in their design and quality. By the turn of the century, production had greatly slowed down. But the kerosene era lingered in parts of rural Canada. In her research, Torontonian Thuro, found that as "late as the 1950s, antique dealers traded new lamps for old, following hydro crews as the network of power lines reached out to farms across the country."

Like most other kinds of antiques, fakes and reproductions are circulating in the marketplace. To avoid buying a 'mistake' look for genuine wear marks on the bottom of the base; tiny scratches or dents of irregular depth and direction. Make sure that the threaded brass collar that holds the burner in place is fastened with plaster, not glue or epoxy. And check the top of

Above: The c. 1870 Marriage or Wedding Lamp, patented by Daniel C. Ripley, in Pittsburgh, is coveted by collectors. The fonts on either side of the match-holder were blown simultaneously by two glassmakers. The match-holder lid sells for several hundred dollars. Collection: Catherine M.V. Thuro. *(Photo: Catherine M.V. Thuro)*

Right: This lamp (known as the Queen Heart, Beaded Heart or Sweetheart) was made by, the Dalzell, Gilmore & Leighton Co., U.S.A., c. 1898. While the illustrated example is in clear glass, lamps have been found in combinations of green and clear, opaque yellow or custard and an opaque light green. Collection: Private. *(Photo: HWF)*

The six wooden oil lamps shown here are extremely rare. They originated in the United States and were made prior to 1880. The two tankard lamps on either side of the photograph have applied pewter handles. Collection: two private collections. *(Photo: HWF)*

the font to make certain that it has not been ground flat. Old pieces either have very smooth tops or jagged edges around the rim.

New lamps recently imported from Mexico are primitive in design and quite pretty. They look free-blown without mold seams but show pontil marks on the base. A few years ago they were sold in Canada for under $6 each but lately some were seen in Ontario at $150 and up.

In the late 1970s an American company made a clear glass oil lamp and impressed "Sept. 18th, 1978" on the bottom. Unfortunately, someone has used an abrasive and removed the "th" and the "19," leaving Sept. 18 78. If you see a lamp with an unusual space between the eight and the seven, you are looking at a faked reproduction.

How To Use an Oil Lamp

- Closely examine the lamp before lighting it. Make sure the wick fills the wick tube.
- Trim the wick to make the corners shorter than the centre portion. Allow about one eighth of an inch of the wick to protrude above the burner.
- Make sure the chimney is suitable for use with an oil lamp as those made for electric fixtures shatter easily when subjected to the greater heat of lamp oil. Check to see that it fits properly into the prongs. Save vintage chimneys for display purposes only. Use reproduction chimneys available at hardware and department stores and in a few antique shops.

One of the pair of silvered-glass candlesticks which Gerald Stevens uncovered. *Collection: Royal Ontario Museum.* *(Photo: ROM)*

- Only use refined lamp oil for burning. It is safer than ordinary kerosene and will not blacken the chimney.
- Make certain the font is filled to 75 percent capacity. There is little danger of explosion unless it is only partially filled and sparks are allowed to ignite the volatile vapours.
- Do not leave the lamp lit when you are out of the room. Remember to treat its flame as you would any other fire.
- After extinguishing the flame turn the wick up high and test it with your fingers to make sure it is cool to the touch.

Misconceptions and Other Problems Related to Canadian Glass

The antique glass market in Canada is in a state of confusion with collectors and dealers seem-

ingly divided into two camps. One group is convinced that certain glass patterns were made in Canada, while the other maintains that these same pieces actually originated in the United States.

To get at the truth I spent six months investigating the entire Canadian glass scene and came away more convinced than ever that a significant portion of antique glass now being sold in Canada as Canadian is, in fact, American.

The late Gerald Stevens (1912-1981) was for some time regarded as the pioneer of Canadian glass research. As a Canadian nationalist he was anxious to prove that the early Canadian craftsmen were just as artistic and talented as their American counterparts and had produced glass objects in Canada before the end of the nineteenth century. It now appears that Stevens, possibly because of little or no formal museological and archaeological training, came to conclusions which, in many instances, may have been incorrect. It is unfortunate that the people who published after him often based their material on his findings and thereby perpetuated errors which in Stevens' case may be forgivable, considering he was the first to seriously deal with early Canadian glass.

One little known incident may effectively illustrate Stevens' lack of scrupulosity when making attributions and authentications. In the early sixties he discovered a pair of silvered-glass candlesticks among some vintage bottles and jars in an old drugstore in Napanee, Ontario. He immediately deduced that they must have been manufactured at the Napanee Glass Works. As a result, numerous collectors purchased similar silvered-glass objects on the assumption that they were Canadian. Later research revealed that Stevens' candlesticks had a type of pressed-glass collar that was never found at the Napanee excavations but was known to have been made at several American glass works.

Kenneth M. Wilson, author of *New England Glass and Glassmaking* (Old Sturbridge Village, 1972), is the former director of Collections and Preservation at the Henry Ford Museum in Greenfield Village and past assistant director and curator of the Corning Museum of Glass in New York State. When we discussed Gerald Stevens' research methods, he expressed concern about the way the Mallorytown excavations had been carried out and the speed with which they were accomplished. "He used a tractor and a two-bladed plough which is hardly professional, and although he stated in one of his books that he had authenticated the pieces, he never said how he did it," Wilson said. "His statements are extremely generalized and not the type of thing a museum curator would be willing to accept." Wilson also wondered why the shards from the Mallorytown excavations were never shown in any of Stevens' books and why he had failed to mention how many he found and what type of objects they had come from.

Wilson found Stevens' theory — that all Mallorytown glass was of the same colour — even more questionable, in view of the fact that "colour is the least reliable measure of authentication. Even mild temperature changes, the position of the molten glass in the container and the ingredients themselves can account for great differences in colour. The quality of soda ash can vary from one place to another, from one company to the next and from time to time," said Mr. Wilson.

Relying exclusively on shards as primary source material further complicates the matter. These broken pieces of glass found by Stevens and others at the excavation sites could have been cullet, a substance that can account for 25 percent of the molten mixture in the production

For years collectors and dealers have incorrectly said that water pitchers in clear glass with opalescent dots were made at Burlington Glass Works, Hamilton, Ontario. Pitchers of this type are known by verification through company catalogues and other American records to have been made in the Ohio Valley. Collection: private. *(Photo: HWF)*

of new glass. In the absence of factory records — early catalogues, notes, advertisements and accounts books — these shards should have been treated as support material, according to Janet Holmes (Royal Ontario Museum) and Olive Jones (National Museum of Man). Commenting on the risk involved in such attributions, they stated in an article in the *Material History Bulletin,* published in 1978, that "when used carefully these methods can add to our knowledge of products from specific factories, but when used without discrimination or by people whose only interest is making specific attributions to specific factories, the conclusions are likely to be questionable."

The late Dr. Arthur G. Peterson, author of *Glass Patents and Patterns* and several other important books on the subject, confirmed that "glassmakers sometimes obtained surplus cullet from other glass houses and from itinerant peddlers who, at one time, collected broken glass as well as rags, scrap metal and even bones. Moreover, glassmakers usually acquired samples of wares made by competitors and many of these were discarded sooner or later. These practises have led to some mistaken conclusions."

Although a lot of pressed glass can be positively traced to American firms, primarily those in the Midwest, some identical pieces could have been produced in Canada at a later date. Pointing to existing records, Eason Eige, a glass specialist and chief curator of Huntington Galleries in West Virginia, maintains that West Virginia glass companies shipped entire rail cars of patterned glass east, west and north, and if some was indeed made in Canada, the molds probably had been designed and manufactured in the United States. "It should perhaps be classified as glass *used* in Canada," said Mr. Eige.

It is known that from 1850 the Boston and Sandwich glass companies and others were selling glassware, lamps and bottles in Montreal. "There is no harm in collecting it as something used in Canada," states Janet Holmes, "although it is more than likely that it was American."

The late William Heacock, author of at least twelve American glass books and editor-publisher of the quarterly *The Glass Collector* blamed the authors of early Canadian glass books for making attributions that were at least 50 per cent incorrect. He specifically cited Peter and Doris Unitt whose *Treasury of Canadian Glass* shows on its cover an opalescent water pitcher claimed to have been made in Burling-

ton, Ontario. It actually originated in Indiana, Pennsylvania, around 1889. The sole evidence for attributing all opalescent glass to the Burlington Glass Works were two colourless shards, each about two inches long, one with opalescent dots and the other with opalescent stripes. Most of the Unitt's findings were based on Gerald Stevens' work and later that of John Sheeter who had participated in the 1969 Burlington digs and had written a series of articles on the private 1968 digs in the now defunct *Canadian Collector.*

During excavations in the summers of 1966, 1968 and 1969 on the site of the former Burlington Glass Company (in business in Hamilton, Ontario, between 1874 and 1897), a fragment was found with a peculiar mark on a handle. Although the experts could only speculate that it *could have been* manufactured at the Burlington plant, many Canadian collectors and dealers chose to regard the conditional conclusion as fact and over the years perpetuate the fable of the so-called "Burlington mark" as absolute truth.

When attaching handles to pitchers and oil lamps, glassmakers would put a blob of molten glass onto the body of the piece, pull it up and out in an arch, loop it back down again and press it into place with a tool used throughout North America. The imprint, resembling a chevron or an inverted feather the size of a thumb print, was decorative as well as functional. Pieces with such marks were made in many parts of the United States. Eason Eige finds it "mind-boggling" that anyone could say with certainty that they were made only in Burlington. Pointing to a cranberry pitcher, claimed to have been produced at the Burlington Glassworks, reproduced on page 274 in the *Book of Canadian Antiques,* edited by Donald Blake Webster, curator of Canadiana at the Royal Ontario Museum, Mr.

Eige states that he knows of at least five factories in the Ohio Valley that could have produced the same pitcher.

At fault too is the Royal Ontario Museum. It was involved in the Burlington digs of 1966 and 1969 but has not yet issued its complete report on these digs to dispel some of the misinformation that has been allowed to proliferate.

One reason why many Canadian glass collectors prefer to remain silent on the matter is that they paid high prices in the past for things supposedly Canadian and now wish to protect their investments. American collectors, on the other hand, are often forced to come to Canada to buy back their heritage. Worst of all, some unscrupulous Canadian dealers are importing glass into Canada and labelling it "Canadian" so that it can be sold at higher prices. "It's a case of a passion being fed by the fuel of profit," states Eason Eige, "with Canadians being the losers more than the Americans because they are paying for something that isn't what it's supposed to be."

Bibliography

Gene, Florence, PO Box 22186, Lexington, KY 40502. (Has published a series of books on depression glass.)

Kaellgren, C. Peter, ed. *A Gather of Glass — Glass Through the Ages in the Royal Ontario Museum*. Toronto, Ontario: Royal Ontario Museum, 1977.

McKearin, Helen and Kenneth M. Wilson. *American Bottles and Flasks and their Ancestry*. Crown Publishing Inc., 1978.

Revi, Albert Christian. *American Press Glass and Figure Bottles*. Thomas Nelson Inc., 1964.

Innis, Lowell. *Pittsburgh Glass 1797-1891*. Houghton Mifflin Co., 1976.

Russell, Loris S. *A Heritage of Light*. Toronto: University of Toronto Press, 1968. (Out of print; copies still available at some antiquarian bookstores.)

Spillman, Jane Shadel. *Glassmaking, America's First Industry*. Corning, NY: Corning Museum of Glass, Corning Glass Center.

Thuro, Catherine M.V. *Oil Lamps — The Kerosene Era of North America*. Wallace Homestead Books, 1978.

Thuro, Catherine M.V. *Oil Lamps: Glass Kerosene Lamps*. Toronto: Thornclife House Inc., 1983.

Weatherman, Hazel Marie, PO Box 4444, Route 1, Ozark, MO 65721. (Has published a series of books on depression glass.)

Wilson, Kenneth M. *Glass in New England*. Sturbridge, MA: Old Sturbridge Village, 1959, 1969.

11

Textiles

Textile collectors are a devoted lot. The things they hoard include old clothing and accessories; purses and scarves; rugs and carpets; bed coverings; tapestries; quilts; upholstered furniture; even dolls' clothing; ecclesiastical embroideries; samplers; pin cushions; beaded objects; and such obscure treasures as saddle bags, and birthing and burial wraps.

Oriental Rugs

New collectors often are confused by the names used to describe rugs. There is no difference between an Oriental and a Persian rug. Oriental rugs come from many places other than Persia; they could be from Turkey, China, Afghanistan, Iraq and Soviet Russia.

After World War II, many people wanted broadloom and threw out their Oriental rugs because they considered them "old-fashioned." Interest was revived in the mid-1970s when it became fashionable to show some floor area, especially dark stained hardwood. As a result, Oriental rug prices which had fallen substantially in the "broadloom" era began to rise, reaching unprecedented heights in the late 1970s, only to fall again late in 1981. The late, Albert Aliman, a respected Toronto dealer, once likened the rug market to the fluctuations in the price of gold. "When it rose, everybody wanted to buy an Oriental rug because they could foresee inflation. Now that gold is down, Oriental rugs are down too." He added that new carpets will continue to be made but as their prices rise "antique carpet prices will go up in sympathy."

"There are many excellent books about Oriental carpets and many more that are notable for their authors' ignorance or their fanciful sales talk," wrote P.R.J. Ford in his book *The Oriental Carpet*. Although his comments were about rug scholarship, he could have been describing rug dealers the world over. The entire business has been likened by some to a "conspiracy of thieves," as it involves thousands of so-called "dealers" and fly-by-night auctioneers who set up onetime sales in hotels and vacant stores throughout North America. Only a small percentage are reliable and trustworthy.

Before you buy, ask a collector whose opinion and judgement you respect to recommend a reputable dealer, one who has been in business for a long time, serving a sophisticated and devoted clientele. Do not let yourself be influenced by flashy and expensive displays or establishments that receive a great deal of publicity. Often those located in humbler quarters are the ones most highly regarded by connoisseurs.

Albert Aliman told collectors to look at sev-

A Kashan from Central Iran, circa 1910 . It measures 78-1/2" x 51-1/2" and is multi-coloured. A blossoming tree coming out of a vase or mountain is an ancient symbol of fertility and well being.

eral pieces before deciding to buy. The collector must know why he wants a particular rug and where it is to be used. If he admires an old piece for its decorative value, it should not be placed in a heavy traffic area for it will quickly deteriorate. But if it is to be used in a living or dining room, it should be strong and durable.

"Take a rug home and put it on the floor," advises Max Allen, the former curator of the Museum of Textiles in Toronto. "Look at it for a week, take the next one home and look at it for another week. Repeat the process until you find the one that suits you and your room best. Choosing a rug in the store is the absolute wrong thing to do; for one thing, the light will be very different from that in your own house."

Before buying an Oriental rug consider the following:

Is it hand- or machine-made?
To determine the difference, separate the fibers and look at the base or round fabric. If you can see the curve of knots tied around the wrap, it probably was made by hand. Generally, knots do not show on machine-made rugs.

Where was it made?
Rugs from Persia (now Iran) and from some part of Soviet Russia are popular. However, to establish their origin requires a discerning eye and years of experience.

What is the condition of the rug?
One in mint condition obviously is worth more than a similar one in a worn state. If you buy from a reputable dealer, he will cover any losses you may incur should the rug deteriorate before its time.

How old is it?
Age is important to establish a price. It takes an expert to determine this accurately. One clue might be its "palette" — when the colours are very bright, the rug is probably contemporary.

What is it made of?
Silk, recognizable because of its lustre, is attractive but not hard-wearing. Wool is strong, and its inherent properties make design and pattern flow easily. As humidity fluctuates, a wool rug can shrink and stretch. Cotton is stable and reliable but because the fabric is harder to work with than wool, the design does not flow as smoothly. When deciding where the rug is to be placed it is imperative to determine the materials used.

Were natural or synthetic dyes used?
The most treasured pieces are those made with natural dyes. The dyes are also a useful guide to determining the age of a carpet.

How many knots per square inch?
Some dealers try to convince their customers that the number of knots per square inch influences a rug's value, maintaining that the more densely knotted are of better quality and, therefore, higher in price. Knot-count is only one aspect of a carpet's character and generally not the most significant when judging its worth.

Is the rug signed or dated?
Those marked with the weaver's name have added interest and importance.

Some Don'ts
- Never buy an Oriental rug for its investment potential alone. The market is fickle, and prices can rise and fall depending on fads, fashions and the state of the economy.
- Never buy because you believe you are getting a bargain. Buy because you love the piece and want to live with it for a long time. And if it is a work of art, hang it on the wall!

Hooked Rugs

"Hooked rugs were those things your grandmother made from old scraps of clothing. They finally got thrown out, along with the Tiffany lamps, about the time somebody decided it would be nice to paint the wooden chairs green," explains Max Allen. Although they were discarded long ago, astute collectors rescued them from obscurity. Their collection, one of the largest in the country, has done much to prove that hooked rugs are an art form, uniquely connected to Canada's early history and culture.

The nineteenth-century housewife hardly associated the rugs she hooked with art or social history. She made them to cover cold floors, to add some decor and colour to her home and, only incidentally, to provide an outlet for her aesthetic impulses.

No one is certain who invented rug hooking, but it is now believed that it developed simultaneously in Quebec and the Maritimes about the mid-1850s. Although dates were rarely worked into the rugs, the Museum of Textiles owns one with 1840 as part of the pattern; it probably was made to commemorate an important event such as a wedding or a birth. However, judging by the materials used, it must have been made after 1910. The earliest reliably dated Canadian rug was hooked by Abigail Smith of New Brunswick in 1860. It is currently owned by the New Brunswick Museum in Saint John.

Rug hooking requires no special talent or training. Rags were dyed and then cut into strips, usually about three eighths of an inch wide; these widths varied according to the thickness of the material. The loosely woven ground fabric was placed on a frame, and the loops of the rags or yarn pulled up through the holes with a small hook specifically designed for the purpose. Burlap grounds were often used. Max Allen says he has seen only four Canadian rugs that were not hooked on a burlap foundation. Often the "yarn" came from unravelled burlap sacks, a method solely employed in this country. Since every scrap of material was utilized, the rugs generally were a combination of various fabrics. Canadian rugs also tended to be more subdued in colouring than those made south of the border. In design, our grandmothers incorporated maple leaves, beavers and even geese, while Americans favoured their patriotic symbols — eagles, stars and stripes, etc.

Two types of hooked rugs existed: commer-

Most hooked rugs were made by anonymous women. However, this example was worked by one of Canada's only documented rug hookers, Maria Beck Warning (1832-1918) of Brunner, Ontario. Collection: Museum for Textiles. *(Photo: HWF)*

cially patterned ones and those drawn by hand. The latter, because of their originality and charm, are dearly coveted by collectors. Design inspiration came from household objects, book and magazine illustrations, pets and even farm animals. There is a story about a Nova Scotia woman who in 1928 hooked the image of a black cat onto crimson ground. When asked how she had created the pattern, she replied:

> I looked in the yard and I looked in the house and I looked in the barn and after a while I saw our cat Malty and I said to myself, he'll be good enough. Then I got my old man to hold him down on this piece of burlap while I drew around him with a pencil. But I didn't know what to do with the tail; he was lying on it, so it didn't show in the picture. But no cat grows without a tail, so my old man held it out nice and straight and I just stuck it on here.

Some women found it simpler to use commercial patterns and Edward Sands Frost, a peddler from Biddeford, Maine, was happy to oblige. As early as 1864 he cut out stencils and printed them on burlap. Later, Wells and Richardson of Montreal, Hambly and Wilson of Toronto, John L. Garrett Company of New Glasgow and the T. Eaton Company of Toronto manufactured and sold patterned burlap to Canadian rug hookers. It takes a trained eye to recognize these commercial designs which, incidentally, are in use today. However, the rugs made from them are neither valuable nor sought by true collectors.

When buying a hooked rug, look for one that is in good condition. Finding someone to repair it is time-consuming and expensive. It should be washed by hand, never in a washing-machine, and dried quickly near a warm furnace or outdoors in warm weather, spread out horizontally or stretched on a screen, rather than hung on a line. If the rug is not to be displayed, keep it rolled up away from bright light. If you want to show it, mount it on a wall as you would a good painting or lie it on a table, rather than on the floor where it can be abused.

Penny Rugs

These small decorative area rugs made from fabric cutouts were popular in the late 1800s and during the early years of the twentieth century. The materials were gaily coloured felt, the kind women's hats were made of, as well as the more subdued gray and black suiting then popular for men's clothing. The cutout shapes in the form of stars, circles, birds, shamrocks and flowers were assembled like overlapping petals and sewn onto backing of burlap, unbleached sacking, linen, felt, or a piece of blanket. Frequently they were embroidered with fancy motifs that resembled people, animals, birds and insects.

For years penny rugs were ignored by collectors. R.A. O'Neil, a Toronto specialist in Canadian country pieces, remembers pickers using them in the early seventies to wrap glass pieces and to protect furniture in transit to antique stores and warehouses. However, today collectors, especially in the United States, are willing to pay several hundred dollars for them providing they are in mint condition and exhibit a pleasing palette and good workmanship. Because of limited demand in Canada, few have appeared in the marketplace which has created the impression that they were not made in large quantities, either here or in the United States. But Simon Waegemaekers, administrator of the Textile Museum in Toronto, believes that "probably one penny mat for every 150 hooked rugs" can be found in practically all parts of the eastern United States and in Canada, although truly fine examples are difficult to locate.

Those from the Maritimes, Quebec and the United States are better colour-coordinated and superior in design, quality and workmanship than pieces from southern, eastern and northern Ontario; so far, none have been found in western Ontario.

Known as "penny rugs" in Ontario, they had different names in other parts of the country. In the Maritimes they were called "felt," "silver dollar," "dime" or "button" rugs (probably because of the size of the appliqued pieces), whereas in Quebec they were known as *tapis de fantaisie* (fantasy rug), *tapis de roulette* (wheel rug made up of circular pieces) and *tapis de languette* (tongue mats made of elongated, floppy pieces).

No one knows where the idea for making these rugs actually came from. According to the curator of the textile division in the Victoria and Albert Museum in London, "there was no direct equivalent craft in Britain." Nor do early women's magazines and pattern books contain instructions for making them. Nettie Sharpe, a prominent Quebec collector, maintains that most French-Canadian women were familiar with the craft during the first quarter of the twentieth century because they were trained to utilize every scrap of available materials. "But like everything else, some women were more artistic than others." The techniques employed to cut out the felt pieces are somewhat obscure. "They could not have used scissors," says Mrs. Sharpe. "The men must have stamped out several layers of fabric for the women to obtain identical pieces of uniform size." In her collection is a four inch-high hand-wrought punch press.

Although the flour sacks used for backing the rugs often show the imprint of the mill from where they came, they do not provide a clue as to where these penny rugs actually originated. Backing material with American flour company labels were often found on rugs in Quebec houses.

Many antique dealers would have us believe that penny rugs were used to cover table tops and chests. "Not so," says Nettie Sharpe. "They usually were placed on top of a store bought rug in front of a piece of furniture, mostly in the parlour, the salon or in low traffic areas."

Because these mats are still relatively unknown as Canadian collectors' items, they might be worth considering, at least until demand for them becomes so great that prices will rise as high as for hooked rugs.

Samplers

Samplers — pieces of embroidery originally designed to record stitches and patterns have been treasured, protected and admired perhaps more than any other antique or heirloom. Long after they were made, used and consulted, they were either carefully stored away or prominently hung and displayed.

Collectors have always found a certain appeal in these charming pieces of embroidery, either as decorative accessories or unusual aspects of antique collecting. But they are more than that. Samplers are among the few old pieces of our material heritage that are often signed and dated, making them remarkable links to the past and vital tools in genealogical research. As well, they are often the only tangible proof that the person who made them ever lived. As instruments for learning about the past, their value is undisputed. Fine old buildings no longer standing nor recorded in drawings or photographs are depicted. Some contain family histories and printed slogans, sayings and verses that serve as constant reminders of the attitudes, ideas, tastes and religious beliefs that dominated early Canadian life.

What is a sampler? The word is derived from the Latin *exemplum* or *exemplar* meaning a thing regarded as worthy of imitation, model, pattern, archetype, a typical specimen or example. In early literature, samplers were referred to by a variety of names such as saumplaire, sawpler, samcloth, sam cloths, sampleth, samplette, ensample, example, exampler and exemplar.

Initially, the fabric or ground was long and narrow with embroidery splashed across in haphazard fashion. No thought was given to appearance. A sampler was a kind of notebook, a place where designs, patterns and stitches could be recorded. If more fabric was needed, it was sewn onto the end, and when the work became too cumbersome to fit neatly into a workbox, it was simply rolled, scroll-fashion, around a piece of wood, parchment or ivory. In some cases, samplers were done by more than one person. This led experts to conclude that they must have been passed on from mother to daughter and added to in the same way as a hand-written recipe collection would have been compiled. In other instances, samplers were willed to friends, relatives and children as they represented a lifetime's work, just as valuable as silver or jewelry.

Most homes in England and continental Europe identified their linens-blankets, chair covers, pillows, curtains and towels with initials, numbers and even stylized monograms and crowns. Fabrics, because they were so time-consuming to make, were valuable possessions and as such carefully accounted for. Hence the importance of knowing how to identify them correctly.

From the late 1500s through the 1600s, England's adult women and certain trained professionals made many of these pieces but with the advent of printed patterns and books, the original purpose was forgotten. By the early eighteenth century the character of the sampler changed dramatically. It became shorter, although it still maintained the eight- or nine-inch widths. Instead of random motifs, stitches and experimental markings, neatly concentrated lines, rows or bands appeared as part of the design; hence the name "band" sampler. At that time, alphabets, numerals and the occasional poem made their debut. The age of its maker dropped, and by the late 1700s sampler-making was taught in Canada at a few schools.

At the turn of 1800s, samplers looked as if they had been designed for framing. Rather than references, they became a record of achievement, and the age of the maker dropped even further. To small children who were forced to make them (they were occasionally worked by boys), samplers became a dreaded experience, a test of coordination, patience and skill. In many ways they represented hurdles to be overcome in the same way as loosing a first tooth, learning to tie a bow or to read. The makers' names and ages frequently were added, especially if the work was good. Sometimes either the teacher's or school's name was included in the text. Not surprisingly, samplers became an accepted tool to teach morals, religion and sometimes even the formation and sequence of letters and numerals. In some cases a young sampler-maker made only one complete sampler but many youngsters were required to make two; the first for marking purposes (a reference to be used for labelling linens) and the second for "good."

To accurately attribute a sampler to one specific country of origin is difficult unless the worker recorded, on the piece, where it was made. English samplers usually were worked on tightly woven grounds and exhibit extraordinarily fine needlework. American examples show imagination and whimsy and are more folk-like in character than Canadian pieces which tend to be plainer and not as well executed as those made in England. However, Canadian Maritime samplers often closely resemble American pieces. Because settlement came so late to Western Canada, examples usually date from the 1860s to the 1880s, although even those are scarce and hard to locate.

Patterns themselves don't reveal much, as they were traded among neighbours, families and friends and were often inherited or copied from an ancestor's work. Crown emblems have for years been thought to indicate a sampler's English origin. However, the evidence is inconclusive because crowns also appear on samplers from other countries including the United States.

In England, sampler-making was in its heyday from about 1750 to 1800; in the United States from approximately 1790 to 1830; and in Canada from 1820 to the 1850s, except perhaps in Western Canada where settlement was later. It would be safe to say that in that thirty-year period more samplers were made in this country than at any other time. The earliest English sampler known is Jane Bostock's, dated 1698; and Lora Standish's, worked sometime before 1655, sets the record in the United States. The earliest known Canadian example is dated 1780, made by eighteen-year-old Marguerite Falardeau when she was a boarder (from December 16, 1779, to January 6, 1781) at the Ursuline Convent in Quebec City. Although in poor condition, her work (measuring 6-1/4 x 5") is still owned by the convent. While some samplers obviously were done at home under a mother's supervision, many more were made at school. Canadian girls sometimes were sent to the United States for their education, others attended ladies' academies in Canada.

The thousands of samplers made in early Canada were cherished and carefully tucked

"Eliza McFee is my name and with my needle I write the same and this is for to let you see the care my parents took of me. Aged 12 years, March 27, Monkstown Day School, Ann McFee T." Written on the back of the frame, in old script, is: "Belongs to Mrs. Edith Eakin, work of her mothers, 110 years ago. Not to go out of the family." *(Photo: HWF)*

Matilda Filbert's sampler sold for a record $41,800 in Sotheby's 1981 benchmark sale. *(Photo: Sotheby Parke Bernet, New York City)*

away in blanket boxes and drawers. However, many more had been brought here in the early years as well as imported more recently. Because it is so difficult to accurately pinpoint the provenance of a particular sampler, those found today should be presumed to be of foreign origin unless they boast the name of a Canadian place and a known Canadian teacher, a school or a documented family history.

Few, if any, authenticated Canadian samplers have come to light at Canadian auctions, and it is therefore difficult to properly gauge the market or suggest a viable price structure. Sam-

plers in the United States have fetched astronomically high prices. The Theodore Kapnek Collection, for instance, auctioned by Sotheby's New York City, in January 1981, surprised even the experts. One piece after another went for double and triple the estimates; 172 lots brought $641,300, excluding the 10 per cent buyer's premium. Matilda Filbert's sampler sold for a record, $41,800 in that benchmark sale. By 1987 that figure would seem like a bargain when a Philadelphia needlework picture sold for $187,000 at Christie's. And shortly afterwards the all-time record price was established by

Estimated to fetch between $20,000 and $30,000 this American sampler by Ruthy Rogers of Marblehead, Massachusetts, c. 1788, realized $198,000 setting an all-time, world-wide record for a sampler. *(Photo: Skinner, Boston, MA)*

"What is Home Without a Mother?" "The Old Armchair;" "After Clouds, Sunshine;" "Eat, Drink and Be Merry" are some still found today.

Worked on heavy perforated paper, originally called bristol board, the designs and patterns were stamped out commercially and subsequently embroidered with a new type of wool which was softer than the traditional crewel yarn. Known as Berlin wool, it came in a variety of unusually bright colours and was available in Canada in the 1850s, brought to England from Germany where it was invented by a man called Philipson. But it was a certain Madame Wittich who was responsible for promoting the new needlework; Mr. Wittich, a printer and presumably her husband, had found a method of blocking out the patterns on paper so that the embroiderer could simply cover it with stitches without previously drawing the design onto the paper. By the 1840s, several stamped patterns were commercially available.

Most of the perforated cards were white but could be purchased in blue, beige, yellow, green, black and pink in various thicknesses, either as whole sheets or in sections. The mottoes were framed, often with aluminum foil backing to give them added depth and sparkle. They also could be made into bookmarks, needle holders, comb-and-brush cases, card containers and letter pouches. The pieces were rarely signed or dated.

As motto work became fashionable in Canada the art of sampler-making regrettably declined and virtually disappeared by the mid-1870s. Samplers had been worked by young girls using the counted-thread technique, usually on a linen ground. Motto making, on the other hand, was a kind of leisure activity enjoyed by adult women who found it easier than petit point embroidery because the background could be left unworked, and the piece was completed in less time. The only negative aspect of the craft

Skinner's in Boston when they disposed of a Massachusetts sampler, done by Ruthy Rogers for $198,000. Canadian samplers have never fetched anywhere near these figures, and it is doubtful they ever will. To date, the highest known price paid for a Canadian sampler is $1,500, with the bulk retailing from $350 to approximately $800.

Mottoes

Mottoes are stitched Victorian motifs and sentimental sayings worked on regularly perforated cards. They were a popular form of needlework from the 1860s to the early 1900s. "Home Sweet Home;" "God Bless our Home;" "Trust in God;"

was that the paper ground was so fragile that one slip of the needle could ruin the entire work.

Many dealers and collectors confuse mottoes with samplers. There is no relationship between them either historically or in originality or workmanship. Mottoes have been available at antique shows and flea markets for many years. They used to be sold framed for twenty-five dollars or even less, and only very recently have collectors begun to pay serious attention to them. Perfect examples now command at least double that figure.

Although mottoes cannot be considered rare art, they are fun to collect for decorative purposes or as reminders of an era that favoured the ornate and the expression of sweet sentimentality through needlework.

Quilts

Many of the early immigrants were totally unprepared for the terrible Canadian winters. Writing to her homeland from the Muskoka bush, one settler described her experience when the temperature reached 40° below zero: "We soon found that all silks, delicate shawls, laces and ornaments were perfectly useless here. As the cold increased we put one thing over another till we must have often presented the appearance of featherbeds tied in the middle with string."

For most of our ancestors, however, surviving the freezing nights was an even more terrifying prospect. To keep family members warm, all kinds of bed coverings were devised. Of those, quilts survived in large numbers and now are of interest to collectors everywhere.

Even though pioneer quilts were based on traditional patterns, they often exhibited unique colour combinatons and intricate workmanship. Their designs elevate some pieces to real art.

A quilt is a textile "sandwich" made up of two layers of cloth with a soft filling of cotton batting, old blankets or raw wool stuffed between them. To hold the three thicknesses together, small ties, pieces of yarn or tiny running stitches (quilting) were used. The stitching kept the padding in place, while at the same time providing an opportunity for artistic expression in both design and execution.

There are three main types of quilts: the whole cloth, where the top and bottom were made from a single piece; the pieced quilt, where the top was pieced or fitted together; and the appliqued quilt, made by sewing small pieces of cloth onto a large piece to form a pattern or design.

American quilts are more imaginative and uninhibited in design than those made by Canadians who worked the same patterns using different colours and stitching. The backing on Ontario quilts, for instance, is generally a practical flannelette, a fabric Americans rarely used. American quiltmakers created pieces with striking-looking borders, whereas Canadian ex-

This a large, slightly stained motto done with Berlin yarn on perforated cardboard. *(Photo: HWF)*

amples show plain borders if any at all. Americans also had a better choice of textiles, while Canadians depended on Great Britain for most of their fabrics.

Quilt prices are high in the United States, especially in New York City where they have been known to reach upward of $10,000. In Canada, quilts sell for $200 to about $1,500.

Bibliography

Aston, Leigh. *Samplers*. London: The Medici Society, 1926.

Bolton, Ethel Stanwood and Eva Johnston Coe. *American Samplers*. Massachusetts Society of the Colonial Daimes, 1921.

Canadian Hooked Rugs 1860-1960, a catalogue of an exhibition organized by Max Allen and Simon Waegemaekers at the McCord Museum in Montreal.

Christie, Mrs. A. *Samplers and Stitches*. London: B.T. Batsford Limited, 1920.

Colby, Averil. *Samplers Yesterday and Today*. London: B.T. Batsford Limited, 1964.

Conroy, Mary. *Three Hundred Years of Canada's Quilts*. Toronto: Griffin House, 1976.

Ford, P.R.J. *The Oriental Carpet: A History and Guide to Traditional Motifs, Patterns* and Symbols. New York: Harry N. Abrams Inc., 1981.

Hooked Rugs: A Canadian Tradition, a catalogue of an exhibition arranged by Allen and Waegemaekers in 1975.

Huish, Marcus B. *Samplers and Tapestry Embroideries*. London: Longmans, Green & Company, in association with the Fine Art Society, London, 1900.

Jones, Mary Eirwen. *British Samplers*. Oxford: Pen-in-Hand, 1948.

Kopp, Joel and Kate. *American Hooked and Sewn Rugs: Folk Art Underfoot*. New York: Dutton & Co. Inc., 1975.

Krueger, Glee. *New England Samplers to 1840*. Old Sturbridge Village, 1978.

Krueger, Glee. *A Gallery of American Samplers: the Theodore H. Kapnek Collection*. E.P. Dutton Co., 1978.

McKendry, Ruth and Blake. *Quilts and Other Bed Coverings in the Canadian Tradition*. Toronto: Van Nostrand Reinhold, 1979.

Ring, Betty. *American Needlework Treasures: Samplers and Silk Embroideries from the Collection of Betty Ring*. New York: E.P. Dutton, 1987.

Swan, Susan Burrows. *Plain and Fancy: American Women and Their Needlework, 1700-1850*. New York: Holt, Rinehart & Winston, 1977.

Waugh, Elizabeth and Edith Foley. *Collecting Hooked Rugs*. Century Company, 1927.

Bette S. Feinstein sells books related to antique and contemporary embroidery and needlework. To obtain a catalogue, write: Bette S. Feinstein, 96 Roundwood Rd., Newton Upper Falls, MA 02164.

12

Folk Art

Once considered the preserve of the specialty collector, folk art has come of age. Not only is it fashionable and collected by the avant-garde, but it is also promoted by art galleries, featured in museum exhibitions, books and in antique shops across North America.

The only problem is that experts can't agree on a definition although almost everyone has taken a stab at it. Some say folk art is created by talented but untrained hands. The work of Nova Scotian Maud Lewis (1903-1970) is a good example. Coming from a poor, rural background and suffering from the crippling effects of polio, Lewis had no formal training. Yet, in the latter portion of her life, she decorated her rural surroundings with paintings of large, bold flowers, birds and butterflies on cookie sheets, walls, windows, blinds and even her front door. She made her humble quarters beautiful by decorating with bright cheerful objects everything in sight, including her stove. "Discovered" in the last few years of her life, she actually made some money selling her work — an unusual occurrence for a folk artist.

Another quality of folk art is that it comes out of a rural craft rather than a fine-arts tradition. Lewis's work certainly did, as did the work of the women who created elaborate quilts and hooked rugs, and the farmers who whittled away the winter nights carving intricate designs into love tokens, jewelry boxes, kitchen utensils and toys.

Some experts have defined folk art as the opposite of fine art while others describe it as naive, delightful, exuberant, imaginative, quaint, bold, sincere and spontaneous. Michael Rowan, a dealer based in Green River, Ontario calls folk art "a decorative, ethnic, traditional form of art, something that is learned from an ancestor." And Bob Starr, proprietor of Town of York Antiques in Toronto, adds that folk art is special because of its 'originality.' To him, a good piece of folk art "has the ability to move a viewer's emotions."

No matter how it's defined, folk art is a catch-all category that includes a wide variety of artifacts such as quilts, baskets, paintings, decoys, weathervanes, trade signs, whirligigs, carvings, pottery, hooked rugs, game boards, calligraphy and some forms of needlework. Often these items, as well as furniture — chests of drawers, blanket boxes, chairs and cupboards — are decorated with painted or carved motifs such as tulips, birds, hearts and geometric shapes.

While experts argue about theory, today's collectors are on a buying spree. Folk art is hot. Once considered merely charming, folk art has now become part of the mainstream art scene.

Bored with our 'plastic' world and the predictability of traditional antiques, collectors are turning to folk art as a unique alternative. They like the distinctive, personal touch folk art gives to a home and they find that the older pieces transport them from the modern world back to a rural or pioneer heritage. Collectors also enjoy the fact that these artifacts were made by hand, not mass-produced like objects available by the ton in today's department stores.

More than anything, however, collectors are delighted by the freshness and whimsy of folk art. Who, for instance, could keep a straight face while examining a painted wooden document box made by Captain Alexander McNeilledge (1791-1874?). It's decorated with beavers and flags and sports inscriptions such as "Township of Ontario/Done in his 74th year/Wear no specks/Use no tobacco/Take only a wee drop as required/Not bad for an old Scotchie." And who wouldn't gasp at the beauty of the Marie-Melanie Quesnell oil painting sold by Sotheby's, Toronto in April, 1990?

While we know about some of our folk artists because their work was signed or came down to us through their families, the identities of most have, sadly, been lost forever. Many folk artists were itinerant workers who moved from town to town painting portraits or carving wooden kitchen utensils, often as payment for lodging. Others made household items for their own use and decorated them because they had the time and felt the urge to beautify their surroundings. These artifacts were rarely if ever signed.

Because folk art has become so popular, great pieces are not only hard to find, but are also rapidly escalating in price. At a 1987 Sotheby's, Toronto standing room-only auction, folk art connoisseurs watched with amazement as a superb early 19th century sheet-metal

Portrait of Marie-Melanie Quesnel, Canadian School (early 19th Century). This work was executed circa 1810. Marie-Melanie Quesnel (1797-1875) was the daughter of the Montreal compser, Joseph Quesnel. She was married twice, first to Jean-Michel Coursol, of the Hudson's Bay Company. Her second husband was Come Seraphin Cherrier, a leading Montreal lawyer and President of the Banque du Peuple. *(Photo: Sotheby's Canada Inc.)*

weather vane, in the shape of a stylized standing bird, from Ste. Placide, Québec, went under the hammer for $9,900. At the same auction, a 19th century parquetry games board, with elaborate maple and mahogany inlay, fetched $1,980. Then in another of their sales, this one taking place in April 1990, an oil on canvas, of Marie-Melanie Quesnel, executed in approximately 1810 by an unknown artist and estimated to fetch between $12,000 and $15,000 went under the hammer for $38,500, a record price for a Canadian folk art painting.

A c. 1880 cutlery box from Lunenburg County, Nova Scotia, made of applewood, ebony, teak and bone. It is a wonderful example of "necessity made beautiful." Collection: R.A. O'Neil. *(Photo: HWF)*

But Rowan says there are still many good accessible folk art buys that might appeal to new collectors. He points out that furniture and artifacts, especially those from Western Canada, are underpriced and are being snapped up. A good decorated western cupboard, dating from the turn-of-the-century, is about $1,500 in his shop — less than half the price of a comparable Ontario piece, and certainly considerably less than anything in the United States.

Sawtooth Borders, a Toronto quilt shop, has a wonderful collection of old Ontario quilts. Proprietor Gloria Rosenberg points out that choice examples can be had for well under $1,000; a 1920 art deco quilt, for example, is priced today at $700; a log cabin design in mint condition is $500. And Alan Clairman, who operates an antique shop in Toronto says he usually displays a whole range of affordable folk art items such as a refinished two drawer Nova Scotia lamp table, priced at $650.

Starr says would-be collectors should consider several points. "First, look for an artifact that is not 'overpainted,' because when you try to remove the 'overpaint,' you'll damage the original paint. Part of the value is in the original surface. Look for an object that predates 1940 and shows a combination of texture, form, craft and art. Such a piece will probably be a good buy." He adds that it will be a great buy for you if it evokes an emotional response.

Unfortunately, fakes do sometimes show up alongside genuine folk art. Because most pieces are unsigned, they are almost impossible to document and quite easy to fake. And it's not just the expensive, large artifacts that are being faked. Butter prints, embroidered samplers, paintings, drawings and even breadboards are being reproduced and passed off as originals.

Another point of controversy revolves

Unusual miniature model of a hearse, Quebec, circa 1870, complete with wooden coffin, the driver seated holding the reins of two carved wood horses painted black, the hearse is hung with black velvet and gold fringe and the horses wear similar blankets, all on a red painted wood stand. The ex- ceptional detailing of this piece suggests that this was a display model, perhaps for an undertaker's shop window. The piece sold at the April 1990 Southeby's auction for $2,900. *(Photo : Sotheby's Canada Inc.)*

around the value of new folk art. Many dealers and collectors insist that contemporary artifacts should not be sold alongside vintage pieces and, in fact, don't even qualify as legitimate folk art. They feel new folk art is done in a copycat manner, that modern artisans are capitalizing on a hot market and their work is forced and contrived. This group strongly feels no genuine folk art has been produced in Canada since the 1930s. (Prior to the 1930s, little was written or known about folk art, and artifacts before that date are generally considered genuine.)

On the other hand, there are respected dealers, like R.A. O'Neil of Toronto, who offer quality contemporary pieces alongside country furniture. "I handle some examples done by artisans like George Desmeules, George Degas, Jacob Roth and Robert Wylie," he explains, "because it's of such high quality, it goes so well with antiques and because I relate to it." O'Neil maintains that such works are good investments and will appreciate over time, much like vintage pieces.

Regardless of the controversies, the collecting of folk art remains a very personal preference; for in the end, every collection of folk art says just as much about the person who selected and bought the pieces as it does about the individuals who created them.

Treen

Treen is an old English word meaning "more than one tree," the letter "n" indicating the plural. Not only has the word disappeared from contemporary dictionaries but the implements themselves have become obsolete. To collectors, however, treen are hand-made wooden utensils associated with food and drink, farming, sewing and playthings. They were either produced by amateur carvers and whittlers or by professional turners, coopers and joiners. Canadian pine is a softwood that was ideal for carving spoons, ladles, paddles, chalices, cups and platters. The hardwoods — maple, cherry, butternut, walnut and oak — were better suited for making butter prints, maple sugar moulds and bowls.

Treen have no hallmarks similar to silver or china. It, therefore, is difficult to determine their age, although weight and colour may provide some clues. As wood ages, it becomes lighter in weight and takes on a rich and mellow patina. Scoops and spoons will show signs of wear, while the smoother texture on handles and darkened wood indicates prolonged contact with skin oils. Wooden pegs and hand-forged nails are other indicators of the pre-factory era.

The recently revived interest in breadmaking has prompted many people, not necessarily treen collectors, to acquire bread boards bearing pressed-in-the-wood mottoes such as *Spare Not, The Staff of Life or Bread*. Similarly, decorated knife handles to match or small butter dishes are sought-after items. Do not buy the butter boards if the glass inserts with which they originally were equipped are missing, as they are almost impossible to replace.

Butter prints and molds often pre-date the bread and butter utensils by one hundred years. Various woods were used to make the prints which came in many different styles and sizes, ranging from a single pat of butter to one- and two pound moulds. They are collected for the itaglio imprint designs stamped or carved into the surface to produce relief imprints on the butter. Typical patterns were flowers, wheat sheafs, fruit, hearts, animals and sometimes the names of buttermakers. American collectors look for eagles, while authentic vintage beaver imprints, because of their scarcity, are highly coveted in Canada. Watch out for later reproductions, as well as for the smaller round butter prints, measuring less than one inch in diameter, which are legitimately sold in contemporary kitchen stores for around $4 or $5 and can be made to appear old by unscrupulous dealers.

Like many other pieces of treen, the earliest prints are the most desirable because they were hand-made. They differ from the machine-made examples in that early designs were often crude with uneven lines carved deeply into the wood. Factory-made pieces, generally produced after the 1870s, appear to be more precise and symmetrical.

The many collectors who have tried to use butter molds and prints in their own kitchens might be interested in the following instructions which appeared in a farm magazine over one hundred years ago:

> When the butter is ready for making up, it is weighed out into the proper quantities and each piece is worked in the butter dish with the ladle into flat round cakes. These cakes are either pressed with the mould or are made to go into the cup of the mould itself. Inside of the cup is a mould with a handle which works through the hole in

the upper part of the cup. The cup is inverted on the table and when this handle is pressed down it forces the mould onto the butter, which is squeezed into a very neat cake. By pushing the handle and lifting the cup the cake of butter is pushed out of the mould. This makes a very favourite mode of putting up fine butter for the market and is well adapted for preparing butter for the table in the houses where neatness of appearance is studied. The moulds when in use should be kept wetted in cold water to prevent the butter from sticking.

Apart from these kitchen utensils some treen collectors specialize in carpenter's tools, farm implements, needlework tools, as well as games and toys. All treen can be displayed in the home, away from sunlight and dampness. They can be waxed with furniture polish, although I prefer ordinary cooking oil. They should never be overcleaned or stripped of their original finish.

A charming treen collection is usually on display in the Canadiana building of the Royal Ontario Museum in Toronto. However, the best one can be found at the Birmingham City Museum and Art Gallery in England. It belonged to the late Edward Pinto who was the author of *Treen and Other Wooden Bygones,* the most comprehensive work on the subject. For other books on this subject consult the bibliography at the end of this chapter.

Decoys

Decoys originally were utilitarian objects. The best are magnificent folk art examples which can range in price from a few dollars to thousands, depending on workmanship, condition, artistic merit, provenance and, of course, the reputation of a particular carver. Not all decoys found today are worth saving. Many are ugly, boring, faked or, worse still, quite contemporary. Some of the more primitive ones possess a simple, almost stylistic beauty, while the detailed and intricate workmanship of others reveals the sophistication of the carver. Both types are sought by collectors who usually are willing to pay high prices for them. Adele Earnest in her book *The Art of the Decoy* maintains that if "the decoy catches the bird in body and spirit we may truly call it art."

Decoys are uniquely North American. They originated when the Indians discovered that it was easier to hunt birds in flight by luring them to dead birds or their facsimiles on the ground. Their decoys were made out of duck skins stuffed with grasses, or they were rough forms fashioned from bullrushes and grass. When the early settlers began to copy them they used wood so that they would look authentic.

There are four distinct decoy categories: ducks, geese, swans and shorebirds. Ducks are seen most often because the birds themselves were the most frequently hunted and found specimens. Those can be divided into two groups: divers — sea and lake ducks with low slung tails — and dabblers — pond ducks that ride with their tails high. Merganser decoys are rare, probably because these birds were not good to eat and emitted an unpleasant odour.

Canada goose decoys are highly priced often around one thousand dollars especially if the carver managed to capture the spirit of the bird. Swans, also, are coveted, but since hunting them was outlawed in North America in the early 1900s most existing specimens likely predate that period.

Shorebird decoys including plovers, snipes, curlews and sandpipers were placed on small sticks and stuck in the ground along the shore. They are rare because laws enacted in the 1920s

This is a c. 1940s carved and painted Canada goose, probably from Quebec, with inset glass eyes, and carved wings. It sold in December 1980 at a Waddington's auction for $640 plus the 10% buyer's premium. Today this decoy might fetch $1,200 at auction. *(Photo: Waddington's)*

This signed, George J Warin decoy which sold at Waddington's, December 1980, for $5, 100 plus 10% buyer's premium, was resold in August 1990 by Decoys Unlimited. An anonymous collector paid $24,4000 U.S. plus a 10% buyer's premium. Its price, compared to the Canada goose on the left, indicates how signature can influence value. *(Photo: Waddington's)*

and 1930s prohibited killing these small creatures. The novice will find it tricky to spot genuinely antique specimens; they must be collected with caution as thousands have been reproduced and faked.

When examining a decoy, look at the underside of the body and at the bill to see if these areas show signs of wear. The nails and the wood should look aged and well marked, and there should be lead weights, inside or on the bottom of the bird. Collectors prefer decoys with the original paint even if it is scraped, cut or damaged. Also, look at the form of the piece — would it qualify as art? Check to see if there is a signature on the belly. If it was made by a well-known and documented carver, the price could be twice or three times as high.

Not all decoys were hand-carved; some were factory-made in the twenties. Mason's of Detroit, Michigan, produced some valuable pieces but stopped manufacturing them in the late twenties. G. & J. Warin (Toronto boat builders) were prominent decoy-makers between 1862 and 1904; Art Chilton of Toronto often signed his work A.C. or A.R.C.; Billy Ellis of Whitby (1875-1963) was most active in the twenties and thirties and sold most of his pieces to Americans for a reported price of four dollars each. Fortunately, many of them are now making their way back to Canada at much higher prices. Other famous carvers were Ken Anger of Dunville, Ontario; D.W. Nickles of Smith Falls, Ontario; Reg Bloom of Picton, Ontario; Orin Halts of Nova Scotia; Orel LeBoeuf of Quebec and

Donald "Ducker" Hay of Belleville, Ontario.

Decoys are still being made today, and while most are honest reproductions, some have been artificially aged. One particular Quebec wood-working shop specializes in Canada geese and literally turns them out by the thousands.

Weathervanes

These sculptural pieces once used by farmers to indicate wind direction have been taken off rooftops and put into collectors' homes.

Some weathervanes were factory-produced, while others were hand-made by farmers. Materials used were tin, zinc, brass, copper and wood. Nineteenth-century American vanes (rarely Canadian) featured Indians, gabriels, animals, fish and ships, whereas trains, cars and airplanes were more prominent in the twentieth century. Some were simple cutouts. However the molded and three-dimensional weathervanes are those most coveted by collectors. The best examples reflect the artistry of their creator and, therefore, can be considered genuine folk art. Competition is fierce and some pieces are fetching astoundingly high prices in U.S. auctions. Those that ten years ago may have cost no more than $500 are now $30,000 or more. Their rarity as well as the high prices have led to hun-

Left: Rare Metal Weathervane, early 19th century, Sainte Placide, Quebec. The bird sold at Sotheby's, Toronto, April 1987 for $9,900. *(Photo courtesy of Sotheby's Canada Inc.)* *Below:* This weathervane was featured in a show-sale put together and sponsored by Toronto artist-collector Fred Tymoshenko in early 1981. *(Photo: HWF)*

Anna Weber (1814-1888) of Waterloo County, Ontario, was not a professional artist. The bulk of her work, done in her old age, was given away to friends and visitors. Collection: Michael Bird and Terry Kobayashi. *(Photo: Michael Bird)*

dreds of weathervanes being secretly removed from rooftops, especially in secluded rural areas. The thieves fly in by helicopter, pick off their bounty and leave.

Compared to the United States, Canadian market activity was relatively quiet until January 1981 when Toronto artist and part-time antique dealer Fred Tymoshenko presented his weathervane collection in a six weeks' show and sale.

Although prices were steep by Canadian standards, they were lower than those charged by Americans. A wooden fish from Nova Scotia was available for $375, while a double-tailed, full-bodied Quebec Chanticler was priced at $3,500. The same price was marked on a rare, late nineteenth century molded zinc running horse made by the Pedlar Company of Oshawa, one of the few documented Canadian weathervane-makers. Among the Quebec examples was an enchanting iron pig painted white ($1,200) and two superior fish vanes — a stylistic and elegant wooden gar ($1,400) and a fullblown iron no-name fish. Although crudely made, the fish was priced at $1,350. There was a Nova Scotia horse dated 1901 ($2,200), and several good American vanes with directional arrows, priced at $2,400 each. Other pieces offered were a typical Canadian beaver, a delightful donkey and an English galley that came from a London church. 1990 prices would likely be double to triple these 1981 prices.

Because good weathervanes are rare, high priced and much coveted, reproductions frequently appear in the marketplace. It is difficult to distinguish between the newly made and the artificially aged examples because legitimate factories still copy vintage pieces, and there will always be unscrupulous people who take advantage of a collecting trend. The best advice for the novice is to buy only from reputable dealers; try to avoid vanes formed in a mould as they seem to be the ones causing most trouble and not to specialize in signed pieces because there are hardly any in Canada.

Frakturs

Fraktur-making was brought to Ontario in the 1800s by the Pennsylvania Dutch and European immigrants. It was a form of decoration used to embellish manuscripts, even prior to the invention of the printing press. Prayers, family registers, house blessings, books and book plates, wedding, birth and baptismal certificates, all were enhanced by this type of illuminated lettering, combined with fancy border designs and motifs — hearts, birds and flowers. The name "fraktur" means the breaking or disjointing of letters, and in his book *Ontario Fraktur* the author Michael Bird stresses that the ornamentation surrounding the alphabets and words also is included in the term.

Fraktur work was done in the 1730s in various Pennsylvania communities but did not reach Canada until the 1820s when some families from there settled in the Niagara Peninsula, Markham and Waterloo County. Many of these Ontario pieces are now in museums, but a large number have found their way into private Canadian collections.

There were many well-known and well documented fraktur artists — Bauman, Hoffman and Hoover among them — but it was Anna Weber (1814-1888) who truly has captured the imagination of Canadian collectors. She came to Canada in 1825 and produced the bulk of her drawings between 1870 and 1880 while living with various Mennonite families. Her work has a fresh, vibrant and almost naive quality. It has been featured in magazine articles and was the subject of a charming book.

Tramp Art

This art form was popularized in North America during the second half of the nineteenth century, although it had existed in Germany and in the Scandinavian countries for decades before that. Tramp art is named after the hobos or tramps who travelled the countryside, making carvings to trade or sell. From ornate chip carvings on cigar boxes, vegetable or fruit crates they made various items, including boxes, banks, pin cushions, item rattles, medicine cabinets, comb boxes, jewelry containers and frames. Sometimes, even large pieces such as dressers or tables were created, many decorated with bits of glass and mirrors, leather, pottery or brass.

These carvings rarely form the basis of a large or significant collection, despite the fact that they have numerous admirers. To own one or two pieces of tramp art is fun but having more could be overpowering.

Today's tramp-art prices vary according to condition, workmanship and design. A small, well-proportioned item might sell from $75 to $200, while larger ones might fetch $500 or more.

Decorated Stoneware

Before the 1900s, utilitarian earthenware and stoneware pottery pieces were part of most lives. They were indispensable in homes, shops and taverns; tradesmen used them for storage; businesses for advertising purposes; and housewives filled them with cider, beer, vinegar, oil or molasses. The vessels were used for making and storing butter, salting meat, pickling and preserving, until mass-produced glass, metalware and plastic containers appeared in the late 1800s and the early part of the twentieth century. At the same time, commercially canned products came on the market, and ice refrigeration became commonplace. These three factors signalled the end of dependency on stoneware products and the decline of a flourishing industry.

In the fifteenth century, people had relied solely on earthenware containers, but because they were porous, fragile and difficult to clean they replaced them with the stronger, longer-lasting and easier to clean stoneware. Whereas a lead glaze had been used for earthenware, stoneware glazes could be made by adding salt to the hot mixture in the kiln. As the clay's silica combined with the sodium it formed a water-tight coating. Since clay was generally a dull gray or brownish colour, the finished pottery was enlivened with decorations, usually stylized animals, birds or flowers, incised or hand-drawn in rich cobalt blue. The pots were marked with numbers to indicate how much they could hold (a crown to indicate Imperial gallons), the name of the pottery that had made them or that of the merchant who had ordered them was also included.

By the 1850s, Canadian stoneware became the preserve of local industries and craftsmen. There were some commercial potteries around Quebec City which produced plain items until the Farrar family from Vermont opened a subsidiary in St. Johns, Quebec, in 1840. Later, the Dion Pottery Works was established in Ancienne Lorette, Quebec, and although some potteries operated in Nova Scotia, the industry did not spread to the rest of Eastern Canada until 1861 when the White-Foley Pottery started in Saint John, New Brunswick. In the *Book of Canadian Antiques,* Donald Webster suggests that by the 1850s there were at least thirty potteries in Western Canada.

The Ontario-German companies made a larger range of containers than their Maritime and Quebec competitors. Names to look for include Justin Morton and Samuel Hart who both came from New York State, Morton settling in Brantford, while Hart immigrated to Picton, Ontario. Samuel Skinner (1860s) sold his business to Samuel Hart who, in turn, left it to his son-in-law George K. Lazier. Known as Hart Brothers and Lazier, the company remained active until 1887. Eberhardt and Burns of Toronto

and the Flack and Van Arsdale Company of Cornwall, Ontario, are also important names to remember. Especially coveted and commanding high prices are pieces made by companies that existed for only a short time, as well as those showing spelling errors or unusual cobalt-blue motifs and decorations.

Bibliography

Ames, Kenneth L. *Beyond Necessity, Art in the Folk Tradition.* Winterthur Books, 1977.

Andrews, Ruth, ed. *How to Know American Folk Art.* E.P. Dutton, 1977.

Bank, Mirra. *Anonymous Was A Woman.* New York: St. Martin's Press, 1979.

Barber, Joel. *Wild Fowl Decoys.* Dover Publications, 1934, 1954.

Bird, Michael. *Ontario Fraktur: a Pennsylvania-German Tradition in Early Canada.* Toronto: M.F. Feheley Publications Ltd., 1977.

Bird, Michael and Terry Kobayashi. *A Splendid Harvest.* Toronto: Van Nostrand & Reinhold, Ltd., 1981.

Bishop, Robert. *American Folk Sculpture.* E.P. Dutton, 1974.

Dewhurst, MacDowell and MacDowell. *Artists in Aprons, Folk Art by American Women.* E.P. Dutton, 1979.

Earnest, Adele. *The Art of the Decoy.* New York: Bramhall House, 1965.

Ebert, John and Katherine. *American Folk Painters.* New York: Charles Scribner's Sons, 1975.

Fendelman, Helaine. *Tramp Art: An Itinerant's Folk Art.* E.P. Dutton, 1975.

Field, Richard Henning. *Spirit of Nova Scotia.* Toronto: Art Gallery of Nova Scotia and Dundurn Press, 1985.

Gates, Bernie. *Ontario Decoys.* Kingston, Ontario: *The Upper Canadian*, 1982.

Good, E. Reginald. *Anna's Art.* Kitchener Ontario: Pochauna Publications, 1976.

Gould, Mary Earle. *Early American Woodenware and Other Kitchen Utensils.* Rutland, Vermont: Charles E. Tuttle Co., Inc., 1962.

Guyette, Dale and Gary. *Decoys of Maritime Canada.* Schiffer Publishing Ltd., 1983.

Harper, J. Russell. *A People's Art, Primitive, Naive, Provincial & Folk Painting in Canada.* Toronto: University of Toronto Press, 1974.

Hemphill, Herbert W., Jr. and Julia Weissman. *Twentieth Century American Folk Art and Artists.* E.P. Dutton, 1974.

Klamkin, Charles. *Weathervanes.* New York: Hawthorn Books, Inc., 1973..

Kobayashi, Terry and Michael Bird. *A Compendium of Canadian Folk Artists.* Erin, Ontario: Boston Mills Press, 1985.

Lipman, Jean and Alice Winchester. *The Flowering of American Folk Art, 1776-1876.* New York: Viking Press, in co-operation with the Whitney Museum of American Art, 1974.

Lipman, Jean. *American Folk Art in Wood, Metal and Stone.* Dover Publications, 1948.

Little, Nina Fletcher. *Country Arts in Early American Homes.* E.P. Dutton, 1975.

Newlands, David. *Early Ontario Potters, Their Craft and Trade.* Toronto: McGraw-Hill Ryerson Ltd., 1979.

Pinto, Edward. *Treen and Other Wooden Bygones.* London: G. Bell and Sons, 1969.

Price, Ralph and Patricia, ed. *T'was Ever Thus, A Selection of Eastern Canadian Folk Art.* Toronto: M.F. Feheley Publications, 1979.

Rhodes, Lynette I. *American Folk Art: From Traditional to the Naive.* Clevcland Museum of Art, 1978.

Thuro, Catherine. *Primitives and Folk Art: Our Handmade Heritage.* Toronto: Thorncliffe House, Inc., 1979.

Toller, Jane. *Turned Woodenware for Collectors, Treen and Other Objects.* South Brunswick and New York: A.S. Barnes & Co., 1976

Trice, James E. *Butter Molds, A Primitive Art Form.* Wallace Homestead Books Ltd., 1973.

Webster, Donald Blake. *Decorated Stoneware Pottery of North America.* Rutland, Vermont: Charles E. Tuttle Co., 1971.

Webster, Donald Blake. *Early Canadian Pottery.* Toronto: McClelland & Stewart Ltd., 1971.

Weiser, F.S., Howell, and J. Heaney, compilers. *The Pennsylvania-German Fraktur of the Free Library of Philadelphia.* The Pennsylvania-German Society, 1976.

See Appendix I for magazines and journals of interest, such as *The Decoy Hunter, The Decoy Magazine, The Clarion, The Upper Canadian, The Maine Antique Digest*, etc.

13

Photographica

Collecting photographs has become a very popular hobby, especially in the United States where images and prints by Julia Margaret Cameron, Edward Weston, William Henry Fox Talbot, Mathew Brady, Alfred Stieglitz, as well as those by hundreds of anonymous photographers, are much in demand. In Canada, despite a few interesting photographic auctions held in the late 1970s, the market is much quieter. Our collectors seem to concentrate on prints by Notman, Henderson, Erb or Karsh.

No one person invented photography. It actually evolved through the efforts of several people. In 1777, Carl William Sheele, a Swedish chemist, experimented with the effects of light on silver chloride, and thirteen years later, Pierre L. Guinard a Swiss glassmaker, improved the method by creating a new type of optical glass. In 1820, Thomas Wedgwood, son of the prominent English potter, and Humphrey Davey almost succeeded in perfecting a photographic process, but their images could not be fixed because they had chosen chemicals that were not light-sensitive enough. However, by exposing silver nitrate to light, they found a way of transferring paintings onto glass.

In 1826, Nicephore Niepce of France managed to photograph a view from his workroom window with an exposure time of eight hours.

He used a simple camera and reproduced the image on an ordinary pewter plate coated with oil. The result was a significant breakthrough and, encouraged by friends and relatives, Niepce signed a ten-year agreement with the French painter Louis Jacques Mande Daguerre (1787-1851).

The two men worked together for four years until Niepce's sudden death in 1833. Daguerre continued to experiment with mercury vapour and salt as a fixative and by 1837 not only was able to reduce exposure times to twenty minutes but also obtained a permanent image showing a portion of his studio. He called his invention daguerreotype.

Reaction was swift, ranging from disbelief to horror. Oliver Wendell Holmes called it a mirror with a memory," and the Paris press praised it for its "prodigious delicacy of details." However, a German newspaper scathingly intoned that "no man-made machine may fix the image of God," and one artist of the day described the new discovery as "the death of painting." The rights to the daguerreotype were bought by the French government who also awarded a 6,000-franc annuity to its inventor and a further 4,000 francs to Isidore, son of Nicephore Niepce.

When daguerreotypes were first shown in America in September 1839, they were received with more enthusiasm there than anywhere else in the world. By the end of the 1850s exposure times had been cut down even further so that they could be used for portraiture in galleries and by itinerant photographers who travelled the countryside.

Daguerreotypes

A daguerreotype image stands out among all others because it is shiny and mirror-like. Produced on a copper plate coated with silver, the surface, sensitized by iodine, bromide and chlorine fumes, was placed in a camera and exposed to light. After developing the image with heated, vapourized mercury, it was fixed. However, it only could be viewed if held up to the light at the correct angle because the unexposed areas of the plate actually were mirrors. Daguerreotype copies could be made by rephotographing the original.

The image was so fragile that when merely brushed with a finger, it could be wiped away forever. For that reason and because of the tarnishing effect of air upon silver, the daguerreotype had to be placed under glass and fitted with a brass cutout and a brass frame. The picture then was placed into a velvet-lined case.

Because only a few daguerreotypes were signed, they are difficult to attribute to any one photographer or location. Images with signatures are, of course, more valuable than those without. The artists who had carefully labelled their work include Edward Anthony, William Southgate Porter, Mathew Brady, Albert Sands Southworth and Josiah Johnson Hawes. Few Canadian photographers took the time to identify their work.

Images showing people in uniform or holding items related to their professions are coveted by collectors everywhere, as are outdoor scenes, famous places or buildings that are no longer standing. Also of interest are pictures of animals, nudes, blacks and Indians. Important people are no less in demand, but the images most often seen are those of unnamed individuals and family groups. In 1859, daguerreotypes began to appear hand-coloured and those too have become quite collectible.

Many daguerreotypes were destroyed during World War I when the glass was needed for gas masks, and the silver and copper had to be melted down. Yet many survived, and their rarity and ultimate price can often be determined by the sizes of plates, the largest being the rarest.

Whole plates	6-1/2" x 8-1/2"
Half plates	4-1/2" x 5-1/2"
Quarter plates	3-1/4" x 4-1/4"
Sixth plates	2-3/4" x 3-1/4"
Ninth plates	2" x 2-1/2"

Daguerreotype cases also are important collectors' items. They were made of leather, wood, papier-mache and a mixture of wood, flour and shellac, which has the appearance of hard rubber or heavy plastic, and were lined in velvet. Many had appealing cover designs of children, flowers, Indians, boats and so on. Antique dealers often have sold these velvet-lined cases as cigarette boxes. Separating them from the images, however, will ruin the chance for any future research, regardless of the significance the cases may have for some collectors.

No attempts must be made to clean or restore daguerreotypes. They should be kept in a cool, dry, dark place, away from direct sunlight.

Calotypes and Talbotypes

In January 1839, William Henry Fox Talbot found a way of photographing on paper. Using a negative-positive process, he first called these new images calotypes, but later, having learned from Monsieur Daguerre, he renamed them talbotypes. They were an improvement over daguerreotypes because several prints could be made from one negative. Whereas Daguerre's images were clear and detailed, Talbot's always looked somewhat misty. By 1840, Talbot also found a way to remove the paper from the camera while it was still blank, treat it and obtain an image, similar to the way we do today. Had Talbot's process been unveiled one month before Daguerre's instead of a few weeks later, the world might have immediately turned to paper photography instead of Daguerre's more complicated method.

Talbotypes never caught on in North America. However, in Scotland the photographic team of David Hill and Robert Adamson used the system to produce images that were remarkable for their warmth and creativity.

Ambrotypes

Frederick Scott Archer introduced his "Collodian process" in England in 1851. It allowed the negative image on glass to be made positive by backing it with a dark material such as velvet, paper, varnish or paint. As Archer had described and published his invention without restrictions or patents, another man, James Ambrose Cutting of Boston, copied his idea, obtaining an American patent in 1854. Later, the daguerreotypist Marcus Root of Philadelphia borrowed Cutting's middle name and called the images ambrotypes. Like daguerreotypes, they were positives — the final picture having been exposed on the plate in the camera with the image reversed.

Neither system could be used to make prints and both had to be housed in cases. But ambrotypes were easier to look at; without the mirror-like surface, there was no glare.

Tintypes

It is thought that tintypes were invented in approximately 1853, although there still is some dispute as to who first came up with the idea — a Frenchman or an American. It was, however, Mr. Hamilton Smith who first made these images in the United States and in 1856 sold the patent to Peter Neff and Victor Griswold who called them melainotypes and ferrotypes. Somehow the name "tintype" was coined later, even though the images were not based on tin at all but on thin iron sheets, japanned black.

Tintypes, just as ambrotypes and daguerreotypes, were direct positives without negatives and with the images reversed. The method not only was cheap and fast but had the advantage that the pictures could be slipped into photo albums or sent through the mail. To operate the camera and process the plates was fairly simple, since with a multi-lens, several images could be shot in one operation.

Collectors actively seek outdoor scenes, large size pictures or any showing things other than faces and families. One drawback to collecting these images is that they rarely were marked with the photographer's name.

Cartes-de-visite

No one is certain who invented the *carte-de-visits;* however, the idea was patented in France in 1854 by Adolphe Disderi. These paper photographs were made from wet plate negatives and pasted onto cardboard. The name *carte-de- visite* probably was chosen because its size (3-1/2" x 2-1/4") came close to that of a visiting card.

CDVs became popular because they were

A *carte-de-visite* of three gentlemen in front of Union Station. J. Esson, photographer, Preston, Ontario. Collection: Private. *(Photo: HWF)*

inexpensive and easy to give to relatives or exchange with friends. Also, for the first time people could buy pictures of famous people. These images are different from all others mentioned so far because many were signed by the photographer, either on the reverse or immediately below the image. Also, because they were on paper, people often took the time to write down the name of the person or the place of the illustration.

Collectors can specialize in one particular photographer's work, series of famous people or images showing different subjects occupations, children or such unusual things as dwarfs and freaks. Millions of these photographs are still available.

Cabinet Photographs

By the mid-1860s, *cartes-de-visite* were out of fashion, and something new had to replace them. In 1866, F.R. Window, an English photographer introduced the cabinet photograph, a print (4-1/2" x 5-1/2") mounted on a card (4-1/2" x 6-1/2") that looked like a large *carte-de-visite*. Almost all bore the name of the photographer, and some even showed his address.

Perhaps the man most responsible for the acceptance of cabinet photographs in North America was Montreal photographer William Notman. Realizing the potential of the larger size, he sent one of his portraits to *The Philadelphia Photographer,* then the most prestigious photographic magazine on the continent, and when it was published in January 1867, Notman received even more recognition.

Stereographs

Stereographs, stereograms or stereoviews originated in the early 1850s when they were taken with two cameras placed side by side. The resulting double images were glued onto cardboard to make them look three dimensional when seen through a stereoscopic viewer. At the beginning of the 1860s a camera with two lenses, approximately one inch apart, became standard equipment for North American and European photographers specializing in stereographs. Soon almost every family owned a viewer and a collection of stereoviews to be looked at and swapped among neighbours, family members and friends.

Oliver Wendell Holmes, the American writer

and physician, is credited with inventing the stereoscope in 1860. About one foot long with a lens mounted at one end and a moveable plate to hold a view card in place, this device comes close to the one used today. The older, more elaborate burlwood models fetch several hundred dollars, while later, simpler machines, even when in good condition, sell for approximately $45 to $75.

Of all the stereograph images, the earliest are readily recognizable because they are on thin paper and usually show neither titles nor other identifications. They also are the most costly and difficult to find. Those made between 1858 and 1865 bear a short title or a manufacturer's name. A revenue stamp on the reverse side of the image pertains to the tax levied on stereoviews by the U.S. government between September 1864 and August 1866. (Canada imposed no such tax.)

William Notman was the first Canadian photographer to produce a series of about five hundred stereoviews. Images can be located today at prices ranging from $6 to $15 each. Stereoview photographers operated in most North American cities and small towns, and many thought nothing of selling their negatives to large publishing houses whose names often appeared on the card. Views by Keystone and Underwood and signed by Underwood are the easiest to locate, while the most elusive and coveted are the older examples showing such unique scenes as disasters, ships, street scenes and those retaining the original labels or marks of certain photographers.

Early Canadian Photographers

William Notman (1826-1891) was not only the most famous Canadian photographer of his time but also the first to earn international repute,

which was rivalled by Mathew Brady, the best-known American photographer of the day.

William Notman was born in Scotland to a family of artist-designers. Lured to Canada in 1856 by Ogilvy Dry Goods of Montreal, he worked for them at first but soon left to open his photographic studio on Bleury Street in Montreal. People flocked there to have their pictures taken by the master. His earliest were daguerreotypes and ambrotypes but because neither used negatives, no documented examples have survived.

In November 1863, John A. Fraser joined the Notman firm, and one year later branch offices were opened in Ottawa and Toronto. Notman's brother James established a gallery in Saint John, New Brunswick, and soon more branches were opened in Halifax, Boston, New York, Albany and Newport, Rhode Island. In 1876, Henry Sandham became a partner, and four years later, when his eldest son William McFarlane joined the firm, it became William Notman and Son.

After Notman had been named Photographer to the Queen in 1861, his career was even more firmly established than before, and many famous people had their pictures taken by him. They included members of the Molson family, Sir Wilfrid Laurier, Sir John A. Macdonald, the Prince of Wales, Jefferson Davis, the Vanderbilts, the Pullmans, Henry Ward Beecher, Henry Wadsworth Longfellow and Canada's governor generals from the 1860s until the end of the century. Notman also travelled extensively, photographing the Canadian countryside and its people.

Catering to the rich as well as to the less affluent at the low price of one dollar for six copies of the same negative, almost everyone could afford to have their picture taken at William Notman and Son. The rich often chose larger

Montreal Snowshoe club, Mount Royal, Quebec, 1877.
(Photo: Notman Photographic Archives, McCord Museum, McGill University, Montreal)

formats or hand-coloured prints which, at times, brought the price to between three and four hundred dollars.

With Notman galleries in so many places, William, the father, could not possibly have taken all the photographs himself, although his name appears on most. Collectors, therefore, must carefully investigate whether their pictures were done by the master or by one of his assistants. In the early 1870s Notman invented "composites," collages made up of several portraits shot in the studio. They were assembled on a large cardboard and rephotographed to appear as one complete work. As many were hand-coloured afterward, a photographer's as well as a painter's skills were required.

William Notman died in 1891, leaving a flourishing business to his sons William McFarlane and Charles. They moved the studio from Bleury Street to Phillips Square in Montreal, and in 1934 Charles sold the firm to Associated Screen News.

In the 1950s, despite the fact that many of the early negatives and plates had been destroyed or severely damaged, Geoffrey and Keith Notman, William's grandsons, together with McGill University, were able to assemble the existing records and plates. In 1956, assisted by *Maclean's,* permanent archives were established at the McCord Museum in Montreal. Curator Stanley Triggs has spent years studying the 400,000 photographic plates and negatives. His book *Portrait of a Period* written in 1967 and published by McGill University Press is currently out of print but sometimes available in antiquarian book shops for about $250. Mr. Triggs has written a second volume (see bibliography at end of chapter.

The Notman archives are open to anyone by appointment. If collectors wish to have their images identified they can send a photocopy and a SASE.

Many other noteworthy people — men and women — made significant contributions to early photography in Canada. Such artists as Eli J. Palmer of Toronto and Thomas Coffin Doane of Montreal, both daguerreotypists, successfully plied their trade and often were mentioned in the newspapers of the time. Unfortunately, not much is known about these two men, nor have images survived that can be attributed to them with certainty. The following are a few whose work stands out from their ubiquitous colleagues.

Duncan Donovan (1857-1933) photographed and documented small-town life in Ontario. He started as an itinerant tintype photographer and later opened his own studio in Alexandria, Ontario. While his work cannot be called inspired, it certainly is representative of its time.

Alexander Henderson (1831-1913) was born in Scotland and immigrated to Montreal in 1855. Five years later he took up photography, first as a hobby and later as a business. His pictures were taken outdoors rather than in the more formal studio setting.

A small but important collection of Henderson negatives and plates, prints and other memorabilia is at the Notman Archives in Montreal. Curator Stanley Triggs hopes to publish a book about this significant, but relatively unknown, Canadian photographic artist.

Humphrey Lloyd Hime (1833-1903) came to Canada from Ireland in 1854. Three years later he became a junior partner in the Toronto civil engineering firm of Armstrong, Beere and Hime. Sponsored by the Canadian government, he joined an expedition to remote parts of Western Canada, working as chief photographer. In the mid-1860s he disassociated himself from his company. And from photography he became involved in finance and later in municipal politics.

When Hime died he left behind a wealth of outstanding pictures, the best of which equalling those taken by the world's great photographers.

Dan Rowe, hockey player, c. 1908. Duncan Donovan, photographer. *(Photo: Ontario Archives)*

Although women had worked with photography since its infancy, they were tolerated more than encouraged by their colleagues. Montreal's Mrs. Fletcher was Canada's first female photographer. She specialized in daguerreotypes and her advertisements appeared in Quebec newspapers as early as 1841. There were about fourteen other women, among them the eccentric Hannah Hatherly Maynard (1834-1918) of British Columbia. After marrying Richard Maynard in England in 1852, they came to Canada and settled in Bowmanville, Ontario. Mrs. Maynard began to study photography, and when the family moved to Victoria, BC, in 1862, she opened her own studio there. By the early 1880s she produced "gems," as she liked to call them — collages consisting of thousands of miniature portraits. Not only did she document life around her, but also experimented with techniques that resulted in surrealistic, comical and, at the same time, beautiful photographic images.

Top right: Assiniboine and Saskatchewan Exploring Expedition, 1858, Red River Settlement. Wigman and an Ojibway half-breed. Humphrey Lloyd Hime, photographer. *(Photo: Public Archives of Canada)*
Right: Hannah Hatherly Maynard, photographer. A peculiar self-portrait, as each of the three women is in the image of Mrs. Maynard. *(Photo: The Provincial Archives of British Columbia)*

Bibliography

Bruce, David. *Sun Pictures: The Hill-Adamson Calotypes.* Greenwich, Connecticut: New York Graphic Society Ltd., 1973.

Darrah, William C. *The World of Stereographs.* Gettysburg, Pennsylvania: W.C. Darrah Publisher, 1977.

Dennis, Landt and Lisl. *Collecting Photographs, A Guide to the New Art Boom.* New York: E.P. Dutton, 1977.

Gernsheim, Helmut. *Lewis Carroll: Photographer.* Dover Publications Inc., 1969..

Gilbert, George. *Collecting Photographica.* New York: Hawthorn Books Inc., 1976.

Haller, Margaret. *Collecting Old Photographs.* New York: Arco Publishing Co., 1978

Jammes, Andre. *William Henry Fox Talbot.* Collier Books, 1972.

Jenkins, Harold. *Two Points of View: The History of the Parlor Stereoscope.* E.G. Warman Publishing Co., 1973.

Newhall, Beaumont. *The Daguerreotype in America.* Dover Publications Inc., 1961, 1976.

Newhall, Beaumont. *The History of Photography.* New York: The Museum of Modern Art, 1964.

Ovenden, Graham, ed. *A Victorian Album: Julia Margaret Cameron and Her Circle.* New York: Da Capo Press, 1975.

Rinhart, Floyd and Marion. *American Miniature Case Art.* A.S. Barnes and Co. Inc., 1969.

Russack, Darrah and Richard. *An Album of Stereographs from the Collection of William Culp.* Doubleday and Co. Inc., 1977.

Sobieszek, Robert A. and Odette M. Appel. *The Spirit of Fact: The Daguerreotypes of Southworth & Hawes, (1843-1862).* Boston and Rochester: David R. Godine, Boston, and The International Museum of Photography, George Eastman House, Rochester, 1976.

Weinstein, Robert A. and Larry Booth. *Collection, Use and Care of Historical Photographs.* Nashville, Tennessee: American Association for State and Local History, 1977.

Welling, William. *Collectors' Guide to Nineteenth-Century Photographs.* New York: Collier Books, 1976.

Canadiana

Greenhill, Ralph and Andrew Birrell. *Canadian Photography; 1839-1920.* Toronto: Coach House Press, 1979.

Harper, Jennifer. *City Work at Country Prices: The Portrait Photographs of Duncan Donovan* Oxford University Press, 1977.

Harper, Russell and Stanley Triggs, ed. *Portrait of a Period: A Collection of Notman Photographs.* Montreal: McGill University Press, 1967.

Huyda, Richard J. *Camera in the Interior: 1858, H.L. Hime, Photographer.* Toronto: Coach House Press, 1975.

Triggs, Stanley. *William Notman: The Stamp of a Studio.* Art Gallery of Ontario and Coach House Press, 1985.

Wilks, Claire Weissman. *The Magic Box: The Eccentric Genius of Hannah Maynard.* Toronto: Exile Editions Ltd, 1980.

For lists of Collector Clubs see Appendix 3, p. 229.
Dealers: Jane Corkin Gallery, 79 John Street, St. 302, Toronto, ON M5T 1X4.

14

Nostalgia, Memorabilia and Collectibles

Collectibles of the Future?

What if you were able to climb into a time machine and return to the 1950s or even '20s and fill a huge container with objects of your choosing? What would you grab? Costume jewelry? Elvis memorabilia? A set of depression glass? Baseball cards?

With hindsight, you could choose items that would make you wealthy, but since that's impossible, lets twist the premise slightly. Let's say instead your goal is to fill that same container with items from the 1990s that will become collectibles of the future.

While collecting for the future is part luck and part enthusiasm it is mostly know-how based on certain collecting trends that seem to hold true year after year. Experience has taught us that signed and dated items are a good bet. As well, a brief biography of the maker and even of the original purchaser accompanied by a sales receipt have proven important. Items still in their original boxes have more value than loose pieces. Of course it's best to have an item in perfect condition but failing that, it is better to have a piece in rough shape than to have one that has been badly repaired. An object is likely more collectible if it began a trend, is unique, was produced in limited quantities or was the first of its kind to employ a new design.

Right now, well-designed 1940s and 50s chrome tables and chairs are the rage. The question is, however, who is making a furniture statement today? Canadian David Lasker, noted design writer, and editor of *Contract Magazine*, a trade journal for interior designers and architects, says that the classic spider table designed and manufactured by Toronto's Tom Deacon of Area Design could be a future collectible. It's Lasker's opinion that an example of this table with its "patinated, aged-looking brass ball feet which are half way to Victorian ball and claw and its thick etched-glass top" should be a priority item in our time capsule collection.

Too, fashion or costume jewelry from the 30s, 40s and 50s is one of the growing new collectibles on the scene today. Designers like Miriam Haskell and Montreal's Sherman sell now for hundreds of dollars more than they did originally. A choice, signed Haskell matching set of earrings, necklace and brooch, for instance, could retail for more than $600 today. When they were initially acquired they probably cost the buyer around $30.

Who are the hot jewelry designers we should be watching for today? Perhaps the pieces done by artists such as Mimi Schulman or Richard Wyman, available for sale in the Art Gallery of Ontario's gift shop. Both these people and some

Toronto Toro hockey memorabilia. The lot includes a booklet, a key chain, a silver ingot, and a badge or emblem. *(Photo: HWF)*

of the others in the gallery are doing innovative, exciting work which could one day become antiques of the future. The real trick to spotting the up and comers in this field is to become immersed in the current craft scene and learn to recognize technical and aesthetic merit.

Second, we should consider objects that have outlived their usefulness; that become defunct because of the discovery of a new invention. Oil lamps were replaced by electricity. Our grandparents threw them out. Today they could be worth between $10,000 and $30,000. More recently, slide rules have been replaced by calculators; mix-masters by food processors and typewriters by computers.

Not to be forgotten are items relating to events that have taken place or businesses that no longer exist. What about expo memorabilia — souvenirs, ashtrays, shopping bags, maps or concert programs? That includes items related to defunct sporting teams or leagues such as the Toronto Toros and the WHA: programs, calendars, logos, watches, team photographs, might one day 'be worth something.'

Baseball cards might just be a good angle to pursue too. The highest reported price so far paid for a baseball card is $110,000 for a T-206 Honus Wagner in top condition. But that record will likely be broken soon when a young American dealer sells what he hopes will be the first $1 million baseball card — a No. 16 in the 1932 U.S. Caramel card set showing New York Giants Hall of Fame third baseman Lindstom.

Next we should consider mass-produced artifacts — things designed specifically to be discarded after use. These items, properly termed ephemera have escalated in value, especially in the last ten years. Early ephemeral items have proven to be worth their weight in gold. Just visit some of the nostalgia shows held throughout the country every fall and spring. In fact, the collecting of ephemera has recently been given the credibility it deserves with the establishment, in November, 1987, of the Ephemera Society of Canada. Founder and President, Barbara Rusch, a collector of Queen Victoria memorabilia, advertising and manuscript ephemera as well as Victorian clothing, has recently started collecting contemporary artifacts too.

Many of the things she has put away are "off-beat but to my mind they are so redolent of the 1980s and 1990s." At the top of the heap is an unopened kit, that looks like a very large capsule-shaped pill, to be used to test for AIDS and "an incredibly graphic brochure printed by the AIDS committee of Toronto."

To Rusch, "anything that's a fad or a very hot issue has the potential to be a future collectible." In that light, along with the AIDS material, she has saved many items having to do with free trade and women's right. "It's not only the material that socks you between the eyes that is collectible," says Rusch, "but the type of articles that show how we live our every day lives that is important."

In other words, consider gathering things such as contemporary store catalogues, colourful advertising pamphlets or brochures such as the ones found in weekend newspapers; advertising signs and tins, calendars, telephone directories, paper shopping bags with interesting graphics, punk clothing items and even character dolls such as E.T., the Six Million Dollar Man, Farah Fawcett and of course, Annie.

Those that have inherited these kinds of materials from their ancestors have done exceptionally well for themselves. For example, a Coca-Cola paper advertising calendar, circa 1915, sold at auction recently for $1,320; a tin Grape Nuts sign, 20 inches by 30 inches fetched $2,200 and a large Anheuser Busch lithographed print featuring a multitude of beer drinkers from around the world brought $2,640 at auction.

Games and toys are another extensive collecting area. Prices for depression era (and later) pieces are skyrocketing, almost daily. For example, a Babe Ruth baseball game, circa 1930, complete with box would retail at about $1,000 and a Jackie Robinson baseball game, circa 1950, with original box, for about $500. In December, 1988 a Connecticut architect established the highest price ever paid for a plastic toy when he bought a plastic Mickey Mouse riding Pluto for $6,000. And not too long ago an original 1959 Barbie doll, with the box it came in, sold to a doll collector for $1,000. U. S.

Given that information, perhaps worth stockpiling today are the early children's hand-held games (you know, the kind with the incessant zings and pings; noises that drove the 1970 and 80s parents crazy) and of course, Pac-Man machines, one of the most popular games of all. Granted, a three or four thousand dollar Pac-Man computer is not a typical collectible — although it might be the equivalent of the 1940s and 50s pin ball machines that are so highly desired by collectors — Pac-Man byproducts such as coffee mugs, t-shirts, game boards, might just do the trick.

If you or your parents had put away that 1930s Shirley Temple doll, which once sold for pennies, you would be able to sell it retail today for about $700. And if you had a Jackie Robinson doll, circa 1949, in a Brooklyn Dodgers uniform with number 42 on the back, Phillips, New York would be able to get you almost $500 for it. All that makes the Brooke Shields doll, marketed in 1982, look like a good bet for the future. Originally available for $8 it has reportedly sold for $20 at some collector toy shows. What will it fetch twenty or thirty years from now? And what, for that matter, will a 1983 Cabbage Patch doll, in its original box with its birth certifcate intact be worth then?

Many people hoard newspapers believing that they have some potential value. With some exceptions, newspapers usually don't. Not even the last Toronto Telegram and the first Toronto Sun, which were published in October, 1971, has much appeal. Almost everyone in Ontario thought the set would be worth a fortune and everyone saved one. Although the pair has been offered at various shows and flea markets for $5 to $30, they rarely change hands. There is no real market for them. Similarly, the American newspapers announcing Nixon's resignation are worth very little because everyone held onto their copy. But the brief report in the back pages of some papers, saying that a break-in took place in Washington's Watergate apartment, is rare. This is the one newspaper that very few people have. The lesson here, of course, is that we should put away the newspapers that no one else considers.

News events present a collecting category all their own. For the 1980s the obvious choice has to be the marriage of His Royal Highness the Prince of Wales to the Lady Diana Spencer. An invitation to the wedding, which took place July 29th, 1981, would be a major find in any 'future treasure chest.' While none are known to have been sold on the open market yet, they certainly will be guaranteed to be worth a tidy amount of money eventually. All kinds of assorted Royal Wedding souvenirs hit the marketplace including dolls, reproduction Lady Di engagement rings, booklets, stamps and coins. If you had the foresight to buy one or two of these, put them into your magic box.

Then there are those who are taken with music, who feel that the sound of any era has to be its soul. To them, music is a whole, separate and clear-cut collecting category. If, in the 1950s you had started collecting Elvis memorabilia, you would have a valuable collection now. For example, an Elvis toy guitar, vintage 1957, which probably originally sold for a few dollars, is now retailing around $700. Beatle dolls are another interesting example. In 1964 they were produced by the Remko company and sold for about $3. Now when they show up at Ameri-can nostalgia shows they have price tags ranging around $850 a piece. Who should we be saving now? Some say Michael Jackson is the name. Remember his dolls and the one handed, glitzy glove that the teenagers bought and stuck into their bedroom mirrors?

What about movie and even television memorabilia? If you had managed to snaffle

Judy Garland's red slippers, the ones she wore in *The Wizard of Oz*, you would have made $165,000 (American) at the June 2nd, 1988 New York City auction when Christie's sold them to a devoted collector. That sale reigned as the highest price ever paid for a piece of movie memorabilia until June, 1989 when someone paid $231,000. for the original annotated film script for *Citizen Kane.*

As far as contemporary material, there are those who are putting their hopes on Star Trek artifacts. Because the show first aired in 1966, and again in 1987 and considering the long life of the reruns, chances are that related collectibles will be a staple for decades. Advice for future collectors? Put away the dolls, posters, T-shirts and the rest of the paraphernalia for any movies and television shows you think has mass, even cultish appeal.

What else is quintessentially of our period? McDonald's of course. Thousands of people are already quietly stockpiling their give-away or promotional items such as the happy meal boxes, hand puppets, cars, games, placemats, glasses and even calendars. Can they really be collectibles of the future?

Yes and no. No, because it is practically impossible to put together the definitive collection as the promotional material varies around the world and even from restaurant to restaurant. Then too, so many millions of these kinds of goods are manufactured and given away, that they could not be considered rare. On the other hand, much of the material is simply discarded, thrown away. The pieces which survive, could possibly, therefore, be worth something.

Gary Reinblatt, Senior Vice President of National Marketing for the company says he has been hoarding McDonalds memorabilia for the last eighteen years and has two large cartons packed away which include items from various campaigns, manager's meetings and conventions. "Not that I have any idea what I'm doing or what I'm going to do with the stuff later," he quips. But Reinblatt makes an interesting point; "Remember that our company is only 35 years old, compared to Coca Cola, which is in its 104th year of business." Inferring, of course, that McDonald's doesn't have a long history to fall back on. He also added the company is only in its third logo now and that if and when the logo changes, there might be a real resurgence in the collecting of McDonalds material because the memorabilia will automatically be placed into a time frame.

Not too many people realize that McDonald's has an extensive employee incentive gift program. Restaurant personnel can select specific items from a special catalogue available only for employees. From time to time, according to Dennis Irwin, the Director of Marketing for Ontario and the Maritimes, this has led to certain hot collectibles. Irwin says that a special telephone was once offered as incentive. Only a few were made. They were not great sellers and lasted over many catalogue printings. As soon as they were gone and no longer available people were after them. He reported that one sold in Europe recently for several thousand dollars.

The key to spotting potential collectibles is to examine your surroundings carefully and save things that no one else might. In addition, you must consider proper storage. "People collecting newspapers or any paper product should store each item in Mylar (a specially prepared conservation product) to keep them from disintegrating" (see chapter 15) She adds that it's important to store paper products in a dark, dry place, otherwise they'll deteriorate and be worthless.

Don't spend too much money either. The treasures you save should be items that are either

This c. 1900 Black Cat Shoe Polish clock which fetched $5,400 plus the 10% buyer's premium at a 1980 Waddington's auction is a wonderful piece of vintage advertising. *(Photo: Waddington's)*

free or very cheap. Once they have been properly sorted, forget about them. Don't expect to sell them tomorrow and make a fortune. You won't but maybe your grandchildren might. And if they don't, well, at least they will have a giggle about what their ancestors hoarded.

Definitions

Goods in the nostalgia, memorabilia, collectibles or ephemera category have often been described as objects that evoke feelings of pleasure, warmth and fond memories; very often childhood related. For the most part they were originally designed as inexpensive, mass-produced, utilitarian items which, in their time, were not thought to be quality goods. Paper dolls, preserving jars, penny banks, sheet music, wind-up toys, tins, postcard, Dinky toys, bubble gum cards and pin back buttons are just a few of the things that qualify. Because they had so little value at the time they originally appeared, they were quickly discarded when their usefulness ended.

It is this scarcity factor and the generally low acquisition price (at least compared to those artifacts that fall into the more costly antiques domain) combined with the warm emotional responses usually provoked by the sight of these items that makes them so coveted. Without question, this area is hot and has more collectors than almost any other area of collecting.

Pin Back Buttons

These small round, usually brightly-coloured plaques are excellent recorders of history, political events, advertising techniques, life-styles and customs. Although made to be ephemeral, they have survived in surprisingly large numbers and still are used to promote political candidates, entertainers, sporting events, products and ideas. Because of their diversity, they may be a novel area of collecting to consider.

Manufacturing methods of pin back buttons have not changed greatly since they were first invented in the United States in 1896. The paper image or photograph is placed on a metal disc and then covered with a thin layer of transparent material — formerly celluloid, now plastic. Only the stamping-out is done automatically now. Various Canadian companies produced pin back buttons; one of the most prolific and whose products have become valued collectors' items was Thomas Whibby of Toronto who began around 1910.

The categories that attract specialist collectors are elections, holidays, comic-book characters, film and rock stars, boy scouts, sports, security and identification badges, royalty, the Prohibition, strikes, advertising premiums and political events, such as the Iranian hostage crisis and referendums.

Some prominent people are known to indulge in button collecting, among them former Premier Richard Hatfield of New Brunswick and former U.S. President Richard Nixon. Bill Kinsman, a former resident of Ottawa, and a collector, found a large framed button collection in the prime ministerial garage shortly after Pierre Trudeau had moved to the residence of the leader of the opposition. "Joe Clark told me it wasn't his so I gathered Pierre must have left it behind," said Kinsman.

The button collection believed to be one of the largest ever assembled in Canada was once jointly owned by Bill Kinsman and the late Max Saltzman, former MP for Waterloo-Cambridge. Apparently, they did try to place it in a Canadian museum but could never get assurance from curators that it would be displayed. Sometime in the mid-1980s after Saltzman's death, the collection was placed in the hands of a Toronto lawyer who was to have it appraised and categorized. At the time this revision was underway (summer, 1990) the collection still had not been disbanded. If and when it's sold, however, the Saltzman collection, as it is widely known, will likely set the price standards for the Canadian market.

At any rate, included in the collection are buttons to commemorate Newfoundland's confederation with Canada and one for Sir Charles Tupper who was prime minister for a brief period in 1896. Especially valued are those issued for Queen Victoria and her 1901 memorial buttons. More recent examples include Trudeau and John Diefenbaker compaign buttons.

Canadian pin back buttons are relatively inexpensive, trading from $1 to about $35 with most hovering around $5. Very often, an eagle-eyed collector can find big bargains in this area.

For instance, one Ontario collector recently picked up a Charles Tupper button for the remarkably low price of $10 Canadian. United States prices are considerably higher; a 1920 dual portrait of presidential candidate James Cox and his running mate Franklin Delano Roosevelt from the Don Warner Collection of Political Memorabilia was auctioned April 4, 1981, by the New England Rare Coin Galleries of Boston, fetching $30,000 plus the buyer's premium of 10 per cent. (Since that sale, a great many similar buttons have surfaced and been sold for significantly reduced prices.) According to several collectors, prices for Canadian buttons (not withstanding those odd ones that appear at antique and nostalgia shows) are generally set by American dealers. For the most part they rarely, if ever, go for more than $40 U.S.

Button collectors in the United States are better organized that Canadian collectors. They hold national, state and regional conventions large enough to fill hockey arenas. As well, they have about a dozen books devoted to the hobby, while we have none. This situation might change shortly with the establishment, in April, 1989, of a Canadian Policital Memorabilia Club (see Appendix 3 for details.) Members are encouraged to contact one another for the purposes of trading rather than selling since, in the words of one knowledgable collector, "most collectors would not know how much to charge for their duplicates."

Tin Cans

People are interested in collecting old tobacco tins, cigar boxes and food containers because they like the ornate and colourful decorations, the archaic-sounding slogans and the quaint lithography. The field is so vast that specialization is almost imperative. Some collect coffee, cocoa or peanut butter tins, while others solely concentrate on aviation, sports or examples featuring native Indians. Many are interested only in trays: miniature examples called tip trays or the larger ones with beer or soft-drink advertisements. Some choose to limit their collections to pieces made in England, America or Canada.

Basically, tins can be divided into two areas: those designed to hold or contain items and those made to be given away as advertising.

Tobacco tins have been favourite collectors' items for a long time, and the manufacturers who created them in Canada were active from the late 1880s to the early 1920s. John Sebert, dean of Canadian tin can collectors, published the histories of four of these companies — Imperial Tobacco, Rock City, Tuckett and Macdonald — in the December 1976 and January 1977 issues of *Tin Type Magazine*. Two pocket - sized containers from Imperial's "Forest and Stream" series are important: one has a lone fisherman and the other shows two men and a dog in a canoe. The latter is more valuable as fewer seem to have been made. Imperial's Taxi tobacco tin (measuring 4 1/4" x 3") is perhaps the rarest Canadian example, fetching hundreds of dollars when offered for sale.

An interesting tin was made by the Quebec-based Rock City Tobacco Company after the turn of the century. Their Torpedo upright featuring a ship has always fascinated collectors. The containers made by the W.C. MacDonald Tobacco Company, established in Montreal in 1858, are the most difficult to find, and most are quite plain. Tuckett Tobacco Company produced posters, paper under glass, tip trays and calendars, but collectors are aware of only one Tuckett-made tin — the Old Squire Pipe Tobacco pocket container.

Next to tobacco tins, small peanut butter pails are equally popular as collectors, items

A selection of high-quality tins gathered from several private collections. *(Photo: HWF)*

because they are so colourful and graphically interesting. They likely were made that way to appeal to children.

Tin cans, trays and signs can be found at flea markets, antique-nostalgia shows and garage sales. (For books and associations on the subject see the bibliography at the end of this chapter.)

Comic Art

If it had not been for the few astute and dedicated pioneer collectors of the late fifties and early sixties, comic art would have disappeared long ago. The movement to preserve comic books, magazines, original art work and related toys began in the 1960s in New York and San Diego when they hosted the first comic-book conventions. In 1977, the first Canadian convention was sponsored by John Biernat, a high school teacher and owner of a Toronto bookshop devoted to comic art.

Who collects this type of memorabilia in

Canada? Biernat believes "mostly kids who neither date, drink or smoke." They go after the less costly, contemporary comic books, whereas the more expensive and older items are bought by adults, "predominantly male school-teachers who, for the most part, don't drink or smoke either." Biernat, who has more than five thousand comics, collects because he finds it "a nice way to recapture a bit of my childhood." Beyond that, he is fascinated by "the shocking anti-Oriental and strong anti-Nazi attitudes displayed in the books published during the forties."

Comics began in the United States with Richard Outcault's creation of *Hogan's Alley,* a strip centred around an ugly character named "Yellow Kid." Until 1933 they appeared in the daily press, simply as "the Funnies," featuring personalities such as Mutt and Jeff, Mickey Mouse and Donald Duck. *Funnies on Parade* by Eastern Color Printing, published in 1933 as an advertising premium was the first actual comic book, made up of reprints from some of the more popular newspaper strips.

The Golden Age of the industry actually began in 1934 with the publication of the ten-cent monthly *Famous Funnies*. Together with several similarly priced reprints, it remained on the newsstands for twenty years. *Action Comics #1* appeared in 1938, featuring heroes specifically created for the strip. According to Robert Lesser, author of *A Celebration of Comic Art and Memorabilia*, four Superman stories first appeared in *Action Comics,* only later to be reprinted in *Superman #1*.

The Silver Age lasting from 1955 to 1960 saw the creation of more superheroes as well as horror stories, science fiction and the first MAD magazines.

From the Golden Age, *Superman #1* comics are the most coveted. A copy in mint condition has a present retail value of $15,000 U.S. Although at least 200 must have survived, no more than 10 are believed to exist today. Early Superman comics are of particular interest to Canadians. In 1938, illustrator Joe Shuster (a former Torontonian and cousin of comedian Frank Shuster), together with his partner Jerry Siegel, drew a building for the Superman strip that closely resembled the old *Toronto Star* building on King Street. Strip character Clark Kent's place of employment, the paper for which he worked, at first was known as *The Star* and later became *The Daily Planet*.

Worth as much or even more than *Superman #1* is first-issue *Marvel Mystery* (1939), followed closely by *Batman, Captain America* and *Wonder Woman*. Golden Age original artwork as well as spin-off toys representing comic-book characters from the same era are rare and almost impossible to obtain, and therefore much coveted. As collectors' items Silver Age comics are less expensive than those from the Golden Age but more costly than the post-1960 Contemporaries that still are in plentiful supply. Novice collectors should start with Contemporaries and work their way backward, making sure the books they acquire have original covers with inside pages intact.

Comics should be stored in non-acidic containers, away from direct light and heat, to preserve the low-grade paper on which they were printed.

In the last few years there has been a surge of interest in cartoon artwork but it wasn't until Christie's and Sotheby's disposed of Disney and Warner animation ceels recently that it became apparent. Prices for strips range from $100 to over $20,000 depending on the strip's age, condition, beauty, etc. Also affecting price are the period they were done in the artist's career and the popularity of the characters. Blue-chip strips include Dick Tracy, especially since the movie's release; Mickey Mouse; Blondie; Pogo and Flash Gordon, to name a few.

Unfortunately, there aren't any collectors' associations yet but there are collector show/sales in and around Toronto and the largest annual event is held in San Diego each year. To find about about these shows contact your local specialist comic book dealer.

Postcards

"By far the worst development of the prevailing pests is postal carditis which affects the heart, paralyzes the reasoning faculties and abnormally increases the nerve." This was how John Walker Harrington, writing in the March 1906 issue of *American Magazine,* described the craze which at the turn of the century was known as philocarty, postal carditis or cartephelia. Today, those addicted to the same mania are referred to as deltiologists or, in the vernacular, postcard collectors.

Between 1900 and 1918 many Canadians, Americans and Europeans hoarded and traded postcards. Interest waned after that only to be reawakened in the early 1970s when long-forgotten albums and card collections appeared in windows and on counters of antique and nostalgia shops.

No one knows for sure when the first postcard was sent. Some experts believe that the pictureless card first appeared in Austria in 1869, while others maintain that private cards were copyrighted in the United States as early as 1861. Yet a third group claims they started in Great Britain in 1870. Most, however, agree that the picture cards mailed during the 1893 Chicago World Exposition led to the craze that dominated the early part of the twentieth century.

While some people are interested in the written messages, the stamps or cancellation marks, most collect because of the pictures on the front.

Canadians prefer cards depicting local history, fishing, nautical, maritime scenes, early views of Western towns, Indians and railway development. They also share a fondness for political and patriotic postcards but are less interested in American and European views.

Special to Canada are Canada's Golden West series (Valentine and Sons, Montreal and Toronto); Habitant Life Studies; and Ter-Centenary of Quebec and Canadian Homestead Life, cards with rural scenes rimmed in gold that often were numbered. Warwick Brothers and Rutter Limited (Montreal and Toronto) specialized in beautiful street scenes and in patriotics; Canadian Postcard Company produced photographic novelties and humourous cards showing gigantic farm animals and fish, as well as oversized fruit and vegetables.

Some collectors concentrate on one particular manufacturer or one series; others choose specific subjects — royalty, expositions, trains, boats, early automobiles, etc. Novices must find an area that appeals to them and then organize their collection, either by storing it in large shoe boxes or, possibly for better protection and viewing, in photo albums. Stacking cards is not advisable because they can warp easily.

Prices for vintage cards normally range between $5 to $8, although political, patriotic and some early photo cards may cost upward of $100.

General Tom Thumb

Tom Thumb collectibles originated with a character created in 1842 by the ingenious Phineas Taylor Barnum for his Barnum and Bailey team of circus performers.

Charles Sherwood Stratton was born in Bridgeport, Connecticut, in January 1838, weighing nine pounds two ounces. He was only twenty-five inches tall and had gained less than six pounds over his birthweight when he became a circus attraction four years later. Barnum had signed him for six weeks, changing his name to General Tom Thumb and adding six years to his age in the belief that the public liked to be duped.

At first, Stratton's parents — an impecunious carpenter and his wife, a cleaning woman — received $7 a week plus board for their son's appearances but the wages soon jumped to $25 a week as this Miniature Man turned into a financial bonanza for them and his promoter. People did not only come to be entertained by him but also bought Tom Thumb souvenirs. When the Little General was just seven years old, he and P.T. Barnum became business partners.

In 1862, Barnum signed on George Washington Nutt, another midget, who became Com-

This *carte-de-visite* shows Mr. and Mrs. Tom Thumb with a child who was hired for the occasion. They never did have a baby of their own. *(Photo: HWF)*

modore Nutt, as well as Anna Swain, "The Nova Scotian Giantess." A third midget, Mercy Lavinia Warren Bump, joined the team as Lavinia Warren. Although she was "courted" by both gentlemen midgets, she was married in 1863 to General Tom Thumb in a well-publicized ceremony. Over two thousand wedding invitations were sent out, and Barnum, together with photographer Mathew Brady, sold thousands of wedding pictures to an adoring public. The additional prints produced by photographers E. and H.T. Anthony from Brady's negatives became veritable collectors' items.

General and Mrs. Tom Thumb travelled all over the world, and wherever they went their souvenirs were sold. Since they had no children of their own, Barnum did not shy away from the ultimate hoax of having them pose for photo-

graphs with babies he had hired.

At fifteen years of age Tom Thumb began to grow again, reaching forty inches and weighing seventy pounds. When he was thirty, he and his wife were millionaires. He died in 1883 at forty-four and some years later his widow married Count Magri, an Italian dwarf. She died in 1919, aged seventy, and in accordance with her wishes was buried next to Tom Thumb in a Bridgeport cemetery.

Tom Thumb toured Canada in 1861, performing at Toronto's St. Lawrence Hall, in Newmarket, Barrie and Bradford, Ontario, as well as in Yorkville's Town Hall. This is what *The Globe and Mail* of October 22, 1861 said about the General's performance:

This miniature specimen of the Genus Homo gave two of his popular entertainments yesterday afternoon and evening. In the afternoon there was a numerous attendance, a great majority of the audience being children. In the evening, the hall was crowded in every part. The General is as sprightly as ever, and sings and dances with great spirit. He looks as might have been expected, somewhat older than he did on his last visit to Toronto and seems somewhat stouter. He appeared in the court costume as worn before Her Majesty, and also in the "garb of old Gaul," and he certainly makes up well as a Highland Chieftain. He also appeared as Napoleon Bonaparte and gave some representations of Grecian Statutes. The Little Gentleman was warmly received by the audience and elicited many plaudits.

In the 1920s, Harry Herzberg, an American lawyer, started to collect circus paraphernalia, including many Tom Thumb items — *cartes-de-*

visites, books, ashtrays, autographs, posters, tickct stubs, programs, handbills, miniature clothing and other tiny articles used by the famous midget couple. Herzberg eventually donated his collection to the City of San Antonio, Texas, and it now is housed in the main library annex. The Barnum Museum in Bridgeport also owns various Tom Thumb objects. The Museum of Northampton in England has in its collection a nine-inch-high leather boot made for the midget in 1844 by Henry Bull of Northampton. The price paid for it at a 1981 London auction was $192. At the same sale the Theatre Museum of London purchased a cashmere waistcoat belonging to Tom Thumb for $312. Alert collectors may still come across Tom Thumb memorabilia.

Sports Memorabilia

Despite Canadians' interest in sports per se, collecting its memorabilia seems to have limited appeal and, therefore, might present an excellent opportunity for beginners. Things, however, are much different in the United States, where collecting sports memorabilia is a passionate hobby for millions of individuals.

Horse-racing, for instance, is an area that has been almost totally ignored by Canadian collectors. In the United States, Derbiana, a term used to describe artifacts connected with the Kentucky Derby, is highly coveted; the Churchill Downs Museum in Louisville owns numerous items reminiscent of the first Derby held there in 1875 — programs, photographs of the winning horses, horseshoes, silk purses, etc. Yet, there is no museum in Canada to house equivalent Queen's Plate artifacts, despite the fact that the event is 15 years older than the Kentucky Derby, 13 years older than the Preakness and 3 years older than the Belmont Stakes,

according to Trent Frayne, noted Canadian horse-racing expert and author of the book *The Queen's Plate.*

A few pieces are at Woodbine Racetrack in Toronto or privately held by racing fans, jockeys and trainers. The archives of the Ontario jockey Club contain numerous items which should be in a museum, including a series of Seagram's paper — underglass lithographs showing Queen's Plate and King's Plate winners between 1891 and 1905. Originally drawn by A.H. Hider, they are available in the open market from $75 to $350. Those owned by the club are never displayed, and according to George Hendre its honorary president, "each time we hang them we receive complaints from members because they contain liquor ads."

If and when the National Association of Canadian Racetracks decides to open a museum, it may encourage private individuals to collect racing programs, news stories, photographs, trophies, ribbons, postcards, membership passes, horseshoes and similar memorabilia.

Baseball Cards

It's only natural that Americans are crazy about baseball memorabilia. After all the game originated in that country the 1870s and flourished, long before it caught on here. Anything to do with this sport is highly collectible to Americans, from early advertising, old uniforms and equipment, autographs, games and of course cards.

Because the market is so active it has become extremely difficult to keep abreast of prices and values. Just look at these figures. Two years ago Guernsey, an American auction company, sold the original painting of Mickey Mantle's 1953 baseball card for $110,000. Then, in 1989 someone bought a Honus Wagner card from Joshua Evans, the proprietor of Lelands Art and Collectibles in Allentown, PA for $110,000, which has to be the highest price ever paid for a baseball card but if Evans, sells his Charles (Lindy) Lindstrom card for $1,000,000 as he thinks he will, that will get the prize. This card, the only one in existence is #16 of the 1932 series. The reason it's so valuable is because the U.S. Caramel Company decided not to fulfill the premium offer on the reverse side and cancelled the card before it ever went into production.

In April, 1990 Guernsey held a spectacular sports memorabilia auction, with over 2,000 lots, in the Pier 90 terminal on the Hudson River in New York City. One day was devoted to baseball memorabilia while another included a combination of all the other sports. The top price in the baseball auction was for two sets of 1914-15 baseball cards issued in Cracker Jacks candy boxes. A collector paid $110,000 for the 320 cards. An 1888 Baseball Card Company game with 71 of the original 72 cards fetched $22,000; a set of ten 1952 unopened Topps wax packs, realized $10,450; and a complete set of 1887 Alan & Ginter Tobacco cards, brought $4,400.

In that same auction, Lou Gehrig's 1939 American League All Star game pin realized $41,800 but the most touching item and probably the one that generated the most attention, was the bat he used in his last season; two years before his death at the age of 35. According to the catalogue he gave the bat to the son of an acquaintance, autographing it with "To Jerry, may you use this to better advantage than I did." Sources reported that it sold to Mark Friedland, a Miami sports collectibles dealer for more than $28,000.

Despite these figures, it isn't too late to jump into this field. Collectors can specialize in Canadian teams and players. Children too can get hooked by just putting their allowance into contemporary cards. After a few years they might have traders or, the way that the market is going, good stock to sell. There are baseball and sports cards show/sales in and around the Toronto area. Local newspapers usually carry advertisements in the want ad sections.

Novice collectors should be warned about the downside of this collecting hobby, especially before buying baseball autographs. Beware of forged signatures. All baseball autograph collectors should have a copy of the *SCD Baseball Autograph Handbook*, which authenticates autographs for all 204 baseball Hall of Fame inductees. (Softcover, $19.95 U.S. plus $5. U.S. handling charges. Available from Sports Books Division, Krause Publications, 700 E. State St. Iola WI 54990.)

Hockey Memorabilia

Although Canadians venerate practically anything connected with ice hockey, they were less than eager to acquire certain important artifacts offered at a Phillips Ward-Price sports memorabilia auction in April 1981. A presentation hockey stick signed by a Stanley Cup-winning Toronto Maple Leafs team brought no more than $80, and a circa-1898 silver-plate hockey trophy from the Halifax Bell-Spalding League went under the hammer for a mere $90. These disappointing results of the sale indicate not that the material was poor but that there are not enough sports collectors in Canada to sustain a quality auction. Or, from another perspective, this area of collecting is underpriced in Canada and might, therefore, be an area for the novice to investigate.

The few people who specialize in hockey memorabilia gather postcards, bubblegum cards, cigarette premiums, calendars, old rule books, game programs and equipment. Old team photo-

A hockey photograph of the Medicine Hat Hockey Team, 1916. Individual portraits of the players were taken in the studio and then placed on a hand-drawn view of the rink. Collection: Ralph Fox. *(Photo: HWF)*

graphs, primarily those taken between 1900 and 1930, are especially coveted. Many show the players in full dress on the ice, although in some instances their photos were taken individually in a studio. The photographer cut out their images and placed them onto a drawing of a rink. These team photos are highly valued, ranging from a few dollars up to seventy-five dollars, depending on condition, size and subject.

Although hockey is a relatively new game, skating has been around for centuries. In the twelfth century an Englishman wrote that "many young men tye bones to their feet and slide on the ice, as swiftly as a bird flyeth in the aire." Later, in the seventeenth century, an artist did a painting, now at the Art Gallery of Ontario, that shows the Dutch playing an unnamed game on frozen canals wearing shoes with blades on the bottom.

Shinny hockey was played in Kingston, Ontario, in the 1850s, but the first organized game took place in the winter of 1885 and 1886. According to *The Hockey Year Book* by George King, published in 1924:

> The first actual game that we have any record of occurred in Captain Dix's rink, which was located on the harbour in front of the city buildings in Kingston. This game was played between teams representing Queen's University and the Royal Military College. The players wore long white duck trousers and used a set of sticks which had been borrowed from an eastern firm, said sticks being expressed

back to the owners after the game. The rink, which was intended for skating purposes only, had a bandstand erected in the centre, and when a player dashed up to the ice he was greatly assisted in his attack by his agility to dodge around the bandstand while en route. A solid rubber ball, which had been cut into a square, was used for the puck.

That puck together with a stick used during that game can be seen at the International Hockey Hall of Fame and Museum in Kingston.

In 1980 and again in 1986, to commemorate this particular Kingston game, 35,000 coins were minted under the auspices of the Historic Hockey Association, the Historic Hockey Committee and the International Hall of Fame and Museum. They were still available in the fall of 1990 and could be obtained by writing to the Museum at Box 82, York and Alfred Streets, Kingston, Ontario, K7L 4V6. For more historic hockey related information, read *Captains, Colonels and Kings* by J.W. Fitsell, published in the mid-1980s by The Boston Mills Press, 132 Main Street, Erin, ON N0B 1T0.

Insulators

Perhaps the least understood collectible is the insulator, that mushroom-shaped glass fixture used to attach wires to supporting poles. Coveted by the select few, they rose in price to unprecedented heights between 1975 and 1977, then plunged dramatically, remaining low for the next five years, only to rise again in the summer of 1982. At that time, American dealers began hounding Canadian collectors to sell what they had acquired in previous binges.

The threadless insulator was invented in 1844 by Ezra Cornell, a construction chief for the Samuel F.B. Morse Baltimore-Washington Telegraph Line who got the idea from a small, round glass knob he had seen bolted to a hotel-room dresser. His new device, named "Bureau Knob" or "Doorknob," consisted of two parts — a thick, square blob of glass attached to the crossarm of the telegraph pole and another glass, mounted on top to hold the cloth-wrapped wire in place. This model soon was followed by a one-piece, bellshaped glass jar, fitted onto a wooden peg; that again had to be redesigned because, during high winds, its mountings were not secure enough to keep the insulators aloft.

The Montreal Telegraph Company was the first to use the threadless insulator in Canada in 1847. Manufacture was discontinued in 1870 when a glass screw became part of the unit. Prior to 1900 the glass for threadless insulators, being of inferior quality, darkened when exposed to sunlight for a prolonged period of time. Due to its manganese contents it turned purple, and the selenium in it resulted in an amber hue.

The most common insulator glass colours found today are clear and green, followed by white, dark and light brown, iridescent and amethyst; cobalt blue is the rarest. A few bear the manufacturer's signature; those made in the early 1900s by Dominion Glass Company of Canada show the imprint "Dominion." Not many threadless models have survived, and collectors therefore concentrate on specific manufacturers or particular colours. The common clear-glass type is priced from about $20 to $50; the rarer coloured pieces could command several hundred dollars, depending on condition and market trends. The threadless purple or cobalt-blue specimens have been known to reach between $1,000 and $2,000.

Although insulators can be found at nostalgia-memorabilia and antique shows as well as flea markets, collectors (sometimes referred to as "polecats") have been spotted trekking along abandoned railway lines and roads in search of hidden treasures.

Toys, Dolls and Teddy Bears

Playthings are collected not only because they bring back childhood memories but also because they are good indicators of life as it was. They represent occupations that no longer exist, fashions that no longer are worn and modes of transportation that have become outdated.

When the pioneer families came to North America, they brought essentials such as seeds, bedding, clothing and tools. Rarely was there room for toys or playthings. At first the children either improvised or managed without; later, as the families were more settled, father would spend the long winter evenings carving dolls, wagons and puzzles for the children. Imports from Germany, France and England became available, and by the 1870s small toy factories began to operate in the United States and to a lesser degree in Canada.

Until the middle of the nineteenth century most playthings were made from wood, and one of the most popular, because it was the only kind considered suitable for Sunday play, was Noah's Ark which came equipped with all the animals. In the late 1850s the first tin plate toys appeared on the market. Although roughly assembled but painted in bright colours, they were a welcome addition to the toy chest. Mechanical playthings followed when European manufacturers discovered a way of stamping out thinner pieces of tin. The earliest wind-up toys were small vehicles or figures whose moveable parts were connected to a clockwork mechanism. By the turn of the century, they became more sophisticated, allowing the figures to perform more intricate movements.

This c. 1910 wind-up toy, wearing its original clothes, was made in France. When wound, it walks, one arm pours the liquor in the glass and the other brings it up to its face. *(Photo:HWF)*

Mechanical banks made from cast iron had their debut after 1870 and continued to be mass-produced in the United States until the 1930s. One intriguing example was a clown that could raise his arm, "swallow" a coin placed on his palm and roll his eyes at the same time. The Shepard Hardware Company of Buffalo, New York, made this and other mechanical banks. Although they only stayed in business from 1882 to 1892, they were one of the most prolific firms. J. and E. Stevens Company of Connecticut produced some very fine banks between 1843 and 1928, among them the famous "Calamity Bank." Patented in 1905, it depicted two football players tackling a third after a coin was placed in the slot. Many more companies made these popular savings devices; however, those still in business today usually copy the older models, which by now have become very expensive and difficult to locate. Collectors should be aware that there are many reproductions and fakes flooding the market.

The Canadian Toy Collectors Society was started in Toronto in 1970 as an Ontario Chapter of the Buffalo Motoring and Miniature Association. Four years later the initial membership had not only grown but its interests had diversified beyond miniature cars to include many other playthings. They now have about one hundred members, mostly men, who meet twice a month in a Toronto hotel to trade and talk about toys. The membership at large includes people from other Canadian provinces, the United States, Europe and Australia. The annual main event is a toy show held each fall in Toronto. For information about the club see Appendix 3, page 249.

Doll collectors are a group unto themselves and in many respects do not seem to follow the creed of most present-day antique collectors whose watchword is "minimal restoration." Pristine dolls still are being prettied up and extensively repaired, and many collections, therefore, are limited to late Victorian and early twentieth-century "fancy" dolls, leaving out the older and more primitive examples.

To say that doll collectors usually are ladies of the "blue rinse" persuasion would be false in view of the many existing clubs, interest groups and magazines that count younger women and even men among their subscribers. Some people are in it for investment purposes, but the majority just enjoy collecting, trading and knowing more about dolls.

Anthropologists believe dolls began as religious idols and sorcerers' magic symbols, although there is evidence that children in Egyptian and Roman times did play with them. French fashion houses used mannikins — a term that has survived — during the seventeenth and eighteenth centuries to model their creations, shipping them to European capitals and North American cities dressed in the latest styles. The following advertisement appeared in a New England newspaper in 1733:

> To be seen at Mrs. Hannah Teatts, Mantua maker at the head of Summerstreet, Boston, a Baby drest after the Newst Fashion of Mantuas and Night Gowns and everything belonging to a Dress, lately Arrived in Capt. White, from London, any Ladies that desire to see it, may either come or send and she will be ready to wait on 'em, if they come to the House it is Five Shillings, and if she waits on them it is Seven Shillings.

As soon as ladies' fashion books made their appearance, these little "Fashion Dolls" or "Fashion Babies" became obsolete and were given to small girls as playthings to be added to their collections of cruder, often homemade, rag and wooden dolls.

It was not until the nineteenth century that dollmaking became an industry in Germany and France. By the 1850s doll heads began to be made of china, papier-mache and bisque. Papiermache consisting of paper pulp, glue and plaster was the cheapest material and because it was so malleable could be used to produce hollow heads, which then were covered with a wax finish and painted. Bodies usually were made from muslin or kid leather and stuffed with a variety of materials, while hands and feet were carved from wood.

During the latter half of the nineteenth cen-

The $38,000 doll sold by Theriault's of Maryland, January, 1983. *(Photo: Theriault's)*

The 'H' Doll's creator was Aristide Marcellin Halpeau, whose company the Barro's Doll Firm of France — he owned it from 1875 until it went out of business in 1889 — introduced the 'bébé' or 'H' doll in 1882. Theriault's sold it in January, 1990 for $100,000, establishing a world record for the sale price of a doll. *(Photo: Theriault's)*

tury until about 1870, the Germans made porcelain, bisque and Parian (a hard material resembling marble) dolls. They exported the heads and limbs to France, until French dollmakers, among them the noted Jumeau family and Casimir Bru, began to make their own, eventually producing some of the most beautiful and life-like examples. Also desirable are later dolls made from rubber and plastic-Kewpies, Shirley Temples, Dionne Quintuplets and Barbies, as well as Canada's own Eaton's Beauties.

The universality of dolls has led to the founding of countless doll museums, the most recent being the Margaret Woodbury Strong Museum at One Manhattan Square, Rochester, New York, that houses an impressive collection of more than twenty thousand dolls.

Theriault's of Annapolis, Maryland, the world's only auction house specializing in dolls, set a world record in February 1981 when at a West Palm Beach, Florida, sale an Oriental-style bisque doll by Casimir Bru was sold for

$16,000. The price was matched by a California collector bidding on an A. Thuillier doll at Theriault's June 1982 Chicago auction. Records were broken in January 1983 by the same auction firm when a California couple successfully bid $38,000 for an A. Marque doll, one of only twenty produced by French sculptor Albert Marque sometime between 1899 and 1915. Because only thirteen of the twenty Marque dolls are accounted for, others might be languishing in some attic. Each of them is signed on the back of the head and bears an incised number beneath the artist's signature. Seven years later, in their January 1990 auction in Orange County, California, they broke their own record disposing of an 'H' doll for $100,000.

Prices for dolls depend on rarity, of course, but condition is still of prime consideration. Dolls that have never been restored, wear vintage costumes and have their original hair are the most valuable. When buying antique dolls, look for manufacturers' markings, quality, workmanship, body restorations and clothing. They should be carefully stored, preferably under or behind glass, and small children should not be allowed to play with them.

Teddy Bears

Americans consistently claim to have invented the teddy bear. They attribute its origin to an incident involving President Theodore "Teddy" Roosevelt who, when confronted during a hunt in the Rocky Mountains by a bear cub someone had tied up, refused to shoot it. A cartoon by Clifford Berryman showing the president with a small bear appeared the next day, November 16, 1902, in the *Washington Post*. On seeing the cartoon, Morris Michtom, founder of Ideal Toy Corporation of New York City, wrote to the president asking him whether it would be impertinent to make a small stuffed bear cub and call it "Teddy Bear." The president had no objection to the idea, and Mrs. Michtom who was handy with the needle helped make many of the samples. One was sent to the president, and in 1903 the other, together with a copy of Theodore Roosevelt's written consent, was taken to the buyer of a wholesale toy firm who bought the entire output. About the same time, the Steiff Company of Germany had exported a small stuffed bear to North America and, therefore, also felt justified in claiming the honour of originating the teddy bear. Other manufacturers soon copied the by now famous toy.

By and large, few collections contain teddy bears made before 1904. To distinguish between a new and a vintage model is not easy: signs of wear and tear, of course, are important; shapes and materials used for stuffing may provide other clues.

After 1906 teddy bears no longer had humps on their backs, and the older German bears had much longer and thinner limbs than those made today. Straw, sawdust and bran stuffings suggest an early manufacturing date. Younger models come equipped with glass eyes, while the older teddies had eyes made of shoe buttons.

"Doc" John Hawkshaw is an avid teddy bear collector. As proprietor of a doll "hospital" in Toronto, he also sells antique and collectible dolls but never displays his collection of teddy bears, the oldest dating back to about 1904.

Competition is fierce among collectors, especially in the United States. In Canada, prices still are comparatively low, and good specimens can be found at flea markets for as little as fifteen dollars. However, teddies in good condition, made by some of the earlier manufacturers, particularly Steiff, can command prices as high as several hundred dollars.

Bibliography

(See Appendix 3 for list of Collector's Clubs and Appendix 1 for the lists of magazines, journals and newsletters of interest to nostalgia collectors.)

Comic Art

Lesser, Robert. *A Celebration of Comic Art And Memorabilia.* New York: Hawthorn Books Inc., 1975.

Williams, Bill and Martin, ed. *The Smithsonian Collection of Newspaper Comics.* New York: Smithsonian Institution Press and Harry S. Abrams Inc., 1978.

Pin-back Buttons

Hake, Ted. *Encyclopedia of Political Buttons, 1789-1976* (three volumes). Dagran House, PO Box 1444, York, PA 17405, 1974, 1977, 1978.

Hake, Ted and Russ King. *Price Guide To Collectible Pin-Back Buttons, 1896-1986.* Pennsylvania: Americana & Collectibles Press, PO Box 1444, York, PA 17405 ($48. U.S.)

Postcards

Anderson, Allan and Betty Tomlinson. *Greetings From Canada.* Macmillan of Canada, 1978.

Miller, George & Dorothy. *Picture Postcards In The United States, 1893-1918.* New York: Clarkson N. Potter Inc. 1976.

Morgan, Hal and Andreas Brown. *Prairie Fires and Paper Moons: The American Photographic Postcard.* Massachusetts: David R. Godine Publishing Co. Inc.; 1981; 306 Dartmouth Street, Boston, MA 02116.

Range, Thomas E. *The Book of Postcard Collecting.* New York: E.P. Dutton, 1980.

Sports

Dunbar, Nancy J., ed. *Images of Sport in Early Canada,* ed. Montreal: McCord Museum and McGill-Queen's University Press, 1976.

Fitsell, J.W. *Captains, Colonels and Kings.* Ontario: Boston Mills Press, 132 Main Street, Erin, ON N8B 1T0.

Frayne, Trent. *The Queen's Plate.* Toronto: McClelland & Stewart, 1959.

Hake, Ted and Roger Steckler. *An Illustrated Guide to Non-Paper Sports Collectibles.* Pennsylvania: PO Box 1444, York, PA 17405.
King, George. *The Hockey Year Book.* Toronto: George King Publisher, 1924.

Tin Cans

Clark, Hyla M. *The Tin Can Book, The Can as Collectible Art, Advertising Art And High Art.* New York: New American Library Inc., 1977.

Hogan, Bill and Pauline. *Canadian Country-Store Collectibles.* Ontario: 16 Haynes Ave., St. Catharines, ON L2R 3Z1, 1979.

Tom Thumb

Barnum, P.T. *Struggles And Triumphs of Forty Years' Recollections of P.T. Barnum.* New York: The Courier Co. of Buffalo, 1877.

Bleeker, Sylvester. *General Tom Thumb's Three-Year Tour Around The World.* New York: S. Booth Printer, 1872.

Photgraphica, vol 7., August/September, 1980, cover story.

Toys, Dolls and Teddy Bears

Anderson, Curtiss. *Jerry Smith's Collections From the American Past*. Hallmark Cards Inc. for Halls in Crown Center, 1976.

Bialosky, Peggy and Alan. *The Teddy Bear Catalog*. New York: Workman Publishing Co., 1980.

Elizabeth, Dorothy and Evelyn Coleman. *The Collector's Encyclopedia of Dolls*. New York: Crown Publishers, 1968.

Hertz, Louis H. *The Toy Collector*. New York: Funk & Wagnalls, 1969.

Husgloen, Kyle D., *ed. The Antique Trader Weekly's Book of Collectible Dolls*. Dubuque, Iowa: Babka Publishing Company, 1976.

Rogers, Carole G. *Penny Banks — A History and a Handbook*. New York: A Subsistence Press Book in association with Dutton, New York, 1977.

White, Gwen. *Antique Toys and Their Background*. New York: Arco Publishing Co. Inc., 1971.

Theriault's Gold Horse Publishing, a division of Theriault's doll and toy auction company, is now producing a wonderful line of doll and toy books. Write for a catalogue: Theriault's Gold Horse Publishing, PO Box 151, Annapolis, MD 21404.

Specialist dealers:

George Theofiles
The Miscellaneous Man
Box 1776
New Freedom, PA 17349
Specialist dealer in posters, select graphic ephemera, publishes regular catalogues of stock.

Joshua Evans
Sports Memorabilia
Lelands Art & Collectibles
4540 Hamilton Blvd.
Allentown, PA
(Moving in 1991 to New York City.)

Ted Hake's Americana Mail Auctions
Box 14444
York, PA 17405
Four subscription catalogues a year, $20 U.S. Sells all manner of nostalgia & ephemera.

15

Conservation and Restoration

Art and antique collectors are the custodians of the artifacts in their possession and as such responsible for researching and recording their histories as well as preserving them for future generations. Many historically important pieces were lost in the past because of neglect, ignorance and short-sightedness. Collectors, like museum curators, have the responsibility of preserving the things in their care.

All materials, new or old, are affected to a greater or lesser degree by extremes in temperatures, humidity, dirt and light. It is essential for the collector to understand these environmental hazards, as well as other more complicated chemical reactions that can be damaging to these materials. He must learn how to control and eliminate them and, if necessary, restore antique pieces which may have been adversely affected.

Framing

The old-time framers used to stretch textiles and tack them onto wooden frames with closely placed nails. Over the years, works mounted in this manner have rusted, discolored and become dry and brittle. Charlotte Zuppinger, noted Toronto textile conservator, points a finger at those who, even now, still improperly wash and stretch textiles. Sometimes she can repair or reverse such damage, but often, it is permanent.

The problem is one of careless framing, and it is not confined to textiles. All fibre-based artworks — prints, photographs, documents and watercolors included — are unstable. Not only are they easily damaged by the environment, but they are also vulnerable to prolonged contact with wood, cardboard or glue. Acidity from these materials migrates onto works of art, leading to deterioration. The only way to counteract this is by surrounding the works with expensive acid-free products.

"Paying for better framing now could easily be one-tenth the cost of conserving and restoring the item later," says John Moore, a Toronto paper conservator and framer. The added expense, which can be twice as much as a routine job, is worth it; proper framing can add years to an artifact's life.

Problems can arise from framers who don't really understand conservation material or how to handle rare artworks. For instance, work not properly sealed between the frame molding and the backboard and without a suitable dustcover produces a condition known as "negative images." This is particularly noticeable on poorly framed gouaches, watercolors, prints and needlework. When air enters, it carries moisture and pollutants, which act upon the acids in the paper backing, causing stains and marks to appear wherever the work presses against a seam in the backing, a knot in the wood or the ridges in corrugated cardboard. In some cases, the actual image is transferred onto the board. Spaces and holes attract household dirt and dust as well as small insects, which can dig into the work and leave lesions. Other problems are caused when the work is brought into direct contact with the glass; flakes of paint can be transferred to the glass, causing irreparable damage.

Similarly, wood, wood pulp and metal must never touch the artwork, nor must it be pasted to the backboard with animal glue, synthetic adhesives, rubber cement or adhesive tape. Framers must use purified starch paste, vegetable-based paste or acid-free tape. The work should be mounted onto 100 percent acid-free board, sometimes referred to as 'museum board,' at least four-ply thick. A 100 percent rag window mat or a pH-balanced cellulose mat, also at least four-ply thick, is placed on top of the museum board so that neither the glass nor the frame can touch the artwork. Generally, these two parts are attached along the top or the left inside edge, using a hinge of gummed cloth tape.

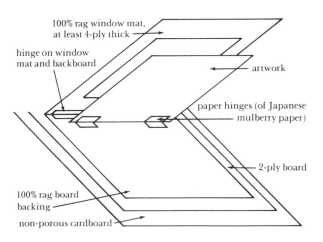

100% rag window mat, at least 4-ply thick

hinge on window mat and backboard

artwork

paper hinges (of Japanese mulberry paper)

2-ply board

100% rag board backing

non-porous cardboard

The artwork should be attached between the window mat and the four-ply board with archival Japanese tissue, generally placed at the upper right and left-hand corners. Any more hinges might create problems, causing the work to buckle as the environment, especially the humidity, changes. The artifact should be allowed to hang freely from the hinges and not have anything touching or pressing against it — the window mat, the glass or the frame. Another two- or sometimes even four-ply sheet of rag board, depending on the size and weight of the artwork, should be placed behind the backboard and, for additional protection, a third layer of nonporous, acid-free cardboard attached. All should be carefully sealed with a dust protector made from nonacidic materials.

Instead of conventional glass, the glazing material should be the new, specially-treated, ultraviolet filtering, (or UF) Plexiglass. However, because of its high buildup of static elecricity, this acrylic plastic should not be used to glaze chalk, charcoals, pastels and certain fancy embroidery because it could cause paint flaking or detachment of loose bits of material. Although UF filters out some normal visible light, it does not completely retard fading. Therefore, use subdued lighting on exhibits at home. The actual frame should be carefully considered too. Wooden frames can cause problems if the wood acids are allowed to transfer or migrate onto the mat or even the artwork. Some framers are now using a special acrylic tape to slow down or counter any adverse reactions. Metal frames or those coated with baked enamel might be best.

According to conservator John Moore, there is no way to tell if the museum mounting you've paid for has actually been done, unless you open the piece afterward. This will, of course, undo much of the work. Therefore, Sandra Lawrence,

A c. 1750 needlework on silk after it was exposed over a period of decades to an acidic paper background and closely placed nails. The edges became discoloured and very brittle. Nothing can be done to repair or restore the damage. *(Photo:HWF)*

Frame Concepts in Toronto and president of the Toronto chapter, explains that all participants are offered courses in framing and conservation given by such experts as Zuppinger and Lawrence. "We are not an anonymous group. People can call me for advice," she says. "And I will also act to settle disputes between our members and the public."

Other Factors Affecting Art & Antiques

Humidity levels in the home should be kept at between 40 and 50 per cent; mildew, which causes 'foxing' (small brown stains), sets in above 70 percent; below 30 percent acute brittleness can occur. Temperatures should be constant at between 68 degrees F and 70 degrees F. To avoid excessive summer heat, rooms should be air-conditioned; modern air filtering systems and humidifiers are important for the maintenance of framed works of art and furniture.

Collectors should also be aware of the impact of sea air on most framed pieces. The tiniest speck of salt with its high moisture content can activate the growth of micro-organisms. Tobacco smoke, too, will leave a residue that can cause discolouration and significant weakening of the textile fibers.

Before buying a framed work of art, ask the vendor to remove it from its frame for examination. If he refuses to do so *before* the transaction is finalized, do not buy the piece. One Canadian collector recently acquired a watercolour-needlework combination from a respected American dealer who specializes in textiles. Before the deal was concluded over the telephone he sent her a glossy photograph (8" x 10") of the piece, and when she questioned some marks, he assured her she had no cause for concern, it was in 'mint condition.' Because of potential insurance problems the vendor insisted

the Art Gallery of Ontario's chief conservator, tells collectors to "ask about conservation or museum-quality framing, question the framer, check his credentials. And get a second opinion. Do a little investigating." She gets miffed when people spend $20,000 on a painting and then balk at a further $500. "Insurance protects the investment; so does proper framing."

Besides word of mouth and referrals from friends, Lawrence suggests consulting those framers who are accredited members of the Professional Picture Framer's Association, which has chapters in Windsor, London, Toronto, Hamilton and soon in British Columbia and Alberta. Angelina Masterangelo, owner of on payment prior to delivery, and the purchaser agreed. When the needlework arrived, she was delighted with it but had certain misgivings when she saw the obvious flaws. Through unforeseen circumstances, three weeks passed before the piece could be examined by a professional textile conservator. When taken out of its frame, signs of earlier restoration became apparent. The silk threads used to reinforce the back of the fabric and repair a few rips were held in place with animal glue.

The interaction of the fragile silk, a biodegradable, organic substance, with the strong and dried-on acidic glue, as well as with the water-soluble colour of the painting, had caused so much damage that it was impossible to restore the piece.

The vendor repudiated all responsibility for the flaws, refusing to compensate the collector who, ultimately, had to look upon the purchase as a somewhat costly learning experience. It had, however, taught the collector to withhold payment until after a work can be thoroughly examined by an expert.

Restoration

Fixing, repairing or restoring antiques has become a complex issue, often debated among museum personnel and connoisseur collectors. Intrinsically, pieces must never be *made* to look like new and nothing of the original work must be removed. Repairs must never be allowed to change the physical appearance of an item or make it into something it was not intended to be. Novice collectors are often guilty of doing just that; converting oil lamps into electrical fixtures, turning armoires into stereo and liquor cabinets; stripping original paint off country furniture; making lamps out of old pumps and vintage decoys; or transforming rare, old telephones into

modern equipment. Any of those actions not only destroy the character and antiquity of a piece but also reduce its value.

Honest restoration such as repairing a major break extends the life of an artifact and makes it usable again, although signs of legitimate wear and tear should not be removed. Yet, the question remains how much restoration is permissible. Most experts condone minor repairs, providing they are fully documented with before-and-after photographs. Novice collectors should not be in a hurry to restore an artifact, especially if there is a chance of eventually selling it or giving it away. Advanced collectors prefer buying pieces in the rough so that they can control the amount of "fixing" which will be done.

Good conservators are difficult to find. They rarely advertise, and dealers are often reluctant to recommend the ones they are using. I visited a number of them at their studios and workshops in the Toronto area, and the results of my conversations are recorded in the following pages. They are not the only professionals in the country but their known competence and ethics can serve as a yardstick for others. If you cannot find an equally qualified expert in your area, the people I mention may be able to recommend someone to you. When writing, enclose a self addressed stamped envelope.

Paper Conservation

In the past, paper conservators rarely were available to private collectors as most were exclusively employed by museums and archives. Besides, collecting prints, photographs, maps, legal documents, early advertisements, letters, broadsides and similar papers is a relatively new field because, traditionally, paper was thrown out.

John Moore is a graduate from Toronto's Ryerson Polytechnical Institute in photographic art. He worked at the Ontario Archives for a while and then completed his studies with a paper conservator from England. After being employed by the City of Toronto Archives for five years he set up his own business in 1981.

The workshop houses every piece of modern equipment to handle the most difficult conservation tasks — a fume hood with activated charcoal filter to eliminate toxic odours, sinks, presses, a copy stand, a vacuum table, drying racks and light tables.

Moore is asked to do a lot of surface cleaning, remove background stains, watermarks and stains caused by tape, grease, oil and fat which attack the pulp of the paper. To treat the scattered brown marks, i.e., foxing, a special bleaching process is required, and stripping off old glue from the backings of maps, photographs and watercolours is an especially delicate operation which must be done before the piece can be mounted on acid-free backgrounds. Moore is also called upon to repair tears, some with parts missing and others that show small "feathers." He believes that a fine line exists between the conservator and the forger. "In some ways it is more difficult with paper because you do fill-ins that are not supposed to be hidden." In other words, the work might look perfect to the naked eye but by holding it up to the light you should be able to detect repairs.

Many paper conservators refuse to undertake certain tasks because of the high risk of damage. That is why paper restoration is so expensive. John Moore's prices are not based on the value of the artifact but on the work involved in restoring it. For example, lifting a paper from its background, removing the old glue and placing the piece onto a new acid-free board can cost upward of one hundred dollars.

Art Restoration

Odon Wagner studied art restoring at an academy in Vienna, Austria. He graduated in 1969 and opened his Toronto gallery shortly thereafter. One part of his business is selling old works of art, restoring them is the other. Over the years he has become a leading authority and consultant on art in Canada as well as in other countries. His work, equally divided between private clients and assignments for public institutions and insurance companies, includes cleaning and restoring watercolours, oil paintings, gouaches, drawings and maps. They may just be dirty or may have suffered fire or other damage.

Like other professional restorers, Wagner and his staff of four try to make repairs invisible to the naked eye but sufficiently noticeable when examined under ultraviolet light. "If a painting has been slashed, we do not overpaint, we merely retouch the slash with hundreds and thousands of small dots." Does restoration devalue a work of art? "Decidedly not," says Wagner. "It depreciates when the damage is done; it regains its former worth when repairs have been made."

Apart from accidental or willful damage, Wagner sighted heat as the major hazard to oil paintings. "Even a 150-watt floodlight is harmful because switching it on and off causes the canvas to expand and contract too much which, in turn, activates an organic disease within the picture." The major destroyers of watercolours are the old, acidic paper and wood backings and, especially in Canada, fluctuating humidity. It can reach 80 to 90 per cent in the summer unless the premises are air-conditioned, dropping to 15 per cent in the winter. Unless levels of at least 50 per cent are maintained so that the ground sizing cannot move up and down between the canvas and the paint layers, heavy cracking, flaking and paint loss are bound to occur. Strangely enough, paint loss generally appears at the bottom of the canvas, near the artist's signature.

Wagner recommends the one-time application of a non-yellowing varnish to protect oil paintings and eliminate the need for further treatments. He deplores the fact that modern artists are not taking advantage of these and other new materials and techniques. "People who buy their works today will have to spend a lot of money in a few years restoring them." Of all the older paintings he has worked on those by Emily Carr have caused the most problems because she used cheap packing paper and gas-based oils. Her works often were mounted on masonite or plywood and removing them from that type of backing and relining the painting is a risky operation.

Although Wagner and his employees come across many sad cases, there are some with happy endings. A man bought an A.Y. Jackson painting in Alberta in 1944. He wanted it cleaned so that he could sell it. "When we took it apart we found another signed piece on the back. We split the canvas and the man suddenly had two paintings instead of one."

Restoration work at Odon Wagner's gallery can take up to 12 weeks during the winter peak periods; 4 to 6 weeks in the summer.

Furniture Restoration

It is not as easy as it looks to refinish a piece of furniture. Many people start the job in their backyards or garages only to find, if they complete it at all, that the end results are less than satisfactory. Worse yet, the piece may have been permanently damaged.

"Sending away your furniture to be stripped by the modern dip or vat method ruins the glue joints, destroys the patina and colour, dries it out, lifts the nap and completely spoils the ther-monuclear structure of wood," according to Craig Black, a specialist restorer of eighteenth- and nineteenth century furniture. He removes overpaint with heat and chemicals which penetrate layer after layer of the paint, down to the original finish. "The vat system is not cheaper than hand-restoring a piece," says Black.

Most experienced dealers and connoisseur collectors are opposed to removing old paint from pine, maple or cherrywood Canadiana pieces. Leaving it on cuts restoration costs in half, and more importantly, the antique is not turned into something it was not meant to be by adding that modern "honey-pine" look. To blend with the original mellow red, brown and blue-green shades, Craig Black prepares a mixture of powdered milk, salt, ammonia and a colour pigment similar to the one used two hundred years ago. Urethanes or plastics are never applied. If hinges, forged nails and locks are missing from the original artifact, he will try to find old ones to replace them; if unavailable, he uses new parts, suitably rusted to fit the antique. Before replacing wooden parts, he makes a mock-up of the item in the appropriate style, and his associate, Michael Lotosky, carves a new one and paints it to match.

Black enjoys working on all early Canadian furniture, but the French-Canadian panelled pieces appeal to him most. "They are beautiful for this climate because the joints are pegged not glued, and the wood can expand or contract in any weather without suffering damage."

Porcelain Restoration

Arnis Berg repairs porcelain, bronzes, ivory, stone, marble and quartz. Most of his private customers ask that their quality pieces be mended invisibly. A museum, however, will request a visible repair job.

Berg does not recommend using repaired precious porcelain everyday because there is no guarantee that it will be water-tight. In theory impregnating a crack with forced-in resin should stop liquid from penetrating. "However," Berg explains, "as I cannot see through the porcelain, I cannot be sure that the entire area has been covered. The repair only can strengthen the piece and prevent the crack from getting longer."

His studio is crammed with interesting objects. While repairing a large blue-and-white Oriental bowl, he came across an earlier restoration from the beginning of the twentieth century which revealed brass pins or staples that had been used to hold the piece together. Other items were a commemorative pitcher with a chip missing from the spout, a marble statue that had lost one finger, ginger beer bottles, mirrors, pottery, bone china plates and crystal pieces. Although most mends were invisible, they did become apparent when examined under ultraviolet light.

Pieces are brought in or shipped from all parts of North America. Most of Berg's customers are antique dealers, moving firms, insurance companies, private collectors.

Textile Conservation

Anything that is created wholly or in part of animal, vegetable or synthetic fibers will disintegrate over time. Humidity, dry conditions, dirt, light, fluctuating temperatures, chemicals in the air, interaction of dyes with fabrics or other dyes can contribute to or hasten the demise of textiles. But because some of the pieces are aesthetically so beautiful and historically so important, most private collectors are as anxious to preserve and repair them as museum curators.

Textile conservation should be done only by professionals. In Canada until quite recently, availability was limited to museums, while private collectors had to send their pieces to the United States for repair or put them away until a qualified person could be found to look after them.

Torontonians are fortunate to have Charlotte Zuppinger whose background in fine arts, specialized training in embroidery at a Swiss school and years of experience teaching embroidery techniques in Zurich, Switzerland, have made her a textile expert. After coming to Canada she worked for fourteen years at the Royal Ontario Museum, taking care of their valuable and historically important textile collection. Mrs. Zuppinger recently retired from her position and now works as a freelance conservator for private collectors across Canada.

The interesting items brought to her workshop include samplers, tapestries, quilts and other textiles, some several years old. Before she begins to work on a piece she will outline the extent of the labour involved and provide clients with a realistic estimate. She attaches to her follow-up report a series of before-and-after photographs as well as swatches, threads and fibers used in the restoration.

Charlotte Zuppinger also washes, cleans and mounts certain textiles for framing but not without first testing their colourfastness with an eyedropper. She prefers washing a piece if it is colourfast rather than having it drycleaned, because she believes chemicals can harm old fabrics. After cleaning, the pieces are pinned to museum board and sized with every thread perfectly vertical and horizontal. Only then will she decide how much conservation work is needed. Mrs. Zuppinger explains:

> The ethics of a responsible conservator require that nothing be removed or added unless it is absolutely necessary to make

"Before" and "after" shots of the American flag which was restored by Mrs. Zuppinger. Collection: Private. *(Photo: HWF)*

the object stable and safe. My only interest is to make certain that any apparent damage will neither spread nor destroy the piece. Unlike furniture where the watchword is "restoration," I am concerned with conservation only.

Caring for Antiques

Silver

Silver tarnishes quickly, reacting with hydrogen sulphide in the air. Allowing a piece to become heavily tarnished is not a good idea since it could leave disfiguring pits on the surface of the metal when it is finally cleaned. Every time a piece of silver is cleaned with a commercial polish the dirt comes off but so too does a small amount of silver, diminishing the silver content and patina over the years.

To avoid having to clean it often, store the silver in sealed, airtight bags. If the piece is to be displayed in a cabinet, you could try using a patent silver keeper, available in some hard-

ware stores or where fine silver is sold. Every time you use your silver wash each piece separately and carefully with warm, soapy water. Also, wash it before polishing to make sure that you have taken off the dust and small bits of grit, such as salt or egg. Never put it in the dishwasher and never store spoons and forks held together with rubber bands as this creates serious oxidation that is very difficult to remove.

One of the best ways to remove tarnish from silver as well as copper and brass is by making a home-made dip. Remember, you should never put more than one piece in the dip at a time, nor should you combine different metals in the same tub.

Put a piece of aluminium tin foil in the bottom of a plastic bowl or bucket and put the metal on top. Dissolve about half a cup of washing soda in two pints of very hot water and pour it over the metal. After a while lift it out and rinse under hot water and dry with a soft cloth. If bits of tarnish still remain polish it by hand with a clean, soft cloth. Should stubborn bits of tarnish still be visible, you then might have to use a commercial cleaner.

Brass

It is safe to try commercial polish on brass however if it is still grungy, mix a tablespoon of salt and a tablespoon of vinegar in a half pint of hot water. Use very fine steel wool and dab the brass with the solution. It shouldn't be necessary to apply too much pressure. Wash in hot water and dry. Some experts also recommend using a rust remover for those very stubborn bits of tarnish.

My cleaning lady once attacked my brass bed with ketchup claiming that it works wonders. Always eager to learn new tricks, I watched but, alas, all that happened was that she made more work for herself and used up half a bottle of condiment sauce. Forget that recipe.

Copper

Neglected copper will acquire green patches. Try the dip recommended for silver. If that doesn't work try the mixture recommended for brass (not the ketchup) although it isn't adviseable to use steel wool. Wash the solution off in hot water and dry carefully.

Furniture

Apply wax to furniture once in a while, not every week. Heavy waxing over prolonged periods of time can harm wood. As well, be careful when you buy furniture that it hasn't been subjected to years of heavy-handed wax. You might consider removing some of the wax build-up with a mixture of four parts mineral spirits to one part linseed oil. Place some of this on a soft cloth and rub on the furniture. It will only affect the wax polish and dirt, not the finish or the veneer.

Sometimes white patches, caused by wet glasses, will etch a white ring into the polish. To remove, apply a liquid metal polish or auto paint cleaner on a soft damp cloth, rubbing slightly. Repolish or wax lightly. Slight scratches can be rubbed out with a metal polish or hidden by polishing with shoe polish.

There are many good wax polishes on the market, to find the one available in your area, ask a reputable furniture dealer. Stay away from spray polishes which often contain harmful additives. You could try making the following beeswax mixture which keeps for a long time in a sealed jar. Put some beeswax in a jar and cover with genuine turpentine for a few days. Eventually the beeswax will dissolve to a thin cream consistency. Put a little of the mixture on a soft cloth and rub in a circular motion. At first put a lot of pressure on the cloth but gradually ease up. Use a clean, soft cloth for one last light polish.

Remember that furniture is just as susceptible to damage from uncontrolled humidity, temperature and light as are art and textiles. Ultraviolet rays can warp, crack and discolour furniture, as well as framed works of art,.

Until recently, antiques had to be kept in darkened rooms or stored in acid-free containers. Now windows can be treated with a film that cuts out between 79 to 99 per cent of the sun's rays. (Currently it is produced by the 3M Company and was developed about twenty-eight years ago, for the space programme). It can be applied to the inside of storm windows. The clear type makes glass shatter-proof; however, most conservators prefer the smoke-coloured variety because it cuts out glare, ultraviolet rays and 33 percent of radiant heat. The film can be applied to all windows in a house in less than one day. Ultraviolet rays also can be eliminated, in this manner, from fluorescent tubing and some firms will apply the film to glass placed over pictures and other art works. For more information about companies specializing in this type of work, contact your local museum or historical site.

The experts I mentioned in this chapter all are excellent craftspersons. However, there are many others in Canada who are just as competent.

Before having a piece refinished, restored or repaired by anyone, check his/her credentials carefully. Don't be afraid to ask questions, obtain references, examine the work they have done. If possible, watch them while they do it. If their workmanship and philosophies are radically different from the professionals mentioned here, think twice about using their services.

Sources of Information
Conservators
Porcelain Marble, China, Figurines, Dolls, Soapstone, Bronze, etc.
Arnis Berg Restorations, 178-1/2 Davenport Road, Toronto, ON M5R 1J2.

Textile
Charlotte Zuppinger's Workshop. (Can only be reached by phone: 416-424-2754 for appointment.

Paper
John Moore, PO Box 26, Station H, Toronto, ON M4C 5H7, or 2186 Danforth Avenue, Toronto, ON M1C 1K3.

Art
Odon Wagner Gallery Limited, 194 Davenport Road, Toronto, ON M5R IG2.

Furniture
Craig Black, 1024 Dupont Street, Toronto, ON M6H 1Z6.

Supplies
Archival supplies, such as 100 per cent museum quality mounting boards, storage and document boxes, envelopes, sleeves for postcards, stereoviews, slides, archival tape, etc., can be purchased by writing to the following:
The Hollinger Corporation, PO Box 8360, Fredericksburg, VA 22404.

APPENDIX 1

Antique Magazines, Journals and Newsletters

CANADA
Antique Showcase
Amis Gibbs Publications Ltd
Hwy. 169, PO Box 260
Bala, ON P0C 1A0
Subscription Information: Published 13 times a year; 1 year, $28; 2 years, $48; U.S. subscribers add $7 a year.
Small magazine format. Contains ads from dealers, auction houses, show promoters and a number of articles, some coverage of shows and auctions. Owned by antique dealers.

Century Home
12 Mill Street South
Port Hope, ON L1A 2S5
Subscription information: published 7 times annually; 12 issues are $30. U.S. subscribers add $12.
This is a glossy magazine with some colour. It features many articles of interest to antique collectors and those involved with furnishing and decorating a vintage home.

The Upper Canadian
PO Box 653
Smiths Falls, ON K7A 4T6
Subscription information: published 6 times a year; 1 year, $18; 2 years, $32.
Newsprint journal. Contains ads from dealers, auction houses, show promoters. Coverage of Ontario and Quebec auctions, shows. Folk art and Country or Canadiana slant. Owned by a dealer, therefore slightly biased towards promoting the marketplace from a dealer's perspective.

The Woodbridge Advertiser
Box 9
Loretto, ON L0G 1L0
Subscription information: published 48 times a year; $20.02 a year.
Newsprint journal style. Contains lists and announcements of country type auctions.

GREAT BRITAIN
Antique Collecting
The Antique Collectors' Club
5 Church Street, Woodbridge
Suffolk, England IP12 IDS
Subscription Information: published 11 times a year; U.S. subscribers, $35; Canadian subscribers, $45.
This glossy magazine is jammed with all manner of auction and show news. Complete with excellent quality articles.

The Antique Collector
National Magazine House
72 Broadwick Street
London, England W1V 2BP
Subscription information: published monthly; Canadian subscribers pay £40 for one year.
This is a glossy, slick magazine full of high quality colour photographs and informative articles pertaining to fine and decorative arts.

Antiques Trade Gazette
116 Long Acre
London, England WC2E 9PA
Subscription information: published weekly. Canadian subscribers pay approximately $50 for one year's subscription. Write for details. Geared to the trade; reporting auctions news, gossip. Contains news of trials, stolen artifacts, new collector groups, etc.

Apollo
22 Davies Street
London, England W1Y 1LH
Subscription rates: $112 to U.S.; £70 to Canada.
Glossy & professional.

Collectors Gazette
The Rosery, New Place
Uckfield, East Sussex
England TN22 5DP
Subscription information: published 10 times a year.
This newspaper is produced for collectors of toys, dolls, models, etc. Founded twelve years ago. Potential subscribers can order from Regent Street Toy Co. Inc, 550 Parkside Drive, Unit 17B, Waterloo, ON N2L 5V4.

The Map Collector
48 High Street
Tring, Herts
England HP23 5BH
Subscription information: £28 to Canada & U.S. air speed service, one year; £54 for two years; £80 for three years.
A quarterly journal for lovers of early maps. This magazine was first published in December, 1977 and has, over the years, become the leading medium of communication between collectors, researchers and dealers. Each issue features articles, news pages, letters, the latest auction prices, a collectors' marketplace, etc. A must for those involved with this aspect of collecting.

THE UNITED STATES
Americana
29 West 38th Street
New York, NY 10018
Subscription information: published 6 times a year; 1 year, $14.97, U.S. to Canada.

This glossy magazine is features American tradition with articles on historic places, antiques, crafts, cooking, preservation and travel.

Antiques
575 Broadway
New York, NY 10012
Subscription information: Send subscriptions to PO Box 1975, Marion, Ohio 43306-2075. Rates are $50 U.S. to Canada.
Also known as *The Magazine Antiques*, this magazine has been the undisputed bible for antique enthusiasts for more than 52 years. It is professional, glossy, full of colour photographs, tantalizing advertisements, and excellent (non controversial) articles.

Antiques & Auction News
PO Box 500
Mount Joy, PA 17552
Subscription information: published weekly; one year, $65 U.S.
Newsprint journal of interest to those who are into collectibles. Jammed with lots of short articles, press releases, syndicated columns, news.

Antiques & the Arts Weekly
c/o *The Newtown Bee*
The Bee Publishing Co. Inc
Newtown, CT 06470
Subscription information: published weekly; air mail service for one year, $160; surface mail for one year, $15. U.S. funds only.
This newsprint journal is stuffed with advertisements, show coverage and other interesting articles, press releases and tidbits.

Antiques & Collecting: Hobbies
1006 S. Michigan Ave.
Chicago, IL 60605

Subscription information: published 12 times a year; 1 ycar, $32 to Canada.
Glossy magazine format, formerly known as *Hobbies*. Of interest to nostalgia, ephemera and doll collectors.

Antique Review
(Formerly called the *Ohio Antique Review*)
PO Box 538
Worthington, OH 43085
Subscription information: published 12 times a year; one year, $20 U.S.; two years, $35 U.S.
This newsprint journal, now into its 16th year of business, has lots of ads, and show/auction coverage of interest to country collectors.

Antique Souvenir Collectors News
PO Box 562
Great Barrington, MA 01230
Subscription information: this 12-page glossy newsletter appears six times a year. The subscription ($18 U.S. to Canada) includes one free 25-word ad in each issue. Newsletters are mailed third class. For first class delivery, add $5 U.S.
The marketplace for antique souvenirs of all types.

The Antique Trader Weekly
PO Box 1050
Dubuque, IA 52001
Subscription information: published weekly; one year, $51 to Canada.
Newsprint journal of interest to nostalgia collectors. Numerous ads for artifacts and shows. Light on article content.

Art & Antiques
PO Box 840
Farmingdale, NY 11737-9740
Subscription information: ten issues, $39 U.S. to Canada.

This is a slick, glossy magazine full of high quality colour photographs, wonderful advertisements and excellent articles.

Art & Auction
250 Wcst 57th Street
New York, NY 10019
Subscription information: published 11 times a year; $42 to U.S.; $54 to Canada.
This is a glossy magazine full of informative articles, auction coverage, advertisements. Lots of colour. Excellent quality photographs.

Barr's Post Card News
Chett Barr, Editor
70 S. Sixth Street
Lansing, OH 52151
This journal carries notices of mail auctions and new book information. They also publish a weekly postcard newsprint journal called *Barr's News*. Write for costs.

The Buyer's Guide
700 E. State Street
Iola, WI 54990-001
Subscription information: published weekly. One year to U.S., $27.95; Canadian subscribers add $40 U.S.
For comic book enthusiasts.

Collectors News & the Antique Reporter
506 Second Street, PO Box 156
Grundy Center, IA 50638
Subscription information: twelve issues a year are $25 U.S. to Canada
This newsprint journal has been on the scene for more than 30 years. According to the editor, they have more than 14,000 subscribers. Articles, calendars, lots of advertisements. Of interest to nostalgia buffs as well as those involved with porcelain and country objects.

Collectors' Showcase
Subscription Service Center
PO Box 837
Tulsa, OK 74101
Subscription information: nine issues a year are $46 U.S. to Canada.
This is a slick, glossy magazine of interest to nostalgia and ephemera collectors.

The Clarion
c/o The Museum of American Folk Art
61 West 62nd Street
New York, NY 10023
Subscription information: published quarterly, and comes free with membership to the museums. Dues are $35 for an individual or $50 for family. Canadians are asked to send an extra $5.00 U.S. to cover higher mailing expenses.

Connoisseur
1790 Broadway
New York, NY 10019
Subscription Office:
PO Box 7154
Red Oak, IA 51591
Subscription information: the magazine does not contain a rate card or information about costs on the mast head. For details write to the subscription office directly but this magazine is available on the newsstands in Canada, the U.S. and Great Britain. (Cost per magazine in Canada is $3.00) Once devoted solely to art and antiques the magazine now contains a variety of articles of interest to collectors, especially those with a great deal of money at their disposal. It is slick, glossy, and full of excellent colour photographs and well-written articles.

The Daze
Box 57JL
Otisville, MI 48463
Subscription information: $5 U.S. to Canada for three years or $18 U.S. to Canada for one year. A single current copy is $2.
This newsprint journal is dedicated to those who love and collect depression glass. The journal is stuffed with advertisements for related reference books, pieces, dealers, shows, auctions, etc. It also has some informative articles and warnings about reproductions and fakes.

The Decoy Hunter Magazine
B. Giacoletto, Editor
901 North Ninth Street
Clinton, IN 47842
Subscription information: publishes six issues a year; $15 U.S. to Canada.

Decoy Magazine
Joe Engers, Publisher
PO Box 1900
Montego Bay Station
Ocean City, MD 21842
Subscription information: publishes six issues a year; $25 for one year, $30 U.S. to Canada; two years are $45 U.S. and $55 U.S. to Canada.
This is a glossy magazine with black and white as well as colour photographs.

Doll Reader
Hobby House Press, Inc.
900 Frederick Street
Cumberland, MD 21502
Subscription information: published eight times a year; $36 U.S. to Canada.
This glossy, slick magazine should be of interest to all doll collectors. Not only are there a great many ads and announcements but the articles and photographs are excellent.

Glass Collector's Digest
PO Box 553
Marietta, OH 45750
Subscription information: published 6 times a
year; one year is $20 U.S.
A small, but thick and glossy digest. Should be
imperative for all those interested in, or curious
about, glass.

IFAR Reports
26 East 70st Street
New York, NY 10021
Subscription information: $50 U.S. to Canada
and U.S., and $65 U.S. for commercial sub-
scribers.
The International Foundation For Art Research
(IFAR) is a non-profit organization which works
to prevent the circulation of stolen, forged or
mis-attributed works of art. The monthly magazine includes the *Stolen Art Alert* in addition to
articles pertaining to art theft, fraud and forgery.
They have been instrumental in many recoveries
and receive frequent inquiries from art dealers,
museums, law enforcement officials, insurance
companies and private collectors from all over
the world, requesting information from their archives. The Stolen Art Alert section of the
maga-zine publicizes information on the most
recently stolen works of art in a specific catalogue form. This is stored in their Art Theft Archive containing, at this date, over 34,000 items.
With this resource, they offer an Art Theft
Search Service as well as an Art Authentication
Service, which exists to resolve controversies
concerning the authenticity of works of art.
These services are available on a fee basis.

The Inside Collector
PO Box 98
Elmont Branch
Elmont, NY 11003

Subscription information: published 9 times a
year; one year is $38 U.S.
This glossy magazine is aimed at those involved
with collectibles, nostalgia & ephemera. The
articles are well-written and the photography is
excellent, mainly colour. Good show and auction coverage.

Kovels on Antiques & Collectibles
PO Box 22200
Beachwood, OH 44122
Subscription information: published monthly;
one year $25; two years, $45 U.S.
Newsletter format. Short articles with pictures.
News about newly published books; warnings
about reproductions and fakes; collecting ad-
vice, buyer's price guide, questions and answers.

The Maine Antique Digest
PO Box 645
Waldoboro, ME 04572-0645
Subscription information: published monthly;
one year, $29 U.S.; two years $50 U.S. Canadian
and foreign subscribers add $12 U.S. per year.
Newsprint journal. Contains marketplace information of special interest to those involved with
folk art and country artifacts. Innovative, a ba-
rometer of Americana. Covers antique shows
and auctions in depth with photographs, reviews
of books etc. Some Canadian coverage.

The McCoy Collectors Newsletter
Sean & Kathy Lynch
12704 Lockleven Lane
Woodbridge, VA 22192
This newsletter has been published since 1986.
Write for details and subscription information.

New England Antiques Journal
4 Church Street
Ware, ME 01082

Subscription information: published monthly; one year, $35 U.S.; two years, $55 U.S.
Newsprint journal very much like *The Maine Antique Digest*.

The New York/Pennsylvania Collector
Wolfe Publications Inc.
Fishers, NY 14453
Subscription information: published monthly; one year, $25; two years, $35.
Newsprint journal with lots of ads, calendars, news coverage.

The Old Toy Soldier Newsletter
209 North Lombard Avenue
Oak Park, IL 60302
Subscription information: published six times a year; one year, $18, bulk rate mail; one year, $28, first class mail. Sample copies, $3.
Continuously published since 1976. Useful articles, big photos, ads and news. Britains and Dimestores in every issue. Total coverage from lead to composition to plastic. New toy soldier releases, show calendar, announcements. Forty plus pages an issue. This is a magazine written for collectors by collectors.

The Pen Fancier's Magazine
c/o Suzie Lawrence
1169 Overnash Drive
Dunedin, FL 34698
Subscription information: $35 U.S. to Canada.
They feature articles about pens, their manufacturers and tips on repairs, etc.

Political Collector
420 Madison Avenue
York, PA 17404
Subscription information: published monthly; $15 U.S. to Canada.
Newsprint journal with computer style printing (slightly hard on the eyes). Involved with almost anything political such as posters, pin back buttons, sheet music, prints, presidential campaign posters, ribbons, etc. The April, 1990 issue had an excellent article by Canadian Scott Wallace, entitled "Anti-Americanism in the 1988 Canadian Election." Illustrating the article were seven free trade related pin back buttons.

Teddy Bear and Friends
Hobby House Press Inc.
900 Frederick Street
Cumberland, MD 21502-1298
Subscription information: published six times a year; $23 U.S. to Canada.
This slick, glossy magazine is a must have for those involved with teddy bear collecting.

The Tin Type Magazine
11970 Borden Avenue,
San Fernando, CA 91340
Write to the editor, Darryl Rehr for information. This magazine is devoted to antique advertising as it appears on tins.

Vintage Fashions
Hobby House Press Inc.
900 Frederick Street
Cumberland, MD 21502-9985
Subscription information: bi-monthly; $28 U.S. to Canada.
This magazine showcases the fashions of yesterday with in-depth articles, and lots of colour photography. If you are interested in vintage clothing, accessories, jewelry, care and repair, then this publication should be sliding through your mailbox regularly.

APPENDIX 2

Auction Companies

The following is a list of major Canadian and American auction companies. Those in the United States have been included to allow Canadian collectors to compare their terms and conditions should they wish to dispose of items that may be of interest to American collectors.

While most of the companies surveyed responded quickly, a few chose not to answer despite repeated letters of inquiry; hence this list is not complete.

These auction companies are not necessarily recommended above all others. Selecting the appropriate gallery must be the responsiblity of the individual collector.

Canadian Auction Houses

BRITISH COLUMBIA
Lunds
Auctioneers & Appraisers Ltd.
926 Fort Street
Victoria, BC V8V 3K2
President — Peter A. Boyle
Commission rate — below $1,000 is 17%; above $1,000 is 15%
Dealer's commission rate — lower for dealers
Buyer's premium — 5%
Reserves and buy-ins — sometimes 5%
Settlement — one week after auction
Insurance — do not charge clients as they hold no special policy for merchandise on premises; separate insurance policy can be arranged through their agent
Photography — no charge
Cartage rates — cartage can be arranged through the auction company. Charge to be deducted from final invoice.
Additional information — in business since 1955.

Maynards
Auctioneers
415 West 2nd Avenue
Vancouver, BC V5Y 1E3
President — Barry Scott
Antiques and Art — Patricia M. Kelly
Commission rate — 12-1/2% to 20%
Buyer's premium — 10%
Reserves and buy-in fees — none
Settlement — 2-3 weeks after auction
Photography — no charge
Cartage — Consignors responsibility financially.

ONTARIO
Christie, Manson & Woods International Inc.
Suite 416, 94 Cumberland Street
Toronto, ON M5R 1A3
President — Suzanne E. Davis
Christie's do not hold auctions in Canada. The Toronto office "acts as liason between our international salesrooms and Canadian clients, for both the buying and selling of property." Despite repeated, request, Christie's, New York did not reply to the survey.

D. & J. Ritchie Inc.
Auctioneers-Appraisers
429 Richmond Street East
Toronto, ON M5A 1R1
Proprietors — Marlene and David Ritchie
Commission rate — 20% for items $500 or less; 10% above $2,000; from $500 to $1500, 10%.
Dealer's commission rate — a special rate can be arranged for dealers who regularly contribute to Richie auctions.
Buyer's premium — 10%

Reserves and buy-in fees — 10% of final floor bid.

Settlement — 35 days after auction

Insurance — no charge

Photography — black-and-white, $25–$50; colour, $125–$400

Cartage — consignors can pay direct or charges can be deducted from final invoice.

Additional information — check with gallery for price of annual subscription, and for catalogues and listings of prices realized. Noted on flyers and catalogues: "A deposit of $20 is required to obtain a bidding number. This amount will be refunded or applied towards purchase upon return of the number." In business for twenty years. Canadian-owned, family-run.

Dupuis Auctioneers & Appraisers

The Colonnade
Suite 431, 131 Bloor St. W.
Toronto, ON M5S 1R1
President — Ronald Dupuis
Commission rate — $5,000 or more, 10%; $1,000 to $4,000, 15%; less than $1,000, 20%.
Dealer's commission — $5,000 or more, 6%; $1,000 to $4,000, $10%; less than $1,000, 15%.
Buyer's premium — 10%
Reserves and buy-in fees — information not supplied
Settlement — 35 days after sale
Insurance — 1.5% of selling price
Photography — black-and-white is $50; colour $150
Additional information — this is the only auction firm in North America that specializes and handles only jewelry.

Joyner Fine Art Inc.

222 Gerrard Street East
Toronto, ON M5A 2E8
President — Geoffrey Joyner

Commission rate — 10% on items sold for $5,000 or more; 15% on items sold for $1,000 to $4,999; 25% on items sold for less than $1,000.

Dealer's commission rate — special rate for dealers

Buyer's premium — 10%

Reserves and buy-in fees — 3% for dealers; 5% for non-dealers

Settlement — 35 days after auction

Insurance — on premise coverage $15 per $1,000 realized; waiver option available

Photography — black-and-white, $50, small; $100, large. Colour $400, small; $800, large

Cartage — arranged, if requested, at seller's risk and expense

Additional information — appraisals for insurance, probate, family division and other purposes; fees on request. Joyner's is the leading Canadian-owned auction firm specializing in sales of Canadian art.

Phillips Ward-Price Ltd.

5A Thorncliffe Ave.
Toronto, ON M4K 1Y4
President — Jack Kerr-Wilson
Commission rate — 15% on lots sold for less than $1,000; 10% on lots sold for $1000 or more
Dealer's commission rate — available on request
Reserves and buy-ins — no charge although there is a minimum charge of $50 per lot whether sold, unsold or withdrawn.
Settlement — 35 days after auction
Insurance — $1 per $100 realized
Photography — black-and-white, 1/2 page or more, $100; black and white, less than 1/2 page, $50; colour, $800.
Cartage — consignors can make own arrangements or else charges can be deducted from final invoice.
Additional information — appraisals are $1,000

per day; $500, per half day, $250 minimum charge, but these figures can vary according to circumstances. Travel and out of pocket expenses are additional.

Robert Deveau Galleries
297-299 Queen Street East
Toronto, ON M5A 1S7
President — Robert Deveau
Commission rate — 25% for articles up to $1,000; 20% over $1,000
Dealer's commission rate — a special rate available on request
Buyer's premium — 10%
Reserves and buy-in fees — none
Settlement — 30 days after auction
Insurance — no charge
Photography — no charge
Cartage — consignors responsible
Additional information — evaluation fees: in metropolitan Toronto and within a radius of 25 miles, $150. Appraisal fees for works of art, antiques and Oriental rugs up to $50,000, 1-1/2% on items exceeding this amount. In business since 1967.

Sotheby's
9 Hazelton Ave
Toronto, ON M5R 2E1
President — Christina Orobetz
Commission rate — 20% of bid price on lots sold for less than $1,000; 15% of bid price on lots sold for $1,000 or more but less than $5,000; 10% on bid price on lots sold for $5,000 or more.
Dealer's commission rate — 15% of bid price on lots sold for less than $1000; 10% of bid price on lots sold for $1,000 or more but less than $5,000; 6% of bid price on lots sold for $5,000 or more.
Buyer's premium — 10%

Reserves and buy-in fees — 5% per lot for the general public and 3% per lot for dealers.
Settlement — 35 days after auction
Insurance — for goods receipted on premises, 1% of bid price or reserve if property unsold; for goods receipted off premises and transported to premises, 1-1/2% of bid price or reserve if property unsold.
Photography — black-and-white, $50 for quarter page; $80 for half page; $100 for full page; colour, $800
Cartage — consignors can pay direct or Sotheby's will deduct charges, plus a 10% handling fee, from final invoice, provided approved cartage company is used.
Additional information — appraisals for insurance and other purposes, fees vary according to the nature and amount of work to be undertaken. Evaluation for auction purposes can also be made at your home.

Waddington, McLean & Co. Ltd.
(Waddington's)
189 Queen Street East
Toronto, ON M5A 1S2
President — Ronald McLean
Commssion rate — catalogue sale: on lots up to $5,000, 15%; over $5,000, 10%; regular sale, 25%
Dealer's commission rate — based on value of consignment
Buyer's premium — 10%, applicable only at catalogue sales
Reserves and buy-in fees — no charge
Settlement — 30 days after auction
Insurance — no charge
Photography — $20, $40, $60 for black-and-white; $500 for full page colour; $250 for half-page colour
Cartage — to be arranged by client or with a cartage company suggested by Waddington's

Additional information — appraisals for insurance purposes, 1% of appraised amount up to $50,000; one-half of a percent thereafter with a minimum of $100 or $750 per day. Appraisals for sale purposes: 1% with a minimum of $100, refunded if sold through Waddington's. Out of town appraisals, $750 per day. In office verbal appraisals, no charge. A wholly Canadian-owned company, in business for 140 years.

NEW BRUNSWICK
Tim Isaac Antiques
97 Prince William Street
Saint John, NB E2L 2B2
Owner — Tim Isaac
Commission rate — 20%
Buyer's premium — None
Reserves and buy-ins — "avoid them unless absolutely necessary"
Settlement — seven days following the auction
Insurance rates — no charge
Photography — catalogues not illustrated
Appraisal fee — $50 per hour
Additional information — in business for 22 years

NOVA SCOTIA
Country Auction Sales
RR 1, Petite Riviere
Lunenburg County, NS B0J 2P0
President — Robert J. Getson
Commission rate — 20% if on location, add 5% for cartage if items have to be transferred to auction hall
Dealer's commission rate — 15%
Buyer's premium — none
Reserves and buy-in fees — seldom put reserve bids on any items unless they are important, nor do they allow buy-ins
Settlement — within one week after auction
Insurance rates — no charge

Photography — no catalogues
Cartage — consignor is responsible
Additional information — in antique business for sixteen years; also deal in secondhand goods and collectibles.

QUEBEC
Hotel des Encans de Montréal
4521 boul. St. Laurent
Montréal, PQ H2T 1R2
President — Martine de St. Hippolyte
Commission rate — 10% for lots over $500.
Dealer's commission rate — 10%
Reserves and buy-in fees — no charge
Settlement — 30 days after auction
Insurance — no charge
Photography — no charge
Cartage — at expense of consignor or can be deducted from final invoice
Additional information — free appraisals Tuesday and Thursdays for sale purposes. One catalogued sale each month. Planning to open an office in New York City with the first sale taking place September 24, 1990 at the Meriden Hotel on 57th Street.

Pinney's Auctions
5627, Rue Ferrier
Ville Mont-Royal
PQ H4P 2M4
President — Oliver Leroy
Commission rate — 5%
Dealer's commission rate — 10%
Buyer's premium — 10%
Settlement — 30 days
Insurance — no extra charge
Photography — no extra charge for black-and-white; colour extra
Cartage fees — at seller's expense
Additional information — "We do appraisals for a fee and we have four catalogue sales a year."

THE UNITED STATES

CALIFORNIA
Butterfield & Butterfield
220 San Bruno Ave at 15th Street
San Francisco, CA 94103
Commission rate — 10% of bid price for lots sold for $7,500 and above; 15% for lots selling at $2,000 to $7,499.
Dealer's commission rate — special rate can be arranged
Reserves and buy-in fees — 5 to 10%
Settlement — 35 days
Buyer's premium — 10%
Insurance — 1 1/2% of the purchase price
Photography — black-and-white: $100 for 1/3 page; $150 for a 1/2 page; $200 for a full page — colour, $350 to $800.
Cartage — consignors can pay direct or we will deduct charges from final invoice.
Additional information — for over 125 years, Butterfield & Butterfield has been Western America's leading auctioneer and appraisers with auction galleries in both Los Angeles and San Francisco.

LOUISIANA
Morton M. Goldberg Auction Galleries Inc.
3000 Magazine Street
New Orleans, LA 70115
President — M.M. Goldberg
Commission rates — 15% and 20%
Dealer's rate — 10%
Reserves — 5%
Settlement — 30 days after sale
Insurance — 1%
Photography — $35 -$100 depending on size
Cartage — at cost
Additional information — annual mailing list, 12 catalogues for $100 a year. U.S.

MAINE
James D. Julia Inc
Box 830, Skowhegan Road
Fairfield, ME 04937
President — James Julia
Commission rates — sliding scale
Dealer's commission rate — sliding scale
Buyer's premium — 10%
Reserves and buy-in fees — no buy-ins allowed but will consider reserves on items of substantial value
Settlement — approximately 35 days after auction
Insurance — no charge
Photography — no charge
Cartage — cartage to be negotiated; charge deducted from final invoice
Additional information — conduct no only general antique auctions but also special catalogued sales of decoys, antique lamps, toys and dolls, advertising, rare glass.

Maritime Auctions
PO Box 322, 935 U.S. Route 1
York, ME 03909
Commission rate — 10%
Dealer's commission rate — none
Buyer's premium — 10%
Reserves and buy-in rates — none, but if an item is withdrawn, consignor pays 5% of estimated low price
Settlement — 14 days after auction
Insurance — no charge
Photography — no charge
Cartage — consignor's responsiblity
Additional information — specialize in nautical maritime and firehouse antiques. In business for 30 years.

MARYLAND
Theriault's
PO Box L5L
Annapolis, MD 21404
Proprietors — George and Florence Theriault
Commission rate — 24% of realized price
Dealer's commission rate — none
Buyer's premium — none
Reserves and buy-in rates — none
Settlement — no later than 35 days after auction. If consignor requires immediate payment, the company will offer the seller fair market price outright, i.e. the estimated auction price, minus 30%.
Insurance — no charge
Photography — No charge for black-and-white; colour, $60; $600 for full-colour catalogue cover. No charge if the company decides to place a colour picture on the cover.
Cartage — transportation included. International fee to be paid by consignor.
Additional information — specialists in auctioning antique and collectible dolls. Accept absentee bids on all lots in catalogue. Also offer free evaluations by mail. In doll auction business since 1977.

MASSACHUSETTS
Richard A. Bourne Co. Inc.
Estate Auctioneers and Appraisers
Box 121
Hyannis Port, MA 02647
President — Richard A. Bourne
Commission rate — 20%, negotiable on major lots
Dealer's commission rate — 20%
Reserves and buy-in fees — none
Settlement — within 30 days of auction
Insurance — no charge
Photography — no charge
Cartage — normally provided by auction house

Additional information — only estate appraisals. Charge, $50 minimum up to $500 per day. No charge for appraisal if estate is consigned to them. Noted for handling antique arms, marine artifacts, decoys, antique glass, antique dolls and toys, paintings, and specialty items within these categories. Hold about twenty catalogue sales a year.

Robert C. Eldred Co. Inc
PO Box 796
East Dennis, MA 02641-0796
Commssion rate — 15% for private consignors
Dealer's commission rate — 10%
Buyer's premium — 10%
Reserves and buy-in fees — 5 to 10% of reserve
Settlement — within 30 days
Insurance — 1% of low side of estimated price
Photography — no charge
Cartage — no charge
Additional information — special area of expertise is Oriental and Japanese art, books, Americana, marine art, fine art of all kinds. In business for over 40 years. In office verbal appraisals for up to three items, free. Written appraisals in office, min. $35 for single item.

Robert W. Skinner
Bolton Gallery
Route 117
Bolton, MA 01740
President — Robert W. Skinner, Jr.
Commission rate — 5% on lots of less than $500; 10% above
Dealer's commission rate — none
Buyer's premium — 10%
Reserves and buy-in fees — none
Settlement — within 14 days after sale; painting auctions within 30 days
Insurance — no charge
Photography — no charge if transport consign-

ments valued at $10,000 or more at no charge; smaller consignments for a nominal fee. Out-of-town or out-of-state cartage negotiable.

Additional information — Appraisals in gallery up to six items, $50 for estates and insurance, $50 per hour to be applied to travel time with a minimum of $200. Will consider partial or full rebate on appraised property consigned for auction. Particular expertise, American furniture, also disposes of antiques, jewelry, toys, dolls, American Indian art and artifacts, and textiles. In business 26 years.

NEW HAMPSHIRE
Richard W. Withington, Inc.
Hillsboro, NH 03244
Commission rate — 10%
Dealer's commission rate — do not sell for dealers
Buyer's premium — 10%
Reserves and buy-in fees — do not allow reserves
Settlement — within 48 hours of auction
Insurance — no charge
Photography — no charge
Cartage — no charge, but not applicable to out-of-town and out-of-state consignments.

NEW YORK
William Doyle Galleries Inc.
175 East 87th Street
New York, NY 10128
Chairman — William Doyle
Commission rate — 10% to consignor for items sold over $3,000; 15% for items sold for $1,000 to $3,000; and 20% for items sold for under $1,000.
Dealer's commission rate — same
Buyer's premium — 10%
Insurance — no charge
Photography — no charge

Cartage — work with recommended truckers. Cost can be deducted from sale price or billed directly to client.
Additional information — full appraisal service except for insurance. Unlike other larger galleries, offer to purchase outright individual items or entire estates. In business for more than 20 years.

Phillips, New York
406 East 79th Street
New York, NY 10021
Commission rate — 10% on goods over $500; 15% under
Dealer's commission rate — special rates negotiable
Buyer's premium — 10%
Reserves and buy-in fees — 5% of reserve price
Settlement — 35 days after auction
Insurance — 1% per $100
Photography — $50 black-and-white; $500, colour
Cartage — consignors pay cartage
Additional information — in business (in England) since 1796.

Sotheby's
1334 York Avenue
New York, NY 10021
Commission rate — 10% for each lot sold for $7,500 or more, 15% for each lot sold for $2,000 or more but less than $7,500 and 20% for each lot sold for less than $2,000.
Buyer's premium — 10% plus tax
Reserves and buy-in fees — 5% if reserve not met
Settlement — 35 days after auction
Insurance — 1–1-1/2% of reserve price
Photography — half page, $200; quarter page, $100; full page $300. Full page colour, $900. Fees vary depending on consignment.

Cartage — vendor's responsiblity.
Additional information — "Experts will provide a verbal evaluation and estimate at no charge. Written appraisals for every purpose can be arranged for a reasonable fee."

OHIO
Garth's Auctions Inc.
Box 369, 2690 Stratford Road
Delaware, OH 23015
President — Tom Porter
Commission rate — 20% on items $50 or over; 25% under $50 of gross proceeds; 14% on merchandise selling for $5,000 and over.
Dealer's commission rate — none
Buyer's premium — none
Reserves and buy-in fees — none
Settlement — 15 business days
Insurance — 1.75% of appraised value
Photography — no charge
Cartage — can be arranged; charges deducted from final invoice
Additional information — in business since 1952. Specializes in Americana.

PENNSYLVANIA
Freeman/Fine Arts Co. of Philadelphia, Inc.
1808 Chestnut Street
Philadelphia, PA 19103
Chairman — Samuel Freeman, II
Commission rate — 10% for lots over $1,000 and 15% for lots selling at $1,000 or less
Dealer's commission rate — same as above
Reserves and buy-in fees — reserves permitted; buy-in at 5%
Settlement — 30 days for catalogued auctions; 14 days for general sales
Insurance — optional; 55¢ per $100
Photography — at our discretion and no charge unless piece withdrawn
Cartage — may be deducted from proceeds

Additional information — any item proven to be unsalable is subject to $25 per item dumping fee. Appraisals for insurance: $250 minimum, $750 full day. Appraisals for estate purposes: $200 min.; $500 full day. In continuous operation since 1805.

Pennypacker-Andrews Auction Centre Inc.
1540 New Holland Road
Kenhorst, Reading, PA 19607
Owner/auctioneer — Cathy M. Pennypacker-Andrews
Commission rate — 15% and 20%
Dealer's commission rate — 15%
Reserves and buy-in fees — 15% and 20%
Settlement — 10 working days after sale
Insurance — no charge
Photography — charge for colour pictures
Cartage — pick-up, pack and transport at consignor's expense, deducted from final invoice.
Additional information — appraisals are 1% of appraised value. Minimum fee is $300.

WASHINTON, D.C.
Adam A. Weschler & Son
Auctioneers and Appraisers
905-9 E. Street, N.W.
Washington, DC 20004
Commission rate — 20% on items up to $500; 15% on items up to $1500; 10% above that amount.
Dealer's commission rate — negotiable
Buyer's premium — 10%
Reserves and buy-in fees — 5% of highest bid received. Consignor pays 15% of the pre-sale estimate if item withdrawn.
Settlement — 30-days after the auction for catalogue consignors. Weekly consignors receive their monies the week following the sale.
Photography — black-and-white, $50; colour, $300.

Insurance — 25 cents per $100 on catalogue items only

Cartage — consignor responsible

Additional information — hold nationally advertised catalogue sales for sprecific categories approximately 20 25 times a year. Non catalogue sales every Tuesday. A family operated business since 1890.

APPENDIX 3

Miscellaneous Clubs for Collectors

(Additional organizations are listed in the individual chapters.)

Arts and Crafts

The Craftsman Homeowner's Club
31 South Grove Street
East Aurora, NY 14052

The Craftsman Home Owner's Club is a modern day society for the Arts and Crafts Era enthusiast. The focus of the Club and newsletter is information regarding the Arts and Crafts lifestyle, not only as it applies to the house and garden but also its philosophy and social action. The newsletter consists of feature articles by Arts and Crafts experts with a good balance of editorial comment and background information. Reprints, ads and excerpts from Arts & Crafts period books and magazines are of particular interest. Four appropriate seasonal issues are planned with a Holiday catalogue in the planning stages. Membership costs $25 U.S. a year and includes special benefits.

Roycrofters-at-Large

PO Box 41
East Aurora, NY 14052

This is a group of interested and concerned persons who find inspiration and delight in the writings of Elbert Hubbard, the crafts and books produced at the Roycroft Shops and the Roycroft Campus Buildings in East Aurora. Members are invited to join to help promote the ongoing Roycroft Renaissance. Membership is $15, U.S., annually which includes newsletters, educational programs, annual convention, etc.

AUTOGRAPHS AND MANUSCRIPTS
The Manuscript Society
350 N. Niagara Street
Burbank, CA 91505
The Society was founded in 1948 as The National Society of Autograph Collectors. Currently they publish a quarterly journal *Manuscripts* and a newsletter sent to members. Membership is $25 U.S.

The Universal Autograph Collectors Club
Chris Wilson, Secretary
PO Box 6181
Washington, DC 20044-6181
This is the largest organization for autograph collectors in the world, boasting over 1,500 members. *The Pen and Quill*, the renowned bi-monthly journal is sent to all members; $18 to Canada.

AUTOMOBILES
Antique Automobile Club of America, Inc.
501 W. Governor Road
PO Box 417
Hershey, PA 17033
This is the oldest and largest automotive historical society, founded in Philadelphia in 1935. Currently it boasts over 50,000 members from all parts of the world. The AACA holds meets and events, tours, meetings, conferences and workshops. There are 375 regions and chapters. Membership is $18 U.S. and includes bi-monthly copies of *The Antique Automobile*, a glossy, professional historical magazine.

Automobile License Plate Collectors Association
Bob Bittner
30 Edwardel Road
Needham, MA 02192

Membership is $22 U.S. to Canada a year — includes newsletter — established in 1954 — 420 members from PEI to BC — and all through the United States.

Georgian Bay Steam, Auto, Gas, Antiques Association
Shirley Corbyn
RR 4
Sunderland, ON L0C 1H0
This year this organization is celebrating their 25th anniversary. First year of membership is $25; after that it is $5; for women & $15; for men. Junior under 18 years is $5.

Vintage Sports Car Drivers Association Ltd.
PO Box 1451
Chicago, IL 60690
Dues are $30 per year and comes with a magazine format newsletter.

AVIATION
The Canadian Aviation Historical Society
National Headquarters
Station A, PO Box 224
Willowdale, ON M2N 5S8
This is a non-profit organzation dedicated to the preservation of Canada's aviation history. Members may be interested in specializing in one or all of the following areas: photography, WW I and II aviation; aircraft registrations; books collections; aviation philately; aircraft restoration, etc. A newsletter is mailed at inver-vals containing an exchange of membership interests. *The Journal*, published quarterly, contains a variety of articles from the very early days of flight to quite recent times. Subjects covered have included ballooning and gliding along with all aspects of military and civil aviation. Membership for one year is $30.

BARBED WIRE
The Kansas Barbed Wire Collectors Association
c/o Chamber of Commerce
PO Box 716
La Cross, Kansas 67548
Membership is $6 U.S. a year, established in 1967, approximately 50 members.

BELLS
The Bell Collectors' Club of Ontario
c/o R. Roy
RR 2
Binbrook, ON LOR 1CO
Membership is $5 a year, payable to R.G. Roy. Currently have about 100 members, established in 1965.

BLUE-AND-WHITE-STONEWARE
Blue & White Pottery Club
224 12th St. N.W.
Cedar Rapids, IA 52405
The Blue & White Pottery Club was formed in June, 1981. Membership includes copies of the newsletter which is published on a quarterly basis; August, November, February and May; free advertising in the newsletter; access to membership lists and an annual convention held every June. Dues are $10. U.S.

BOOKPLATES
The American Society of Bookplate Collectors and Designers
605 N. Stoneman Avenue #F
Alhambra, CA 91801
Quarterly publications entitled: *Bookplates In The News,* established in 1970 and the *Year Book* now number fifty volumes published since 1922. Membership is $45 and includes both publications.

BRICKS
The International Brick Collectors Association
Dr. Ronald P. Anjard, Sr.
10942 Montego Drive
San Diego, CA 92124
This organization has over 300 international members who participate in two annual swap meets and enjoy the journal which is published six times a year focussing on brick technology, history, collecting and collectors. Membership is $10. U.S.

BUTTONS
The National Button Society
Lois Pool, Secretary
2733 Juno Place
Akron, OH 44313
Membership is $15 U.S. and includes National Button Bulletin, which is printed five times a year. This club boasts more than 2400 members.

CANDY CONTAINERS
Candy Containers Club of America
PO Box 1088
Washington, PA 15301
or write to:
Virginia L. Plunkett
Public Relations Chairperson
RR 5
8 Southview Drive
Boonton Township NJ
Dues are $18 a year which include the cost of the bi-monthly publication called *Candy Gram.* They hold a convention each year and have a membership of 400.

Antiques

CAROUSEL ANIMALS
The American Carousel Society
Craig Knight
1015 Munich Street
San Francisco, CA 94112-4505
Membership is $15 U.S.

CAST IRON SEATS
The Cast Iron Seat Collectors
Charlette Traxler
RFD 2, Box 40
Le Center, MN 56057
There are about 500 members in the United States, Canada, Ireland, England, Wales, Australia and New Zealand. Believe it or not, there are currently four books available on the subject. Membership of $10 U.S. includes the yearly meetings, held in the summer in conjunction with a threshing show, and a newsletter with many want ads, articles, etc. As well as seats, collectors in this club are also interested in cast iron corn planter lids, tool boxes and covers, windmill weights and drill box ends and tools of all kinds.

CIGARETTE PACK COLLECTORS
The Cigarette Pack Collectors Association
Dick Elliott, President
61 Searle Street
Georgetown, MA 01833
This club was formed in 1976 with six members. Today it boasts more than 250 members, worldwide. Most members concentrate on full packs of obsolete U.S. brands, but there are also collectors of cigarette advertising, international brands, tins, books and premiums. Since 1976 there have been three conventions in North Carolina. Dues are only $5 a year, U.S., which includes a subscription to the bimonthly newsletter, *Brandstand*.

COMPACTS
The International Compact Collectors Club
PO Box "S"
Lynbrook, NY 11563
Members are involved and engrossed in the collecting of ladies powder compacts. The newsletter, published quarterly, appropriately called *Powder Puff* features three important columns under the following headings: Seekers, Sellers & Swappers. So far, of the 300 members, 4 are Canadian; in planning stages now is the 1991 NY convention. For details, dates, etc. write to the club directly. Membership is $20 U.S. to Canada.

CLOCKS AND WATCHES
National Association of Watch & Clock Collectors
Chapter 33
c/o G. Gibbins
16 Nursewood Road
Toronto, ON M4E 3R8
Membership: $30 for chapter membership and $32 for National membership. (Must be a member of the National Association to belong to local chapter.) There are also chapters in Belleville, London, Montreal, Ottawa and Vancouver.

National Association of Watch and Clock Collectors, Inc.
514 Poplar Street
Columbia, PA 17512-2130
Annual dues are $25 U.S. Add surface or air mail, to this amount. Surface to Canada is $7 US extra or $22 U.S., air mail. Membership includes subscription to the bulletin, participation in National Conventions, etc. More than 32,000 members around the world.

COCA-COLA MEMORABILIA
Ontario Cola Collectors
1548 Glenhill Crescent
Mississauga, ON L5H 3C5
Established in 1982 this group has about 65 active members. Membership is $8 per year and includes a newsletter.

COOKIE CUTTERS
The Cookie Cutter Collector's Club
Ruth Capper
1167 Teal Road S.W.
Dellroy, OH 44620
Membership is $6 U.S., established in 1972; approximately 600 members; quarterly newsletter entitled *Cookie Crumbs*, sent to members.

DECORATIVE ARTS
The Canadian Society of Decorative Arts
Box 4, Station B
Toronto, ON M5T 2T2
This is a non-profit national organization founded to promote the applied arts and design in Canada, particularly of the twentieth century. Allying architects, artists, designers, crafts-men, curators, collectors, scholars and the general public, the Society was created to support exhibitions, collections and study of these arts across the country. The *Bulletin*, published four times a year in English and French, illustrates and reports on important exhibitions, collections, meetings and issues in Canada and abroad. Membership is $35 a year.

DISNEYANA
The Mouse Club
2056 Cirone Way
San Jose, CA 95124
The Mouse Club began in 1979 and judging from a selection of their reading material this is a very enthusiastic, fun-loving, devoted group of collectors who host an annual convention, complete with a show/sale and publish a monthly magazine. Membership is $22 U.S.

DOLLS
Madam Alexander Doll Club
PO Box 330
Mundelein, IL 60060
Write for details and costs.

The Ottawa Dollcraft Guild
31 Hillview Road
Nepean, ON K2H 5G6
Membership is $12 a year which includes a bi-monthly newsletter.

The United Federation of Doll Clubs
2814 Herron Lane
Glenshaw, PA 15116
This is an international organization of clubs and members-at-large for doll collectors. It began over 50 years ago with the founding of the National Doll & Toy Collectors Club in New York City. As this club expanded to include clubs all over the country, it provided the nucleus for what would soon become The United Federation of Doll Clubs. UFDC is divided in 17 Regions with a Director for each. Region 16 is the International Region which services collectors outside the USA. There are about 17,000 members. To belong to UFDC a person must be 18 years of age or older and must have a collection of at least 10 dolls. Membership includes a subscription to the doll magazine *Doll News*, which comes out quarterly. National dues are $15 per year for club members and $17.50 a year for members at large (more to Canada.)

DOORKNOBS
The Doorknob Collector
PO Box 126
Eola, IL 605 19-0126
Membership to Canada is $20 U.S. which includes a newsletter, published six times a year and ranges from 8 to 14 pages per issue. The club was formed in 1976, has about 180 members and holds an annual convention.

EPHEMERA
The Ephemera Society (Canadian branch)
Barbara Rusch, President
36 MacAuley Drive
Thornhill, ON L3T 5S5
Membership costs $25 a year which includes the Canadian newsletter as well as the bulletins produced by the sister American organization. The Society was established in 1987 and meets every other month in Toronto.

The Ephemera Society
PO Box 37
Schoharie, NY 12157
This is the founding Ephemera Society on which the Canadian branch is modeled. Write for costs and details.

FANS
Fan Association of North America (FANA)
505 Peachtree Road
Orlando, FL 32804
FANA currently has about 300 members; 225 from North America and 75 scattered throughout the world. Dues are $20 U.S.; $25 to Canada; membership includes a quarterly bulletin. There is a FANA Assemblage, held in various locations throughout North America, once a year for four days. Previous meetings have been in New York City, Washington DC, Boston, Dallas, Philadelphia and Vancouver.

The Fan Circle International
Dawn Dyer
79A Falcondale Road
Bristol, England BS93 JW
The Fan Circle International is a society established in 1975 to promote interest in and knowledge of the fan. In 1982 it was granted charitable status. Membership is world-wide, the majority of members residing in Europe, Australia and the U.S.A. Members receive copies of the bulletin, published 3 times a year, containing articles on a wide variety of topics such as the care and conservation of the fan; the fan's place in social history; prices fetched at the auction sales; reports on exhibitions and relevant books. There are also articles and correspondence from members, advertisements and notices about forthcoming sales and meetings. The advent of the new Fan Museum in Greenwich — the first museum in the world devoted solely to the fan, will provide a great deal of input into the bulletin. Membership to Canada and the U.S. is $23 a year.

FLOW BLUE
Flow Blue International Collectors Club
291 E. Jefferson Street
Brooksville, FA 34601
Yearly dues $30 U.S., includes newsletter *The Blueberry Notes*, published about 6 times a year.

GAMES
American Game Collectors Association
4628 Barlow Drive
Bartlesville, OK 74006
The American Game Collectors Association (AGCA) maintains an archive of games, game instructions and historical information about games and their manufacturers. It accepts donations from people who want to see their games preserved and used by game researchers. As

well, the AGCA publishes a newsletter, *Game Times*, three times a year. Dues are $20 U.S.

The American Antique Deck Collectors Club
(playing cards)
PO Box 1002
Westerville, OH 43081
Membership dues: $15 U.S.; includes copies of quarterly publication, *Clear the Decks*. As well, the club holds three or four mail auctions a year.

GLASS
The American Cut Glass Association, Inc.
3228 S. Boulevard, Suite 271
PO Box 1775
Edmond, OK 73083-1775
This is a non-profit organization devoted to the study and research of American Brilliant Period Cut Glass. It was formed in 1978 by 35 cut glass enthusiasts and today has a membership of 1,200, plus. The newsletter, *The Hobstar*, published ten times yearly, contains information and educational articles and photos on all aspects of cut glass. They also have available for purchase, reprints of catalogues from thirteen of the old glass cutting companies. There are sixteen regional chapters through the United States and their annual conventions feature programs on glass conducted by well known speakers, exhibits of rare pieces, an auction and a dealer's show. Membership is $25 U.S.

Glasfax (District III)
John Waba
907-35 Widdicombe Hill
Weston, ON M9R 1P2
There are two active groups, one based in Toronto and the other in London, Ontario. Write to this address for details and costs.

Glass Knife Collectors
c/o Adrienne Escoe
PO Box 342
Los Alamitos, CA 90720
This newly formed organization will publish a newsletter, *The Cutting Edge*, for glass knife enthusiasts shortly. Write for details and costs.

Heisey Collectors of America, Inc.
PO Box 4367
169 West Church Street
Newark, OH 43055
Membership is $25 U.S. plus $15 yearly dues. ($40 the first year and $15 thereafter) Membership includes the 24 page monthly publication, *Heisey News*, which contains informative articles, profiles of former employees, information on reproductions, Heisey for sale, questions and answers, new finds, dealer directory and club news.

The Lilliputian Bottle Club
13271 Clinton Street
Garden Grove, CA 94543
Club membership is $15 U.S. and it includes a bi-monthly bulletin.

The National Early American Glass Club, Ltd.
Membership Chairman
PO Box 8489
Silver Spring, MD 20907
The NEAGC is involved in the study and appreciation of glass, regardless of type and period. Membership includes *The Glass Club Bulletin* published three times annually; *Glass Shards* which is published twice annually and access to their National Glass seminars which are held every spring in various cities across the U.S. Individual membership is $15 U.S.

NATIONAL GLASS CLUBS
PO Box 416
Cambridge, OH 43725
The national glass collecting clubs listed below have each been organized to help the collector and is dedicated to the education of the collector and the preservation of their particular type or manufacture of glassware. If interested in any of the societies or clubs listed, write to the National Glass Clubs, address above, for information and details.

Collector clubs belonging to the National Glass Clubs are for collectors of Fenton Art Glass, Depression Glass; Imperial Glass and Duncan Glass.

The Sandwich Historical Society
PO Box 103
Sandwich, MA 02563
They hold meetings once a year; publish a newsletter, *The Cullet*, and a scholarly journal once a year. Write for details.

GRANITEWARE
National Graniteware Society
PO Box 326
Albarnett, IA 52202
Yearly membership dues are $12 U.S. including quarterly newsletter.

HATPINS
The International Club for Collectors of Hat Pins and Hat Pin Holders
15237 Chanera Avenue
Gardena, CA 90249
Founded in 1977 by Lillian Baker, the author of the definitive book on the subject, this organization currently has more than 400 members, world-wide. Membership provides an official membership card and the monthly newsletter called *Points*, as well as a 32 page pictorial journal. *Points* is mailed the first of each month except for June when the Pictorial Journal is issued. (July and August are dark.) Conventions are held during 'even' years. Seminars are on the 'odd' years and both take place at various locations in the United States. Initially the dues are $35 U.S., which includes a one-time assessment for office expenses. After that there is a yearly renewal fee of $25. (And, out of interest, some collectors are beginning to refer to this collecting area as 'hatpinology.')

INFANT FEEDERS
The American Collectors of Infant Feeders
Jo Ann Todd, Secretary-Treasurer
5161 West 59th Street
Indianapolis, IN 46254
Membership is $25 U.S., and it includes a quarterly newsletter appropriately entitled, *Keeping Abreast* which runs between 40 and 50 pages. It's currently in its 17th volume. Some members collect nursing bottles, while others are heavily into infant and invalid feeders. Most enjoy the additional collecting of go-withs which consist of pictures, puzzles, sterilizers, bottle warmers, post cards, advertisements or just about anything related to infant feeding.

INKWELLS
Society of Inkwell Collectors
5136 Thomas Ave South
Minneapolis, MN 55410
Membership is $22.50 which includes a subscription to *Stained Finger*. This newsletter includes profiles of collectors, featured inkwells, repair and cleaning, networking, auctions, classified market place.

IRONS

The Smoothing Iron Collectors Club

c/o A.H. Glissman

4400 Park Drive

PO Box 215

Carlsbad, CA 92008

The Midwest Sad Iron Collectors Club (3915 Bay St., Des Moines, IA 50317) is the only formalized meeting group in the U.S. (None in Canada.) This club was founded in 1984 in Minnesota with 24 family names. Now it boasts over 260 names in 37 States, Australia, Canada, England, France and Holland. A convention is held annually. Between meetings members will be kept abreast of the hobby of sad iron and trivet collecting through a periodic newsletter that will serve as an information exchange. Yearly membership dues are $10 U.S. per family.

KALEIDOSCOPES

The Brewster Society

Suite 602, 100 Severn Ave

Annapolis, MD 21403

The society was established in 1986 and currently has about 600 members. They publish a quarterly newsletter and have a yearly convention, usually in Kentucky. Membership is $25 a year and $5 U.S. extra for Canadians.

LIGHTING

Aladdin Knights of the Mystic Light

(Aladdin coal oil mantel and early electric lamps, as well as a few others.)

J.W. Courter

Route 1

Simpson, IL 62985

This club has published their newsletter, *The Mystic Light* since 1973. Write for costs of membership and information about their annual convention.

The Historical Lighting Society of Canada

PO Box 561, Station R

Toronto, ON M4G 4E1

They publish a bimonthly bulletin called *The Illuminator*. Write for more details on membership costs, etc.

Night Light

Bob Culver

38619 Wakefield Court

Northville, MI 48167

For collectors of miniature oil lamps. The quarterly newsletter will keep members up-to-date with collecting, buying and selling, and the marketplace. Membership is $10 U.S.

The Rushlight Club, Inc.

Suite 196, 1657 The Fairway

Jenkintown, PA 19046

The club was founded in 1932 in Boston and is one of the oldest organizations dedicated to the study of one phase of antiquity. The purpose is to "stimulate an interest in the study of early lighting including the use of lighting devices and lighting fuels, and the origins and development of each by means of written articles, lectures, conferences, exhibition ... and its object shall be to collect, preserve and disseminate information and data obtained through these studies." Annual dues are $20 U.S. Membership includes a quarterly newsletter, providing information on Club and member activities, meeting notices, special projects and events. Reprints of early pamphlets or catalogs are distributed to members as part of their membership; an annual Directory of the membership is sent out; an extensive reference library is maintained at the Old Academy Library at Wethersfield, Ct.; and a quarterly publication called *The Rushlight*, devoted to technical articles, research, photographs, illustrations and the history, development and application of lighting, lighting fuels, accessories, etc. is mailed to members.

LOVE TOKENS
The Love Token Society
Lloyd Entenmann
130 Cornell Road
Audubon, NJ 08106
The Society was formed after a conversation between two love token enthusiasts in 1971 and has grown and flourished since then. A bimonthly newsletter, appropriately called *The Love Letter* is mailed to all members. Included are articles, news, names of new members, advertisements, and events. Two coloured slide programs on Love Tokens and Love Token Jewelry may be borrowed to show at meetings, the only charge being the postage. One of the first objectives of the group is to promote interest in numismatics, particularly in the field of 'Engraved Coins.' Membership is $10 U.S.

LUNCH BOXES
Lunch Box Collecting
Box 481
Cambridge, MA 02140
Annual membership is $20 U.S. and it includes the new magazine, *Hot Boxing*, which has lots of ads, market tips, features and profiles, auctions prices, and so on.

MAPS
The Hermon Dunlap Smith Center for the History of Cartography
The Newberry Library
60 West Walton Street
Chicago, IL 60610
Annual North American membership is $8 U.S. Includes *Mapline*, the quarterly newsletter.

MARBLES
The Canadian Marble Collectors Association
Craig Gamache
23-271 Wellington Crescent
Winnipeg, MB R3M OA1
Membership is $10 per year and members receive the newsletter called *Swirls* four times yearly. Only 35 members so far since the organization was just recently formed.

MATCHCOVERS
The Rathkamp Matchcover Society (RMS)
c/o John C. Williams, Secretary
1359 Surrey Road
Vandalla, OH 45377-1646
RMS was organized at the home of Ken Riggs in Pocasset, Massachusetts, in 1941. The name of the group honours Henry Rathkamp, one of the best known hobby pioneers in the 1930s and the collector who came up with the idea of an annual gathering. Membership in RMS is open to all collectors who have an interest in the hobby. Dues are $12 for the first year, $10 thereafter. Members receive a roster of over 1500 collectors; six club bulletins a year; tips for new collectors and a list of local clubs. An annual convention is held each August.
Similar Canadian clubs can be contacted by writing to the following:

Northern Lites
2770 Aquintaine Ave., #817
Mississauga, ON L5N 3K5

Phillu-Quebec
Mr. Aube
8220 Oregon
Brossard, PQ J4Y 2J7

Southern Ontario Match Cover Collectors
Box 219
Caledonia, ON NOA 1AO

Trans-Canada Match Cover Collectors
2/1505 Upper Middle Road
Burlington, ON L7P 4M5

MILITARY ITEMS
Association of American Military Uniform Collectors
Don Darmos
1200 N. Quarry Road
Amherst, OH 44001
Membership is $17.50 U.S. and includes a copy of *Footlocker*, the quarterly newsletter.

MUSIC RELATED ARTIFACTS
(See sheet music listing under PAPER)
The American Musical Instrument Society
c/o Shrine Music Museum
414 East Clark
Vermillion, SD 57069-2390
The American Musical Instrument Society is an international organization founded in 1971 to promote study of the history, design, and use of musical instruments in all cultures and from all periods. Each year the Society publishes an issue of the *AMIS Journal* and three issues of the *AMIS Newsletter*. The *Journal* presents scholarly articles on the history, design and use of musical instruments; the Newsletter disseminates information on worldwide activities, book lists and comments and short articles of general appeal to curators, collectors, performers and others interested in musical instruments. Regular membership is open to individuals upon payment of annual dues of $25 U.S. Members receive the *Journal* and the *Newsletter* as well as mailings about activities of the Society.

NIPPON CHINA
International Nippon Collectors' Club
22 Millpond
No. Andover, MA 01845
Membership is $25 U.S. and this includes a quarterly newsletter.

NUMISMATICS
The Topical Numismatics Society
3708 Nipomo Ave.
Long Beach, CA 90808
This group consists of collectors whose coins and bank notes are based on themes or topics such as birds, reptiles, fish, ships, etc. In other words they collect money solely for the sake of the art work on it. It is the only association of collectors devoted to all aspects of topical numismatics. Contact them directly for information about membership, costs, etc.

OCCUPIED JAPAN ITEMS
The Occupied Japan Collectors Club
c/o Florence Archambault
29 Freeborn Street
Newport, RI 02840
Membership of $15 U.S. includes the montly newsletter published 11 times a year.

PAPER ITEMS
(Including adverting, books, newspapers, poster, prints, sheet music, sports cards and post cards.)

The Big Little Book Collector's Club of America
Larry Lowery, President
PO Box 1242
Danville, CA 94526
This club holds two meetings a year, publishes a guide, and a bimonthly newsletter called *The Big Little Times*. Membership to Canada is $10 US a

year, and they they currently have about 500 active members.

Deltiologists of America
(Postcard collectors)
PO Box 8
Norwood, PA 19074
This is an international postcard society for postcard collectors, dealers and enthusiasts. Members receive six bi-monthly issues of *Postcard Classics*. Membership is $15 U.S. for six issues (1 year); $27.50 U.S. for 12 issues, (2 years).

The National Sheet Music Society
Marilyn Brees, Secretary
1597 Fair Park Avenue
Los Angeles, CA 90041
Membership includes a 40 word listing in the newsletter (published 10 times a year) and yearly directory as well as a free listing in their 'market place.' For U.S. and Canada dues are $15 U.S. This Society was established in the late 1950s and its aims include the increase and dissemination of knowledge about America's music and teaching the historical and cultural value of this music, believing that "the story of a nation is told in its songs."

Newspaper Collectors Society of America
Box 19134
Lansing, MI 48901
Established in 1884 this society currently has more than 335 members. Dues are $23 U.S. to Canada. Available for $1 U.S. (Cash) is a handy booklet, entitled *A Primer on Collecting Old & Historic Newspapers* by Rick Brown. It is filled with advertisements, information, advice and data about reprints, the papers that novice collectors might be 'taken' with. It also includes a price guide for British and American newspa-

pers. Membership in NCSA is $18 to Canada, U.S. funds and it includes a newsletter.

The Toronto Postcard Club
PO Box 6184, Station A
Toronto, ON M5W 1P6
Membership in Canada is $10; to USA $15 and overseas, $20. Included is the Newsletter called *Cardtalk*, published three times a year. In addition Cardmart, is published for advertisements only. There are four other Canadian clubs based in Burlington, Ontario; two in Halifax, Nova Scotia; and Vancouver, BC. For addresses and more information write to the Toronto Postcard Club, attention President, Wilf. Cowin.

PENCILS
The American Pencil Collectors Society
Arthur T. Iberg
491 Pike Drive E
Highland, IL 62249
Membership dues, which includes a subscription to *The Pencil Collector* newsletter (published since 1955) is $7 U.S. Each member received a copy of the current membership directory with more than 300 names and addresses.

PHONOGRAPHS
The Antique Phonograph Collectors Club
502 E. 17th Street
Brooklyn, NY 11226
Established in 1973 this organization boasts 2,000 members. Membership of $18 U.S. to Canada includes copies of their quarterly newsletter entitled: *The Antique Phonograph Monthly*.

The Canadian Antique Phonograph Society
Bill Pratt, Treasurer
122 Major Street
Toronto, ON M5S 2L2
In its 23rd year, this organization currently has

241 members. They meet eight times a year on Sundays between 1 and 5 p.m., and the programme consists of some area of collecting and an auction. Annual membership dues are $15 which covers the cost of producing and distributing eight newsletters which notify members of upcoming programmes and other events, describe past auction results and provide articles of interest to the phonograph and record collector.

The Michigan Antique Phonograph Society
2609 Devonshire
Lansing, MI 48910
The Michigan Antique Phonograph Society (MAPS) was established in 1976 and currently has about 550 members. Membership of $16 U.S. a year includes the newsletter appropriately entitled *In the Groove,* giving members a source of information about technical and historical subjects, advertisements, announcements, etc. The Constitution indicates the purpose of the Society which is to provide information and entertainment for people interested in collecting and restoring antique phonographs, music boxes and their records, cylinders or discs and to assist the newcomer to the hobby by promoting authentic restoration and repair of damaged or worn machines; to rescue old records before they are destroyed and lost.

Photographica
American Society of Camera Collectors, Inc.
4918 Alcover Ave.
North Hollywood, CA 91607
Send out monthly bulletins; have two shows a year, and charge $20 U.S. for membership.

The Calgary Photographic Historical Society
PO Box 3184, Station B
Calgary, AB T2M 4L7
Write for details and costs.

Club Daguerre-Darrah
2662 Victoria
Wichita, KS 67216
Write for details and costs.

The Photographic Historical Society of Canada
PO Box 115, Postal Station S
Toronto, ON M5M 4L6
This organization is a very active group promoting all aspects of Photographic history in Canada. They publish their magazine *Photographic Canadiana* five times a year and hold monthly meetings and two fairs each year. National Society membership is $24 a year; National and Toronto membership is $32.

National Stereoscopic Association
(Devoted exclusively to Stereo Photography and Stereoviews.)
PO Box 14801
Columbus, OH 43214
Membership to Canada is $46 U.S. *Stereo World* magazine is published bi-monthly with 40 or more pages in each issue. Lavishly illustrated, this journal provides high-quality reproductions of stereo views on coated paper.

Western Canada Photographic Historical Association
Box 33742
Vancouver, BC 90607
Write for details and costs.

Political Artifacts
American Political Items Collectors
Joseph Hayes, Secretary
PO Box 340339
San Antonio, TX 78234
The American Political Items Collectors, founded in 1945, is a non-profit membership

organization dedicated to the study and preservation of materials relating to political campaigns of the United States of America. All types of items are collectible: buttons, ribbons, posters, glassware, canes, autographs, photographs, prints, ballots, jewelry, sheet music, books and pamphlets. A growing segment of the hobby is the collection of cause items such as women's suffrage, prohibition, war and liberty bonds and labour organizations. Membership includes APIC newsletter, Keynoter as well as a monthly subscription to the Polical Bandwagon, access to meetings and much more. Canadian dues are $26 U.S.

Canadian Political Memorabilia Club
Grant Harper, President
303-2020 Urquhart Road N.W.
Calgary, AB T2N 4C5
This newly formed club, established in April, 1990, sends a newsletter to members, about once every two months. Annual dues are $5. Most members collect political buttons and pins but some are involved with political postcards, posters, stickers, political speeches/tapes, literature, etc.

RADIOS

The Antique Wireless Association, Inc.
Box E
Breesport, NY 14816
This non profit club, established in the early 1950s boasts approximately 3500 worldwide members. Membership of $10 U. S. includes access to the *Old Timers Bulletin,* published quarterly. In addition, the association sponsors several annual historical 'meets' in the U.S. and Canada.

The Ontario Vintage Radio Association
T. Catton
197 Humberside Ave.
Toronto, ON M6P LK7
A prerequisite for admission to and continued membership of the Club is that all members must take an active part in the meetings and activities of the club. The group is interested in the promotion and preservation of Canada's wireless (radio) history. Annual dues are $10 and they meet four times a year.

The New England Antique Radio Club
RR 1, Box 36
Bradford, NH 03221
The club began in 1988 with three members and has grown to a current membership of 425. They are dedicated to the restoration, collection, preservation and enjoyment of antique and collectible radios and TV's. Membership is $10 annually and entitles one to a one year subscription to the quarterly newsletter, the *Estcutcheon*, as well as the opportunity to reserve table space at the quarterly Swap and Sell Meets. These Meets generally feature over 75 tables of old radios, TV's, parts, books, magazines and other related items and draw crowds of over 600 people.

SALT AND PEPPERS

The Salt & Pepper Novelty Shakers Club
Irene Thornburg
Membership Coordinator
581 Joy Road
Battle Creek, MI 49017
Membership is $15 U.S. and includes a quarterly newsletter. 718 members to date.

SCALES

The International Society of Antique Scale Collectors

Bob Stein, President
11 North Canal Street, #380
Chicago, IL 60606

A prerequisite to membership in ISASC is an interest in antique scales and/or weights. There are two types of memberships: active and associate. Active members are scale collectors and associates are those who are involved with scales in a field of endeavor such as scientific, teaching, writing, publishing etc or whose regular activity has to do with scales in some general way, be it academic, journalistic or custodial. All members receive a membership directory, which is updated annually, and a quarterly magazine called *Equilibrium*. As well, the Chairman's newsletter is mailed to all members four times a year. Each issue contains news about the Society's activities and other matters of interest. Dues for both categories of membership are $40 per calendar year.

SNUFF BOTTLES

The International Chinese Snuff Bottle Society

2601 North Charles Street
Baltimore, MD 21218

The Chinese Snuff Bottle Society of America, Inc was formed in 1968 as the first society to honor snuff bottle collectors and to publish scholarly articles about snuff bottles. Members are entitled to the quarterly Journal presenting high quality articles as well as information about collectors and collections throughout the world, a membership directory by state and country as well as dealer listings and a dynamic convention held in a different location each year. Membership is $65 U.S. and $12 U.S. a year extra to Canada.

SOUVENIR CHINA

The Souvenir China Collectors Society

PO Box 562
Great Barrington, MA 01230

This organization is interested in all types of souvenir ware — plates, cups, pitchers, pin trays, salt and pepper shakers — as well as glassware, spoons, paperweights and woodware. Reflecting this broad interest, the official publication entitled *The Antique Souvenir Collectors News* is packed with articles about manufacturers, rare finds, collecting tips, classified ad section. Write to the club for details regarding membership.

SPOONS

The Minoru Spoon Club

7671 Minoru Gate
Richmond, BC V6Y 1R8

Established in 1977 as the BC Spoon Club, the name was changed in 1982, to the Minoru Spoon Club. The informative little newsletter entitled *Input*, appears 10 times a year. Dues are $9 a year to Canada; $10 for the USA and $15 overseas. The group is interested in the history and make-up of spoons. Judging by a sample newsletter there is a Canadian souvenir spoon thrust.

Spoony Scoop Newsletter

Mrs. Margaret Alves
84 Oak Ave.
Shelton, CT 06484

For hobby souvenir spoon collectors. Yearly dues are $10 U.S.

TEDDY BEARS

Good Bears of the World

PO Box 8236
Honolulu, Hawaii 96815

Membership is $13 US and includes copies of quarterly publication known as *Bear Tracks*.

TELEPHONES
Antique Telephone Collectors Association
Box 94
Abilene, KS 67410
Membership is $30 a year, U.S.; established in the early 1970s and have over 2,000 International members. Monthly newsletter.

THIMBLES
Thimble Collectors International
c/o Dorothy Friend
1300 Lake Shore Drive
Chicago, Il 60610
(Or to the president, Mrs. Rose Kerchner, 631 Abington Ave., Glenside, PA 19038.)
Dues are $20 to Canada. Membership includes a quarterly bulletin.

Titanic Collectibles
The Titanic Historical Society, Inc.
PO Box 51053
Indian Orchard, MA 01151-0053
The Society will be of interest to those who are curious about the history of great ocean liners of the past, particularly the White Star Line. For the yearly membership of $25 U.S., one receives access to research staff, free admission to the Marine Museum at Fall River, four current issues of *The Titanic Commutator*, with original photos, articles, announcements, advertisements, etc.

TOOLS
Early American Industries Association
PO Box 2128
Empire State Plaza Station
Albany, NY 12220-0128
For nearly 60 years the EAIA has served the needs of people interested in tools and trades of yesteryear. They publish periodicals and reference works about early American tools, crafts and industries; offer related publications to its members through a Book Sales program; published *The Directory of American Toolmakers*, containing information on over 10,000 North American makers and dealers; sponsors meetings to exchange information and tools; maintains a lending library of related materials and holds annual meetings. *Chronicle* is published quarterly providing excellent articles and a section for members to write in their comments and questions. *Shavings* comes every two months with current news, information on regional tool collector groups and notices of antique tool sales catalogues and auctions. Individual membership is $22 annually. Canadian applicants please add $5 and make payment in U.S. funds.

TOOTHPICK HOLDERS
The National Toothpick Holder Collectors Society
Audrey Trumbold, Secretary
PO Box 204
Eureka, IL 61530
Membership is $10 U.S. and includes a monthly bulletin with information on pattern identification, reproductions and new issues, price trends, reference material, questions and answers. As well, an annual convention is held the second full week-end of August. Membership set around 600 people.

TOYS
Canadian Toy Collector's Society Inc.
PO Box 636
Maple, ON L6A 1S5
Membership is $30 initially and $25 each subsequent year. There are 300 members, who meet once a month in Toronto. A newsletter is published with informative articles, news and a section with want ads, free to members. The

Society holds a very large toy show, in Toronto, every fall. Members are interested in a wide variety of topics including dolls, trains, wind-ups, dinky cars, etc.

TOY TRAINS
Train Collectors Association
National Business Office
PO Box 248
Strasburg, PA 17579
Yearly dues are $20 U.S. and there is also a one time initiation fee of $25 U.S. Newsletter is included in membership as is a glossy quarterly magazine. Currently boast 23,000 members.

Lionel Collectors Club of America
Dienzel C. Dennis, Secretary
1425 Ruthbern Road
Daytona Beach, FL 32014
The LCCA was founded in 1970 and currently boasts about 6500 collectors. Members receive a copy of the bi-monthly newsletter, *The Lion Roars,* devoted to all aspects of Lionel collecting and operating. In addition the group also publishes a bi-monthly 'buy and sell' bulletin called the *Interchange Track.* An annual membership roster is published to assist the membership. All publications are covered by annual dues. Membership is $30 a year. This consists of a $20 annual fee and a $10 initiation fee.

Wallace Nutting Collectors Club
George Monro
186 Mountain Ave.
North Caldwell, NJ 07006
Write for information re costs of membership, newsletter. No response to this author's requests for information.

WHISTLES
Air Horn and Steam Whistle Enthusiasts
Richard J. Weisenberger
2655 N. Friendship, Lot 18
Paducah, KY 42001
The Horn and Whistle is the official journal of this organization and is published bi-monthly. Members are dedicated to the history, development, preservation, as well as the technical advancement of horns and whistles presently used in marine, industry, railroad service and general signaling and warning applications, with an emphasis on safety. Subscription payments may be made only by draft on a United States bank or by International Postal Money Order, payable in U.S. dollars. Annual subscription rates are $18 to Canada and the U.S.

WHITE IRONSTONE CHINA
The Tea Leaf Club International
PO Box 904
Mount Prospect, IL 60056
The play on words of the Newsletter title, *Tea Leaf Readings*, sometimes leads people to think that this is a group who reads tea leaves. "Not so," says the editor of the newsletter, Julie Rich. "We collect white ironstone china decorated with a copper (or gold) lustre leaf. It was made in England, primarily in Staffordshire, some in Scotland and in the United States. The first potter who registered it was Anthony Shaw (1856) as Lustre Band and Sprig."

The club was organized to educate, stimulate and maintain an interest in the collection of Tea Leaf Ironstone China and Variants as well as to promote the interchange of information between members in various parts of the world. Membership is $20 U.S. The newsletter is published five times a year and contains informative articles as well as activities of the organization and its members.

Antiques

Willow Pattern China
The Oregon Willow Club
Box 1360
Oakridge, OR 97463
Membership in the club is $5 U.S. with free
news and sources lists. Interested collectors may
want to subscribe to *American Willow Report*, a
bi-monthly Willow pattern china newsletter.
Their address is: P.O. Box 900, 48354 E. First
Street, Oakridge, Oregon 97463. It is jammed
with all manner of information, articles, adver-
tisements, etc. Subscription is $15 a year, U.S.

WORLD'S FAIR ITEMS
World's Fair Collectors Society Inc.
PO Box 20806
Sarasota, FL 34236-3806
Members in the society, established in 1968,
have varied interests. Some collect from only
one event, such as the 1893 Columbian or the
1967 Montreal fairs. Others hunt for specific
types of items such as dolls, books, glassware,
tickets, toys, thimbles, spoons, marbles, maps,
literature, films, videos, etc. Membership to
Canada is $13 a year, U.S. and includes the bi-
monthly *Fair News*, which contains news about
Fairs, members and upcoming events of interest.
Every new member is listed with his or her collecting interest in and is entitled to a free classified ad in each issue. The Society sponsors
periodic exhibits and courses in different parts
of the U.S.

INDEX

Printed in Canada